New Religious Movements and Counselling

There are many different ways in which minority religions and counselling may interact. In some cases there can be antagonism between counselling services and minority religions, with each suspecting they are ideologically threatened by the other, but it can be argued that the most common relationship is one of ignorance – mental health professionals do not pay much attention to religion and often do not ask or consider their clients' religious affiliation. To date, the understanding of this relationship has focused on the 'anti-cult movement' and the perceived need for members of minority religions to undergo some form of 'exit counselling'. In line with the series, this volume takes a non-judgemental approach and instead highlights the variety of issues, religious groups and counselling approaches that are relevant at the interface between minority religion and counselling.

The volume is divided into four parts: Part I offers perspectives on counselling from different professions; Part II offers chapters from practitioners directly involved in counselling former members of minority religions; Part III offers unique personal accounts by members and former members of a number of different new religions; while Part IV offers chapters on some of the most pertinent current issues in the counselling/minority religions fields, written by new and established academics. In every section, the volume seeks to explore different permutations of the counsellor-client relationship when religious identities are taken into account. This includes not only 'secular' therapists counselling former members of religion, but the complexities of the former member turned counsellor, as well as counselling practised both within religious movements and by religious movements that offer counselling services to the 'outside' world.

Sarah Harvey has been a researcher at Inform since 2001 and is studying for her PhD at the School of European Culture and Languages, University of Kent, on the subject of 'natural' childbirth.

Silke Steidinger has been an Assistant Research Officer at Inform since 2006. She is also a UKCP-registered attachment-based psychoanalytic psychotherapist (qualified at The Bowlby Centre) and also works as a mentalisation-based therapist at an NHS Personality Disorders Service. Currently she is doing an MA in Information Experience Design at The Royal College of Art.

James A. Beckford, a Fellow of the British Academy, is Professor Emeritus of Sociology at the University of Warwick, Vice-Chair of the Board of Governors of Inform and a former President of the Society for the Scientific Study of Religion.

INFORM

THE INFORMATION NETWORK ON RELIGIOUS MOVEMENTS

Routledge Inform Series on Minority Religions and Spiritual Movements

Series Editor: Eileen Barker

London School of Economics and Political Science, UK

Inform is an independent charity that collects and disseminates accurate, balanced and up-to-date information about minority religious and spiritual movements.

The Routledge Inform Series addresses themes related to new religions, many of which have been the topics of Inform seminars. The series editorial board consists of internationally renowned scholars in the field.

Books in the series will attract both an academic and interested general readership, particularly in the areas of Religious Studies, and the Sociology of Religion and Theology.

For a full list of titles in this series, please visit www.routledge.com/religion/series/AINFORM

Legal Cases, New Religious Movements, and Minority Faiths
Edited by James T. Richardson and François Bellanger

The Public Face of African New Religious Movements in Diaspora
Imagining the Religious 'Other'
Edited by Afe Adogame

'Cult Wars' in Historical Perspective
New and Minority Religions
Edited by Eugene V. Gallagher

Visioning New and Minority Religions
Projecting the future
Edited by Eugene V. Gallagher

Fiction, Invention and Hyper-reality
From popular culture to religion
Edited by Carole M. Cusack and Pavol Kosnáč

New Religious Movements and Counselling
Academic, Professional and Personal Perspectives
Edited by Sarah Harvey, Silke Steidinger and James A. Beckford

New Religious Movements and Counselling

Academic, Professional and Personal Perspectives

Edited by
Sarah Harvey, Silke Steidinger and James A. Beckford

Routledge
Taylor & Francis Group
LONDON AND NEW YORK

First published 2018
by Routledge

2 Park Square, Milton Park, Abingdon, Oxfordshire OX14 4RN
52 Vanderbilt Avenue, New York, NY 10017

Routledge is an imprint of the Taylor & Francis Group, an informa business

First issued in paperback 2019

British Library Cataloguing-in-Publication Data
A catalogue record for this book is available from the British Library

Library of Congress Cataloging-in-Publication Data
A catalog record for this book has been requested.

ISBN: 978-1-4724-7271-7 (hbk)
ISBN: 978-0-367-88157-3 (pbk)

Typeset in Bembo
by codeMantra

Contents

List of contributors

James A. Beckford, a Fellow of the British Academy, is Professor Emeritus of Sociology at the University of Warwick, Vice-Chair of the Board of Governors of Inform and a former President of the Society for the Scientific Study of Religion. His main research interests are chaplaincies and relations between religion and the state. His publications include *Cult Controversies* (1985), *Religion in Prison. Equal Rites in a Multi-Faith Society* (1998, with Sophie Gilliat), *Social Theory and Religion* (2003), *Muslims in Prison: Challenge and Change in Britain and France* (2005, with D. Joly and F. Khosrokhavar), *The SAGE Handbook of the Sociology of Religion* (2007, edited with N.J. Demerath III) and *Migration and Religion* (2 edited volumes, 2015).

Pedr Beckley studied at London University gaining his first degree in Chemistry and Food Science and then worked in the Food Industry before returning to study in Bristol where he read Theology. He was ordained in 1979. His interest in new religious movements began in London as an undergraduate, when he met some of the early arrivals in Britain of the Jesus People and the Unification Church ('Moonies'). This interest continued and, with the founding of Inform, he became the Diocese of Sheffield's adviser on NRMs – a post that he has now held for 25 years. His publications include *Unlocking the Future* (Lion Publishing, 1989) and *Mission in a Conspiracy Culture* (Grove Books, 2002).

Simon Cooper worked as a pastor for a local congregation (roughly 200 people) for the Unification Movement in West London until 2014 (43LG community church). It's a very mixed congregation in respect of age, ethnic background and career paths. He is also the media spokesperson for the movement in the UK, recently having worked with Firecracker films and Channel 4 in the making of a successful documentary about the second generation of the community's journey towards marriage. Now in his mid 40s, he is married and has five children between the ages of seven and sixteen. Simon studied English Literature at Newcastle and Law in London and was, between 2008 and 2012, the national director for the Unification Movement in the UK. He now works full time for a claims management company but continues to play an active voluntary role in his church community and was recently involved in a restructuring process and sits on the newly established National Council for the UK Unification Church.

Joe Copestake left Oxford University in 2013 with an MSt in the Study of Religion (Distinction). His dissertation was entitled 'How do Muslims in the UK understand mental health?' He was a founder of the Oxford Student Mindfulness Society: the country's first student-run society offering secular mindfulness for well-being, which in its first year attracted 250 students to its events. He has been active in several student support and mental health campaigning organisations in Oxford. He also has a Buddhist practice of several years, particularly Insight Meditation and the Plum Village tradition. A former intern at Inform, he has spent the past three years working at AQA and Reed and studying towards an MA in Social Research Methods (Social Policy) at Durham University, all with the goal of connecting his aforementioned interests to the charity sector.

Vivianne Crowley lectures in Psychology of Religion at Nottingham Trent University, UK, and is a member of the Faculty of Pastoral Counseling and Chaplaincy, Cherry Hill Seminary, Columbia SC, USA. She was formerly Lecturer in Psychology of Religion in the Theology and Religious Studies Department, King's College London. She is a Chartered Psychologist and received her PhD from University College London. Her current research interests are in psychology of religion, mindfulness-based interventions, Jungian psychology, and contemporary Paganism.

Wendy Dossett is Senior Lecturer in Religious Studies at the University of Chester, and Principal Investigator of the Higher Power Project. She is a former Associate Director of the Alister Hardy Religious Experience Research Centre. She has research interests and publications in Japanese Buddhism, religious education, and in spirituality and recovery from addiction. She has worked in a residential drug and alcohol addiction rehabilitation centre, and has undertaken field research amongst those in twelve step recovery programmes. Findings of the Higher Power Project are published in 'Addiction, Spirituality and the Twelve Steps' in *International Social Work*. May, Vol. 56, No.2, 2013, and 'Reflections on the Language of Salvation in Twelve Step Recovery' in H. Bacon, W. Dossett, & S. Knowles (Eds.) (2015), *Alternative Salvations: Engaging the Sacred and the Secular*. London: Bloomsbury Academic.

Linda Dubrow-Marshall is a clinical and counselling psychologist, registered with the Health and Care Professions Council and a registered counsellor/psychotherapist with the British Association for Counselling and Psychotherapy. She is the Programme Leader for the MSc Psychology of Coercive Control and also for the MSc Applied Psychology (Therapies) programmes at the University of Salford. In the USA, she is a licensed psychologist in Pennsylvania and is registered with the National Register of Health Service

Psychologists. She co-founded RETIRN, the Re-entry Therapy Information and Referral Network in the USA and subsequently in the UK in order to provide specialist mental health services to individuals and families with involvement with NRM's or other high demand groups.

Roderick Dubrow-Marshall is a Lecturer in Psychology in the School of Health Sciences and is a Visiting Fellow in the Criminal Justice Hub at the University of Salford where he is also Programme Leader for the MSc Psychology of Coercive Control. Formerly Deputy Vice-Chancellor at the University of Derby and Pro Vice-Chancellor at the University of Central Lancashire, Rod gained his BA and PhD in Psychology at the University of Nottingham and he went on to be Dean of Faculty at Buckinghamshire New University and at the University of South Wales. His research specialities include the psychology of undue influence and cults or extremist groups (where he has developed the 'Totalistic Identity Theory' as an evidence-based theory to combat and reduce ideological extremism and ideologically driven violence), organisational behaviour and healthiness and the social psychology of identity and prejudice. A graduate member of the British Psychological Society, he is also a member of the Board of Directors and Chair of the Research Committee of the International Cultic Studies Association (ICSA, the formerly American Family Foundation) and is a co-Editor of the International Journal of Cultic Studies (www.icsahome.com). Rod also co-founded the Re-Entry Therapy Information and Referral Network (RETIRN) UK in 2004 (with Dr Linda Dubrow-Marshall) and he is a member of the Board of Directors of the Buxton International Festival (www.buxtonfestival.co.uk) where he interviews authors each year as part of the Festival's literary series.

Abi Freeman was formerly a member and spokesperson of The Family International (TFI), previously known as the Children of God. She joined the movement in her teenage years, subsequently living in TFI communities in England, Iran, Turkey, the Indian Subcontinent and various parts of Europe including Eastern Europe, until moving out of the community with her husband in 2007. She is no longer involved with TFI aside from personal friendships with some former and current members. Trained and qualified as a teacher/lecturer, she writes and edits books on topics ranging from faith to loss, and volunteers with various health-related charities.

Lorna Goldberg, LCSW, PsyA, Board member and past president of ICSA (the International Cultic Studies Association), is a psychoanalyst in private practice and Director of the Institute for Psychoanalytic Studies. In 1976, she and her husband, William Goldberg, began facilitating a support group for former cult members that continues to meet on a monthly basis in their home in Englewood, New Jersey. In 2009, she received the Margaret T. Singer Award from ICSA. Lorna has been a member of ICSA's Board of Directors since November 2003 and served as President from 2008 to 2012.

She has published numerous articles about her therapeutic work with former cult members in professional journals, most recently: Goldberg, L. (2012). “Influence of a Charismatic Antisocial Cult Leader: Psychotherapy With an Ex-Cultist Prosecuted for Criminal Behavior”. *International Journal of Cultic Studies*, (Vol. 2), 15–24. Goldberg, L. (2011). “Diana, Leaving the Cult: Play Therapy in Childhood and Talk Therapy in Adolescence”. *International Journal of Cultic Studies*, (Vol. 2), 33–43. She also wrote a chapter on guidelines for therapists in the book, *Recovery from Cults*, edited by Michael Langone (1995). Lorna has co-written with William Goldberg, a chapter on psychotherapy with targeted parents in the book, *Working with Alienated Children and Families* (2012), edited by Amy J. L. Baker and S. Richard Sauber. Most recently, Lorna is the coeditor, along with William Goldberg, Rosanne Henry, and Michael Langone, of a book (in press), *Cult Recovery: A Clinician's Guide to Working with Former Cult Members and Their Families*.

Sarah Harvey, Researcher at Inform since 2001, has an undergraduate degree from the University of Manchester in Comparative Religion and Social Anthropology and a Masters degree from the London School of Economics and Political Science in Social Research Methods (Sociology). She is studying for her PhD at the School of European Culture and Languages, University of Kent, on the subject of ‘natural’ childbirth. She is co-editor, with Dr Suzanne Newcombe (2013), of *Prophecy in the New Millennium: When Prophecies Persist* Aldershot: Ashgate, has guest-edited a special issue of *The Pomegranate: The International Journal of Pagan Studies* (volume 11, no. 1, 2009) and has written numerous other encyclopaedia entries and short articles.

Nicola Laaninen lives in Orange County, New York with her husband and three children. She joined the Unification Church in San Francisco in August of 1978, and returned to England in 1981. She was kidnapped from the streets of London, was restrained and subjected to a deprogramming. She later returned to the Unification Church supported by her parents and brothers. She has since distanced herself from the church and its politics but still regards the theology as a beginning point to answering many of her questions. She has a beautiful family, good friends, and memories that are all an integral part of her involvement with the Unification Church.

Maitreyabandhu was ordained into the Triratna Buddhist Order in 1990. He has written three books on Buddhism: *Thicker than Blood: Friendship on the Buddhist Path* (2001), *Life with Full Attention: a Practical Course in Mindfulness* (2009) and *The Journey and the Guide: A Practical Course in Enlightenment* (2015) all with Windhorse Publications. Maitreyabandhu is also a poet and has published two collections with Bloodaxe Books: *The Crumb Road* (2013) and *Yarn* (2015). He lives and works at the London Buddhist Centre.

Alastair Pearson works as a Family/Systemic Psychotherapist in an inner London Child and Adolescent Mental Health Service, having originally trained as a social worker. He has a long-standing interest in religion and spirituality, establishing a private practice focussing on difficulties arising from involvement in New Religious Movements, an account which has been published in the systemic press. He is a trustee of the Institute of Family Therapy and member of the Diversity, Equality and Inclusion committee of the Association of Family Therapy and Systemic Practice.

Eric Roux has occupied many functions in the Church of Scientology for more than 20 years, including lecturing on the Scientology religion at many levels. He is currently the President of the Union of the Churches of Scientology in France. He has worked on the topic of religious freedom for many years at national and international levels. He has been a speaker on this topic at many events, including at the OSCE, Council of Europe, US capitol and more, and works on various interfaith platforms. He has been President of the European Interreligious Forum for Religious Freedom since 2013.

Charlotte Shaw is Head of Research at Phenomen Trust. Her pursuit of understanding the place of new religious movements in society has spanned both academic and media industries. Charlotte completed her PhD at the University of Oxford, where she focused on two NRMs in London. The project achieved international recognition, resulting in awards including The Abrahamic Studentship and The Edward Schillebeeckx Prize. This success followed two awards from the AHRC for her MSt research on NRMs in New York City. Charlotte also contributes to media projects and has been involved with numerous features on new religion for the BBC and CNN.

Silke Steidinger has been an Assistant Research Officer at Inform since 2006. The primary focus of her work is researching religious groups for the Inform database and cataloguing the Inform library. In 2004, she received an MSc in Religion in Contemporary Society (Sociology) from the London School of Economics, the focus of her dissertation being on death in New Religious Movements. In 1999, she received a BA (Hons) in Religious Studies from King's College London. She has been practising as a UKCP registered attachment-based psychoanalytic psychotherapist (qualified at The Bowlby Centre in 2014) and has worked at Tower Hamlets National Health Service Personality Disorders Service since 2014. Currently she is doing an MA in Information Experience Design at The Royal College of Art.

Joseph Szimhart has been a Cult Intervention Specialist since the early 1980s. He has an undergraduate degree from the University of Dayton in Ohio, a Certificate in Painting from the Pennsylvania Academy of Fine Arts, and completed a course in social psychology at Ursinus College,

PA. He taught art courses at St. John's College in New Mexico and at the New Mexico State Penitentiary. Since 1998, he is employed as a crisis caseworker at Montgomery County Emergency Services, a psychiatric emergency hospital in Pennsylvania. The work of pioneer modern artists piqued his interest in the Theosophical Society and related new religious movements (NRMs) including the Agni Yoga Society and Church Universal and Triumphant (CUT). His radical experience with CUT from 1978 to 1980 drew him into cultic studies and the fringe field of cult intervention. He has presented papers many times at conferences regarding NRMs, including twice with the Association of Sociology of Religion and many times with the International Cultic Studies Association. As a media consultant, he provided the story for *A Mother's Deception* starring Joan Van Ark (1994) and was the subject of the feature article "New Age Exorcist" in *DETAILs* Magazine (Sept. 1991). He was acquitted in 1993 by a jury trial in Boise, Idaho of all charges for allegedly kidnapping a member of a NRM. He maintains an art studio at *Goggleworks Art Center* in Reading, PA. His first novel *Mushroom Satori: The Cult Diary* was published through Aperture Press in 2013.

Acknowledgements

The editors thank all of Inform's staff, governors and management committee and, in particular, Eileen Barker, founder of Inform. Inform staff Dr Amanda Van Eck, Dr Suzanne Newcombe and Sibyl Macfarlane were very supportive and expertly managed Sarah and Silke's time away from routine responsibilities to work on this volume. The Inform staff and governors put together the Inform seminar on the subject of New Religious Movements and Counselling held in May 2013 – efficiently organised by Sibyl – where many of the papers were first presented. We would like to thank all of the speakers and participants at this event, as fruitful discussions during the day directly contributed to the final volume. We would also like to thank Dr Hamish Cameron who helped organise that seminar and read through many of the first drafts.

We would like to thank all of the contributors to the volume – both those who presented at the 2013 conference and have stuck with the volume throughout and those who came on board more recently.

The editors would also like to thank their families and friends for their support.

1 Minority religions and counselling

An overview

James A. Beckford and Sarah Harvey

The web of relationships between minority religions and counselling is dense and fascinating. In some cases, there are antagonism and suspicion between them, with each side accusing the other of being hostile. More often the relationship is one of ignorance, especially as counsellors and other mental health practitioners tend to avoid paying much attention to religion in general or to their clients' religious views and commitments. At the same time, many minority religions discourage their followers from seeking help from 'secular' counsellors. In other words, neither side is 'literate' about – or sensitive to – what the other has to offer. Misunderstandings, talking at cross purposes and stand-offs are not uncommon. An additional complication is that some minority religions – just like mainstream faith organisations – have developed their own forms of counselling and pastoral care which are grounded in their particular beliefs and values. Some may even present themselves primarily as counselling or therapeutic groups. This can exacerbate tensions with counsellors who are unsympathetic to some or all minority religions.

All the contributors to this volume aim to bring their professional expertise and personal experience to bear on the complicated and evolving web of relationships between minority religions and counselling. They come from widely differing backgrounds, and their different ways of looking at the interactions between religion and counselling are not all compatible with each other. There is pain, and there is puzzlement, but there is also pride in having overcome serious difficulties. The mixture of accounts given by counsellors, clients and their close relatives as well as by academic researchers is unique and, in places, troubling to popular preconceptions or prejudices.

The origins of this book can be found in preparations for a one-day seminar held in London on 18 May 2013 by Inform (Information Network Focus on Religious Movements).[1] The preliminary discussions among Inform's Governors and members of its research staff recognised that questions about counselling had run like a hidden thread through many of the activities in which Inform had been involved since its foundation by Professor Eileen Barker in 1988. For, although Inform has never offered to provide counselling, it was quite common for enquirers to ask for advice about the counselling services and providers that might be available to people affected in a wide variety of ways by minority religions, new religious movements (NRMs) or 'cults'. Indeed, numerous participants in Inform's twice-yearly public seminars and occasional conferences had talked about counselling from different points of view. And Inform's researchers had sometimes had dealings with counsellors while conducting their investigations into how individuals, families and therapists had been affected by minority religions, as well as with counsellors who had allegedly recruited their clients into religious or spiritual movements. The decision to devote a seminar specifically to counselling and NRMs was, therefore, a recognition of the importance of tackling the many issues that arise in the interplay between them.

In keeping with Inform's commitment to providing a public space for discussion of all issues concerning NRMs, this book provides a platform for views that are not necessarily shared by all contributors or indeed by all researchers at Inform. Like all of the volumes in the Routledge-Inform series on Minority Religions and Spiritual Movements, this book is unique in its presentation of different perspectives on a certain issue, in this case counselling. As a result, the voices of members of certain movements are juxtaposed to those of ex-members, opponents or critics, counsellors and academics. Some of the narratives are personal; others are more analytical; and yet others suggest practical advice.[2] But there is a shared concern with the ethical and practical issues that arise when people who are, or have been, affected by minority religions engage with counsellors and *vice versa* – and when minority religions themselves engage in activities that may qualify as counselling. This all helps to make the book unique for bringing together such a variety of perspectives and voices.

Minority religions, 'brainwashing' and counselling

Minority religions or NRMs are anything but uniform or monolithic (Barker 1989, 2013). Their diversity and changeableness are beyond doubt. And so is their tendency to be caught up in a range of controversies which put them in the headlines from time to time (Beckford 1985, 1993). These controversies arise from allegations that NRMs are responsible for actions and processes that are either illegal or immoral. Journalists and programme makers typically portray NRMs as controversial for reasons that include authoritarian forms of leadership, economic exploitation of members, sexual abuse by leaders, political intrigue and abuse of members' children. Common to most such allegations is the charge that leaders exercise influence and power over their followers in ways that are excessive, fraudulent and unaccountable. 'Brainwashing', 'coercive persuasion', 'mental manipulation' and 'mind control' are just a few of the popular catch-all terms that have been used to characterise the processes whereby undue influence is supposedly wielded in NRMs (Hassan 1988) – terms that are forcefully rejected by scholars such as Robbins and Anthony (1979, 1982), Bromley and Richardson (1983) and Barker (1984). And right at the centre of these controversies is the general accusation that such abuse of influence and power generates so much distress for members, ex-members and their close relatives or friends that they turn for help to – or are referred to – counselling and therapy.

Beginning in the 1960s in the USA, these claims about brainwashing and mind control in NRMs became powerful drivers of campaigns and movements to monitor, control or outlaw the activities of religious and spiritual groups often labelled as 'cults' or 'destructive cults'.[3] Powerful support came from psychologists (Singer 1979) and psychiatrists (Clark 1979; West and Singer 1980; Clark et al. 1981; West 1990) who, in turn, had drawn inspiration from the work of the distinguished American psychiatrist Robert Jay Lifton's (1961) book *Thought Reform and the Psychology of Totalism* as practised by communist forces on allied prisoners during the Korean War and on prisoners held in China in the 1950s. The influence of these ideas was strong in predominantly Christian 'counter-cult' movements (Chryssides 1999; Cowan 2002) as well as in non-religious 'anti-cult' campaigns (Introvigne 1995).[4] These ideas about brainwashing also shaped the various forms of counselling and psychotherapy that developed in connection with attempts to provide a rationale for the forcible removal of members from NRMs (kidnapping and 'deprogramming'), to offer arguments that might help members to make their own decision to leave the movements ('exit counselling') and to assist ex-members and their close relatives and friends to recover from the experience of membership ('thought reform counselling') (Langone 1993). Arguments about brainwashing have also led to legal controversies in various parts of the world (Richardson 1996) and to disputes about the deployment of brainwashing claims in official reports on NRMs in Europe (Richardson and Introvigne 2001). Yet, notions of brainwashing still have their defenders (Zablocki 2001; Kent 2008). And no truce has yet been signed in the so-called cult wars (Gallagher 2016).

Therapies and controversies

A further twist in the argument occurs at this point. In an inversion of claims that counselling and psychotherapy can facilitate recovery from the distress allegedly inflicted by controversial NRMs, it is also charged that those NRMs which offer their own forms of counselling or therapy to their own members are only likely to do so as a way of reinforcing their undue influence. In short, controversial NRMs are widely accused of, on the one hand, causing the kind of distress that requires the assistance of counsellors and, on the other, of practising forms of counselling that blight their members' lives (Singer, Temerlin and Langone 1990). Even relatively non-controversial religious and spiritual groups can find themselves implicated in public disputes about the merits or demerits of any of the therapies that they offer if they depart from prevailing norms of biomedical paradigms and practices. The interface between NRMs and counselling is truly complex and contentious. There may even be rivalry between them (Kilbourne and Richardson 1984).

Many of the chapters in this book explore the interface between NRMs and counselling but they also raise broader questions about the varieties of 'counselling' on offer and the highly variable extent to which counsellors, like psychiatrists, are trained to take account of the religious and the spiritual in their therapeutic practice. According to a British psychiatrist, psychiatry has

> traditionally held a certain antipathy towards religion … Where religion has been addressed by clinicians, it has been generally in terms of its differential diagnosis from psychopathology. Clinicians are far less religious than the patients who consult them. There is a 'religiosity gap' between the two groups.
>
> (Dein 2009: 1)

Nevertheless, in recent decades, many psychotherapists and counsellors – especially in the USA[5] – have come to recognise the importance of engaging with their clients' expressed religious beliefs and experiences (Blando 2006; Koenig 2013). Some also argue that it can be helpful for therapists to communicate their own religious viewpoints to clients in certain circumstances provided that they do not seek to impose their faith on them (West 2011, 2012). Indeed, Kenneth Pargament (2007: 9), among many other distinguished authorities, offers 'a number of good reasons to take the spiritual dimension of life far more seriously and to integrate it far more fully into the process of psychotherapy'. And a 'position statement' issued by the Royal College of Psychiatrists in the UK (2013: 6) recognises that

> there is now a sufficient body of evidence to suggest that spirituality and religion are at least factors about which psychiatrists should be knowledgeable, insofar as they have an impact on the aetiology, diagnosis and treatment of mental disorders. Further, an ability to handle spiritual and religious issues sensitively and empathically has a significant potential impact upon the relationship between psychiatrist and patient.

In the opinion of a French observer of British psychiatry (Champion 2013: 17), we should now be talking about a 'new presence' of the religious in psychiatry and mental health care.

But a number of contributors to this volume show that problems can arise if therapists or counsellors wish to challenge clients' spiritual or religious beliefs and practices. Further difficulties arise if spiritual or religious material is introduced into therapy in ways that could be considered problematic for clients, therapists or their supervisors. The training and supervision of therapists or counsellors therefore has a direct bearing on how these problems are framed and managed. Particularly difficult issues have arisen in connection with, for example, allegations that counsellors or medical doctors have 'coached' clients to concoct and to disclose false memories of distress supposedly suffered at the hands of unscrupulous leaders of minority religions or so-called Satanic abusers (La Fontaine 1998, 2003).[6]

But questions are often raised about how therapists or counsellors can acquire the information needed for them to make sound judgements about the advisability or inadvisability of trying to integrate religion and spirituality into therapy, especially with regard to the diversity of expressions of religions and spiritualities found in many countries (Ruff and Elliott 2016). Other questions are raised by contributors to this volume about the advisability or inadvisability of practising therapies tailored specifically for people adversely affected by minority religions. There is no doubt, then, that the controversies are not only about NRMs; they can also arise in connection with other forms of religion and spirituality as well as with the very theories and practice of counselling.

Changing contexts

It is also important to recognise that the societal contexts in which debates about minority religions and counselling have developed have changed in several significant respects. First, the twenty-first century has seen the blossoming of popular interest in a wide swath of beliefs, experiences and activities categorised as 'spiritual' (Spalek and Imtoual 2008; Cadge and Konieczny 2014). This is an extremely vague category which includes all manner of New Age sensitivities, alternative therapies, holistic diets, astrological predictions and fitness regimes. It may be an exaggeration to think of these developments as a 'spiritual revolution' (Heelas and Woodhead 2005), but there is no doubt that awareness of them has seeped into aspects of mainstream life such as employment (Grant, O'Neil and Stephens 2004), health care (Orchard 2001; Culliford 2002), nursing (Gilliat-Ray 2003), ecological movements (Bloch 1998; Kearns 2007) and sports (Parry et al. 2007). As a result, levels of familiarity with the spiritualities conveyed by many new and minority religious groups have increased to the point where they are less likely to be regarded as weird or threatening than was the case when NRMs were really new. Indeed, some forms of counselling and therapy now embody aspects of spirituality previously stigmatised as 'cultic' or 'New Agey', thereby aggravating concerns in some quarters about encroachments of mammon into spirituality (Carrette and King 2005). But in general, a process of rapprochement is taking place between spiritualities, new and minority religions and the everyday world in many liberal democracies – albeit slowly, unevenly and in the face of persistent objections.

A second contextual change involves the growth of religious and spiritual diversity, notably in countries that have experienced immigration from parts of the world where liberal forms of Christianity are not the dominant expressions of religion. The global circulation of students, workers and accompanying family members mainly from East Asia, South Asia, the Middle East, Africa and South America has not only boosted religious diversity in Europe,

North America and Australasia, but has also created successive generations of descendants who are continuing to put down 'religious roots' in their countries of settlement (Beckford 2015). Equally important are the global electronic media and networks which now cut across national boundaries, disseminating religions and spiritualities that find themselves 'at home' virtually everywhere in the world. This nourishes all manner of both original and hybrid versions of cultural traditions, aspects of which can find their way into host cultures where they continue to evolve. Neo-Hindu movements and strands of Kabbalah are prime examples of these developments (Altglas 2005, 2014). And these global flows of religions and spiritualities have, in turn, helped to shape new ideas about health and well-being. Again, some of the results have given rise to concerns about abuse and exploitation, thereby boosting the demand for counselling and therapies. But, on the other hand, innovative ideas about religions and spiritualities have also flowed into novel forms of counselling and therapy such as mindfulness-based cognitive therapy (Crane 2009; Herbert and Forman 2011) or Ayurvedic Yoga and self-healing (Stiles 2007). The increase of all these aspects of religious and spiritual diversity in the early twenty-first century has gone some way towards blunting the sharp antagonism that was widely levelled against new and minority religious movements in the final third of the twentieth century. In effect, the would-be target of anti-cult sentiment has become so broad, diffuse and embedded in everyday life that it largely evades serious censure in many countries – with the notable exceptions of countries such as China, Russia and France where moral panic about new spiritual and religious movements remains potent.

A third series of changes affecting the interplay between minority religions and counselling or psychotherapy have occurred in the context of law and regulation. In contrast to countries such as China and Russia, most liberal democracies have adopted constitutional devices for protecting the freedom of religion and have signed up to international legal instruments that defend the right of their citizens to hold, or not to hold, religious beliefs (McCrea 2010; Sandberg 2011, 2014). Some states have gone even further in maintaining that all religions must be treated equally. This is far from saying that all legal systems and courts of law respond to religious cases in the same way; indeed, the religion cases coming before the European Court of Human Rights, for example, illustrate wide disparities between states in their treatment of religions (Richardson 2004, 2015; Durham 2013; Kirkham 2013; Lykes and Richardson 2014; Richardson and Bellanger 2014). But the general point is that, at least in theory, the constitutional and legal apparatus for protecting religions and spiritualities has become more robust in many – but not all – regions of the world. Over the course of modern history, minority religions have been in the forefront of efforts to construct this apparatus (Wilson 1996; Peters 2002); and some of them are far from reluctant to seek legal remedies for their problems. Admittedly, there are still difficulties in a wide range of countries including China, France, Greece, Russia and Turkey. Nevertheless, the complex interface between minority religions, spiritualities, psychiatry, counselling and psychotherapy is now framed by laws, human rights doctrines, international religious freedom protocols, professional codes and judicial processes which have helped to moderate levels of contention in many countries.[7] As a result, the level of 'vigilante' attempts to kidnap and forcibly deprogramme members of minority religions has declined substantially in liberal democracies. And the deployment of notions of brainwashing and mind control in support of deprogramming has also been largely eclipsed by more subtle notions of exit counselling and mind reform counselling.

Structure of the book

In view of the wide variety of forms that counselling can take, the first section of the book explores different perspectives on the connections between counselling and minority religions. The three contributors to this section offer personal reflections on the particular circumstances in which they found themselves either providing or trying to facilitate counselling for people affected by minority religions. **Pedr Beckley's** chapter on his experiences as a diocesan adviser on NRMs in the Church of England and as a non-professional counsellor and adviser highlights the Church's ambivalence towards such advisers. Nevertheless, the three examples that he describes of his own work as a counsellor and adviser in connection with widely differing cases underline the ways in which the challenges facing counsellors have changed over time, partly as a consequence of demographic shifts and partly in response to the greater importance currently attached to mental health. His realistic conclusion is that 'advisory work is extremely complex' and that 'there can be untidy loose ends'. Then follows **Silke Steidinger's** chapter about her joint roles as a professional psychotherapist both in the National Health Service (NHS) and in private practice, and as a researcher at Inform. Her work bridges clinical practice and academic research on NRMs in a unique fashion. Recognising that there are still difficulties in the stance of some psychotherapists and counsellors towards minority religions, she explains the personal and academic settings in which her interest was aroused in NRMs – especially in questions about the extent to which recruits to NRMs can be said to exercise agency. Her initial training in the social scientific approach of *Verstehen* and, subsequently, in attachment-based psychoanalytic psychotherapy has given her insights both into the social forces that dispose some people to join NRMs *and* into the emotional responses of recruits and their close relatives and friends. But she insists that 'the therapist is no longer seen as 'the healthy expert' administering 'the cure' to a sick patient. Instead, therapy is seen as a co-created relationship and journey of joint discovery with focus on the client'. Contrary to the claims advanced by 'cult specialists', her argument is that a narrow focus on the dangers supposedly presented by certain minority religions is less important than offering, on the one hand, therapies that can 'strengthen individuals to protect themselves from abusive relationships as an on-going part of life' and, on the other, the kind of objective information and empathetic support provided by Inform. This section ends with **Alastair Pearson's** outline of the development of systemic psychotherapy, which emphasises the changing contexts in which ideas about psychotherapy have developed. The engagement between psychotherapists and religion, in particular, has become more positive in recent decades; this includes a growing awareness among therapists of the need to cultivate their own self-reflexivity towards questions about religion and spirituality. His own experiences of being a member of the Evangelical Free Church as a child and of distancing himself from it on the way to becoming a professional systemic psychotherapist have convinced him that 'It is crucial that people experiencing distress in relation to an NRM have access to therapists who are competent to respond to the range of complex mental health, family and social problems that may need addressing'.

The second section of the book focuses closely on the approaches adopted by various forms of psychotherapy and counselling towards working with people adversely affected by minority religions. The range of views and practices is wide, but there are also points of strong agreement on the kind of problems to which therapists can respond positively. To begin with, **Lorna Goldberg**, who integrates both psycho-education and psychodynamic psychotherapy into her professional practice, stresses the need to take account of the similarities and differences between first-generation and second-generation former members of 'destructive cults', i.e. people recruited into NRMs and people who grew up as children in NRMs. An extended case study of a first-generation former member of an NRM identifies the many psychological difficulties that can be brought to awareness if therapy proceeds as a 'collaborative process' and if 'clients feel free to have different beliefs than the beliefs of their therapist'. The role of 'cult education' in this process is to overcome the mystification that often surrounds recruitment to NRMs and to enable former members to understand the undue influence and deception to which they had been subjected. Exploration of early childhood experiences is the second phase of this integrated therapy which aims to help first-generation former members 'to live more productively in the present' while being aware of 'how the cult past as well as life prior to the cult is constantly affecting them and shaping their present life'. The approach to counselling that is presented in the chapter by **Linda and Roderick Dubrow-Marshall** is designed to meet the needs of a wider group of people adversely affected by minority religions. It includes not only former members but also continuing members and the families of those who have left or who remain in high-demand religious movements. In all cases, the counselling aims to counter the harmful effects on clients' self-identity of exposure to the excessive forms of commitment that are typically demanded of members. The holistic model of counselling, which is shared by practitioners associated with the Re-entry Therapy, Information and Referral Network (RETIRN), stresses the distinctiveness of the psychological causes and effects of participation in various kinds of high-demand and extremist movements. The RETIRN model also identifies specific processes of counselling which seek to remedy the damage done to clients' self-identity by cultivating 'unconditional positive regard in families, supportive and respectful interventions, and a non-judgemental psycho-educational model'. The objective is to help former members of abusive movements to adjust to life outside them, recognising that their psychological problems may be different in critical respects from those experienced by people facing other mental health difficulties – and that the appropriate form of counselling should also reflect this distinctiveness. A much more philosophically oriented approach to counselling people impacted by controversial NRMs is outlined in **Joseph Szimhart's** chapter on his four-part 'orbiting' model. It presents members of minority religions as 'flies' who are 'bottled up within high demand relationships' and therefore in need of an 'exit coach' who can show 'the limits of living in the bottle' and can persuade them that the environment outside the bottle is relatively safe. Drawing on his own experience of participating for about five years in the Summit Lighthouse movement, an arm of the Church Universal and Triumphant, Szimhart began helping people to leave other movements in which they felt trapped. Having intervened in more than 500 cases, including incidents in which members of minority religions were held for several days against their will, he emphasises the importance of establishing rapport with clients and persuading them to trust him. Taking two case studies, he explains the themes that he challenges in the course of his interventions: transcendent attraction, exclusive authority, circular tension and exit perils. He does so by employing 'ordinary language' to help clients to see that the 'transcendent wholeness promised' by their religious groups is actually 'more like a hole – a bottled up life'.

The experiences of members and former members of minority religions are the focus of the book's third section, but the complex connections with counselling remain a guiding thread. Some chapters examine counselling from the viewpoint of members or former members of religious movements, while other chapters analyse the movements' own practices that can be likened to counselling. As in other sections of the book, the diversity of experiences, approaches and practices is unmistakeable and, in some cases, surprising. To begin with, **Vivianne Crowley** draws on recent research to explore two sides of an important dilemma that can arise in therapeutic relationships. On the one hand, practitioners of Paganism may have misgivings about revealing their Pagan beliefs or practices to counsellors or psychotherapists, fearing that commitment to Paganism might be regarded as a symptom of psychological disorder. On the other hand, counsellors or psychotherapists who happen to be Pagans may also have misgivings about disclosing their spiritual beliefs to their clients. Despite an improvement in official guidance to mental health professionals about the need for sensitivity towards clients' religion and spirituality, ambivalence and misunderstanding remain widespread towards minority expressions of religion. This can make therapeutic encounters difficult, although Pagan therapists are clear that disclosure of their beliefs needs to be negotiated during their training as well as in their professional practice. Crowley argues that one way forward is for Pagan therapists to set up their own referral system for Pagan clients. She suggests that another 'beneficial development would be for counsellors and psychotherapists to be better informed about contemporary Paganism' as well as other religious and spiritual worldviews. **Eric Roux's** chapter is concerned much less with questions about disclosure. As a scientologist, he is more intent on establishing the differences between auditing in Scientology and counselling as commonly understood. He places auditing in its historical context as a religious practice or set of exercises that seek to guide a person's immortal spirit (the 'thetan') towards higher levels of spiritual awareness and freedom. The practice of Scientology auditing cannot therefore be combined with any other forms of psychological or psychotherapeutic methods. Roux regards any pastoral benefits that might follow from auditing as incidental rather than intentional. His conclusion is that 'Scientology auditing is more than a form of counselling, it is undoubtedly a method of salvation'. In **Simon Cooper's** chapter, we find a more instrumental and positive attitude towards psychotherapy as a resource that has helped him at various times to cope with problems arising from his family's opposition to his membership of the Unification Church (UC). His personal account of his recruitment, his marriage to a fellow member, his improving relationship with his parents and brother, his work in the UC and his positive experience of counselling based on Transactional Analysis is intensely self-reflexive and self-critical. Although he is aware that tensions are common between psychotherapy and aspects of religion, he is adamant that 'Therapy in its different forms has helped my faith to mature' and that he may decide to avail himself of it again in the future now that his teenage children who were born into the UC are starting to question their own beliefs. He does not want to react against them if they fail to think like him. And this raises a general question about the changing relevance of counselling at different stages of an individual's life and of a family's development.

Abi Freeman's chapter is a personal account of the type of counselling practised in one particularly controversial NRM. As a former member of the Children of God – now known as The Family International (TFI) – she describes the distinctive form of counselling that was practised in its communal centres as well intentioned but occasionally 'intrusive and arguably harmful'. Before most of the residential communes were disbanded in 2010, 'personal shepherding' could be practised without training on, and by, any member of the community and was considered superior to other forms of counselling. It could even be imposed by leaders on members suspected of disobedience, spiritual problems or 'negative thinking'. Reports on counselling were not kept confidential. Nevertheless, Freeman acknowledges that many ex-members grieve for the intensely communal life that they lost when they left the movement. This is why, in her view, 'grief counselling can be a helpful model for supporting' ex-members. Her chapter also hints at more general questions about the institutionalisation of counselling practices which have virtually no grounding in public understandings of how counselling should be defined and regulated. To add a further layer of complexity, the very notions of member and ex-member are made problematic by **Nicola Laaninen's** chapter about her complex and changing relationships with the UC. Her narrative is not about accepted forms of counselling but is about the harmful practice of deprogramming in which some self-styled counsellors were involved in the 1970s and 1980s. Three years after her recruitment to the UC, she was arrested in California for overstaying her visa and sent back to the UK where she was abducted and subjected to two attempts at deprogramming by ex-members of the movement with the ambivalent complicity of her parents on the first occasion. Nevertheless, she returned to the UK whilst restoring her good relationship with her parents, although her relationship with the UC eventually changed considerably. And, although she taught UC theology to her own children, she has 'no desire for [her] children to be involved in the UC'. Indeed, she finds the movement's 'political engine' 'quite flawed'; and she is 'uninspired' by its recent developments. Her ambivalence towards the UC is in sharp contrast, however, to her condemnation of deprogramming and of the strains that it placed on her family. The shift to **Maitreyabandhu's** chapter marks a dramatic change of mood and focus. As an ordained member of the Triratna Buddhist Order since 1990 and the co-founder in 2004 of the London Buddhist Centre's (LBC) 'Breathing Space', he outlines a Buddhist approach to mindfulness. Denying that this approach amounts to a 'scientific theory, psycho-educational tool or mental health intervention', he claims that the human mind is constantly engaged in 'self-talk' which diverts us from our human depths and feeds our appetite for habitual preoccupations – just as YouTube tries to tempt viewers with clips related to the ones that they have already chosen to watch. Cultivating a 'fit mind' through mindfulness training involves abandoning the 'inner YouTube' for the sake of 'directly felt experience' – pleasant, unpleasant or neutral – and of the kind of 'discriminating intelligence' which keeps things in perspective and encourages people to 'get on with the things that really matter'. But his conclusion is that mindfulness training in settings as different as schools, General Practitioner (GP) surgeries and prisons will only be effective if it is practised in conjunction with Buddhist ethics and positive emotions. If mindfulness is not, therefore, a stand-alone practice or merely a relaxation technique, Maitreyabandhu leaves open the question of whether mindfulness is likely to be effective in non-Buddhist forms of counselling.

The fourth section of the book brings together some recent academic research on the multifaceted connections between minority religions and counselling. Each of the three chapters highlights emergent issues in long-running concerns with therapies, theologies and philosophies. Appropriately for the book's closing section, fresh questions are raised, but no claims are made about the definitiveness of answers. **Charlotte Shaw's** chapter, for example, tackles the relatively unexplored topic of 'emotional transformation' in two different new religious and spiritual groups in London – the Shanti Yoga Centre and The Sufi Order – which draw inspiration from eclectic sources. Comparing the different ways in which both of these groups try to facilitate the transitions that participants claim to make from feelings of anxiety and stress to feelings of 'hope, acceptance and peace'. Both groups generate their own distinctive narratives and techniques that shape participants' outlooks in terms of, for example, 'positive energy' and 'positive ethos' as well as the kind of 'felt experience' that features in mindfulness practices. Participants also acknowledge that the collective support provided by the groups is part of their therapeutic regimes, although notions of counselling or psychotherapy are not necessarily explicit. This research raises a general question, then, about the definition of counselling and related therapies in the context of spiritual and religious groups. **Joe Copestake's** chapter explores the issues that can arise when either a counsellor or a client holds religious or spiritual beliefs – more specifically Buddhist beliefs about non-attachment, which differ in significant respects from those deployed by non-Buddhists. He argues that the contrast between (a) attachment theory in psychology (as it is applied in many forms of secular counselling) and (b) Buddhist ideas about 'not self' can be sharp, albeit to varying degrees in different traditions of Buddhism. There is a risk that Buddhist meditation teachers in some traditions stress equanimity at the expense of 'warmth and kindness' and a concern with 'ethics, community, doctrine and ritual'. For this reason, many Buddhists seek 'secure attachment' to others by meditating in groups as well as individually. In other words, there can be a productive overlap between attachment psychology and Buddhism. Indeed, Copestake's view is that there is nothing in Buddhism which, in theory, excludes the fostering of good relationships and secure attachment. For him, there are 'fascinating points of contact between Buddhism and attachment-based counselling'. The final chapter, by **Wendy Dossett**, takes the discussion of spiritualities and counselling on to a different terrain – Twelve Step communities that have elaborated their own versions of the ideas that gave rise to Alcoholics Anonymous in the 1930s and subsequently to many other 'mutual aid fellowships'. Her research has analysed the accounts that participants in these groups give of the connections that they perceive between spirituality and managing addictions. Their accounts reflect sharp differences and tensions between the expertise of professional counsellors and their own experiences; the remunerated basis of much counselling and the voluntary nature of mutual aid work; and the time-bound basis of counselling sessions and the freer availability of Twelve Step encounters. The philosophies that underlie forms of counselling are also regarded as incompatible with Twelve Step-based therapies to the extent that the former imply that mutual aid activities engender feelings of powerlessness rather than empowerment. Dossett argues that these differences come to a head in disputes about whether addiction is basically a disease or a 'spiritual malady'. Indeed, some Twelve Step programmes are accused of being cult-like for being dogmatic and claiming exclusive truth, whereas their defenders claim that the spiritual or religious basis of mutual aid fellowship significantly enhances the quality of participants' lives. The wider tensions and collisions between competing views of spirituality, religion and counselling are all exposed in these controversies.

In keeping with Inform's practice of providing opportunities for the exchange of a wide spectrum of views on matters connected with minority religions, the chapters in this volume offer differing ideas about counselling which, in turn, reflect the contributors' different perspectives and experiences. Some of the contributors are trained professionals in the fields of psychotherapy and counselling, others draw mainly on their personal experiences with minority religions, while the academic contributors focus more on theoretical ideas and explanations. Bringing these varied perspectives together in a single volume helps to make it uniquely valuable.

Notes

1 Inform is an educational charity that seeks to collect, assess and disseminate reliable information about minority religions. www.inform.ac. We would like to acknowledge Dr Hamish Cameron's help in facilitating the seminar and preparing the texts for publication.
2 However, this book is far from a 'practical guidebook' or 'how to manual' for counselling former members and their relatives. For one such guidebook, see the International Cultic Studies Association publication *Cult Recovery: A Clinician's Guide to Working with Former Members and Families* edited by Goldberg et al. (2017).
3 Barker (2016) characterises these initiatives as the 'cult-awareness movement'.
4 For accounts of anti-cult activities, see Shupe and Bromley (1994), Melton (2004), Shupe and Darnell (2006) and Barker (2016).
5 But see www.counsellingandspirituality.co.uk for an example from Scotland of collaboration between counselling or psychotherapy and faith or spirituality. See also the website of 'BACP Spirituality', a division of the British Association for Counselling & Psychotherapy at: http://bacpspirituality.org.uk/.
6 For the case of Carol Myers, see www.justiceforcarol.com.
7 For attempts to capture the general shape of relations between religions and states, see Grim and Finke (2006), Fox (2008) and Durham (2013).

References

Altglas, V. 2005. *Le nouvel hindouisme occidental*. Paris: Éditions CNRS.
Altglas, V. 2014. *From Yoga to Kabbalah. Religious Exoticism and the Logics of Bricolage*. New York: Oxford University Press.
Barker, E.V. 1984. *The Making of a Moonie*. Oxford: Blackwell.
Barker, E.V. 1989. *New Religious Movements. A Practical Introduction*. London: HMSO.
Barker, E.V. (ed.) 2013. *Revisionism and Diversification in New Religious Movements*. Farnham: Ashgate.
Barker, E.V. 2016. From cult wars to constructive cooperation—well, sometimes, in: E.V. Gallagher (ed.) *'Cult Wars' in Historical Perspective: New and Minority Religions*. London: Routledge, pp. 9–22.
Beckford, J.A. 1985. *Cult Controversies. The Societal Response to New Religious Movements*. London: Tavistock.

Beckford, J.A. 1993. States, governments and the management of controversial new religious movements, in: E. Barker, J.A. Beckford and K. Dobbelaere (eds) *Secularization, Rationalism and Sectarianism*. Oxford: Clarendon Press, pp. 125–43.

Beckford, J.A. (ed.) 2015. *Migration and Religion*. 2 vols. Cheltenham: Edward Elgar Publications.

Blando, J.A. 2006. Spirituality, religion, and counseling. *Counseling and Human Development*, 39(2), 1–14.

Bloch, J.P. 1998. Alternative spiritualities and environmentalism. *Review of Religious Research*, 40(1), 55–73.

Bromley, D.G. and J.T. Richardson (eds) 1983. *The Brainwashing/Deprogramming Controversy: Sociological, Psychological, Legal and Historical Perspectives*. New York: Edwin Mellen Press.

Cadge, W. and M.E. Konieczny 2014. 'Hidden in plain sight': the significance of religion and spirituality in secular organizations. *Sociology of Religion*, 75(4), 551–63.

Carrette, J. and R. King 2005. *$elling Spirituality. The Silent Takeover of Religion*. London: Routledge.

Champion, F. 2013. La nouvelle présence du religieux dans la psychiatrie contemporaine L'exemple anglais. *Archives de Sciences Sociales des Religions*, 163, 17–38.

Chryssides, G. 1999. *Exploring New Religions*. London: Cassell.

Clark, J.G. 1979. Cults. *Journal of the American Medical Association*, 242(3), 279–81.

Clark, J.G., M.D. Langone, R.E. Schecter and R.C.B. Daly 1981. *Destructive Cult Conversion: Theory, Research, and Treatment*. Weston, MA: American Family Foundation.

Cowan, D.E. 2002. Exits and migrations: foregrounding the Christian counter-cult. *Journal of Contemporary Religion*, 17(3), 339–54.

Crane, R. 2009. *Mindfulness Based Cognitive Therapy*. Hove: Routledge.

Culliford, L. 2002. Spirituality and clinical care. *British Medical Journal*, 325, 1434–35.

Dein, S. 2009. The faith of patients. Annual Meeting of the Royal College of Psychiatrists. Liverpool. Available at: www.rcpsych.ac.uk/pdf/Dein%20The%20Faith%20of%20Patients.x.pdf. Accessed 18 February 2017.

Durham, C.W., Jr. 2013. State reactions to minority religions: a legal overview, in: D.M. Kirkham (ed.) *State Responses to Minority Religions*. Farnham: Ashgate, pp. 3–13.

Fox, J. 2008. *A World Survey of Religion and the State*. Cambridge: Cambridge University Press.

Gallagher, E.V. (ed.) 2016. *'Cult Wars' in Historical Perspective: New and Minority Religions*. London: Routledge.

Gilliat-Ray, S. 2003. Nursing, professionalism, and spirituality. *Journal of Contemporary Religion*, 18(3), 335–49.

Goldberg, L., W. Goldberg, R. Henry and M. Langone 2017. *Cult Recovery: A Clinician's Guide to Working with Former Members and Families*. Bonita Springs, FL: International Cultic Studies Association.

Grant, D., K. O'Neill and L. Stephens 2004. Spirituality in the workplace: new empirical directions in the study of the sacred. *Sociology of Religion*, 65(3), 265–83.

Grim, B.J. and R. Finke 2006. International religion indexes: government regulation, government favoritism, and social regulation of religion. *Interdisciplinary Journal of Research on Religion*, 2, 1–40.

Hassan, S. 1988. *Combatting Cult Mind-Control*. Rochester, VT: Park Street Press.

Heelas, P. and L. Woodhead 2005. *The Spiritual Revolution. Why Religion Is Giving Way to Spirituality*. Oxford: Blackwell.

Herbert, James D. and E.M. Forman (eds) 2011. *Acceptance and Mindfulness in Cognitive Behavior Therapy: Understanding and Applying the New Therapies*. Hoboken, NJ: John Wiley & Sons.

Introvigne, M. 1995. The secular anti-cult and the religious counter-cult movement: strange bedfellows or future enemies?, in: R. Towler (ed.) *New Religions and the New Europe*. Aarhus: Aarhus University Press, pp. 32–54.

Kearns, L. 2007. Religion and ecology in the context of globalization, in: P. Beyer and L. Beaman (eds) *Religion, Globalization, and Culture*. Leiden: Brill, pp. 305–34.

Kent, S.A. 2008. Contemporary uses of the brainwashing concept: 2000 to mid-2007. *Cultic Studies Review*, 7(2), 99–128.

Kilbourne, B. and J.T. Richardson 1984. Psychotherapy and new religions in a pluralistic society. *American Psychologist*, 39(3), 237–51.

Kirkham, D.M. (ed.) 2013. *State Responses to Minority Religions*. Farnham: Ashgate.

Koenig, H.G. 2013. *Spirituality in Patient Care. Why, How, When, and What*. 3rd ed. West Conshohocken, PA: Templeton Press.

La Fontaine, J. 1998. *Speak of the Devil*. Cambridge: Cambridge University Press.

La Fontaine, J. 2003. Satanic abuse: lessons from a controversy, in: J. A. Beckford and J. T. Richardson (eds) *Challenging Religion*. London: Routledge, pp. 91–101.

Langone, M.D. (ed.) 1993. *Recovery from Cults: Help for Victims of Psychological and Spiritual Abuse*. New York: W.W. Norton & Co.

Lifton, R.J. 1961. *Thought Reform and the Psychology of Totalism: A Study of 'Brainwashing' in China*. New York: Norton.

Lykes, V. and J.T. Richardson 2014. The European Court of Human Rights, minority religions, and new versus original member states, in: J.T. Richardson and F. Bellanger (eds) *Legal Cases, New Religious Movements, and Minority Faiths*. Farnham: Ashgate, pp. 171–201.

McCrea, R. 2010. *Religion and the Public Order of the European Union*. Oxford: Oxford University Press.

Melton, J.G. 2004. The fate of NRMs and their detractors in twenty-first century America, in: P.C. Lucas and T. Robbins (eds) *New Religious Movements in the 21st Century*. New York: Routledge, pp. 229–40.

Orchard, H. (ed.) 2001. *Spirituality in Health Care Contexts*. London: Jessica Kingsley.

Pargament, K.I. 2007. *Spiritually Integrated Psychotherapy: Understanding and Addressing the Sacred*. New York: Guilford Press.

Parry, J., M. Nesti, S. Robinson and N. Watson 2007. *Sport and Spirituality: An Introduction*. Abingdon: Routledge.

Peters, S.F. 2002. *Judging Jehovah's Witnesses. Religious Persecution and the Dawn of the Rights Revolution*. Lawrence, KS: University of Kansas Press.

Richardson, J.T. 1996. 'Brainwashing' claims and minority religions outside the United States: cultural diffusion of a questionable concept in the legal arena. *Brigham Young University Law Review*, 4, 873–904.

Richardson, J.T. (ed.) 2004. *Regulating Religion. Case Studies from around the Globe*. New York: Kluwer.

Richardson, J.T. 2015. Managing religion and the judicialization of religious freedom. *Journal for the Scientific Study of Religion*, 54(1), 1–19.

Richardson, J.T. and F. Bellanger (eds) 2014. *Legal Cases, New Religious Movements, and Minority Faiths*. Farnham: Ashgate.

Richardson, J.T. and M. Introvigne 2001. 'Brainwashing' theories in European parliamentary and administrative reports on 'cults' and 'sects'. *Journal for the Scientific Study of Religion*, 40(2), 143–68.

Robbins, T. and D. Anthony 1979. Cults, brainwashing and counter-subversion. *Annals of the American Academy of Political and Social Science*, 446, 78–90.

Robbins, T. and D. Anthony 1982. Deprogramming, brainwashing, and the medicalization of deviant religious groups. *Social Problems*, 29(3), 283–97.

Royal College of Psychiatrists 2013. *Recommendations for Psychiatrists on Spirituality and Religion. Position Statement PS03/2013.* London: Royal College of Psychiatrists.

Ruff, J.L. and C.H. Elliott 2016. An exploration of psychologists' possible bias in response to evangelical Christian patients: preliminary findings. *Spirituality in Clinical Practice*, 3(2), 115–26.

Sandberg, R. 2011. *Law and Religion.* Cambridge: Cambridge University Press.

Sandberg, R. 2014. *Religion, Law and Society.* Cambridge: Cambridge University Press.

Shupe, A.D. and D.G. Bromley (eds) 1994. *Anti-Cult Movements in Cross-Cultural Perspective.* Garland, TX: Garland Publishing Inc.

Shupe, A.D. and S.E. Darnell 2006. *Agents of Discord: Deprogramming, Pseudo-Science, and the American Anticult Movement.* Rutgers, NJ: Transaction.

Singer, M. 1979. Coming out of the cults. *Psychology Today*, January, 72–82.

Singer, M.T., M. Temerlin, and M.D. Langone1990. Psychotherapy cults. *Cultic Studies Journal*, 7(2), 101–12.

Spalek, B. and A. Imtoual (eds) 2008. *Religion, Spirituality and the Social Sciences. Challenging Marginalisation.* Bristol: Policy Press.

Stiles, M. 2007. *Ayurvedic Yoga Therapy.* Twin Lakes, WI: Lotus Press.

West, L.J. 1990. Persuasive techniques in contemporary cults: a public health approach. *Cultic Studies Journal*, 7, 126–49.

West, W. 2011. *Exploring Counselling, Spirituality and Healing.* Basingstoke: Palgrave Macmillan.

West, W. 2012. Addressing spiritual and religious issues in counselling and psychotherapy. *Thresholds*, Winter, 12–17.

West, L.J. and M.T. Singer 1980. Cults, quacks and non-professional psychotherapies, in: H. Kaplan and B. Sadock (eds) *Comprehensive Textbook of Psychiatry.* Baltimore: Williams and Wilkins, pp. 3245–58.

Wilson, B.R. 1996. Religious toleration, pluralism, and privatization, in: P. Repstad (ed.) *Religion and Modernity. Modes of Co-existence.* Oslo: Scandinavian University Press, pp. 11–34.

Zablocki, B. 2001. Towards a demystified and disinterested scientific theory of brainwashing, in: B. Zablocki and T. Robbins (eds) *Misunderstanding Cults. Searching for Objectivity in a Controversial Field.* Toronto, ON: University of Toronto Press, pp. 159–214.

Part I

Perspectives on counselling

2 From the curious to the criminal

Diocesan Advisers' requests for counsel and help

Pedr Beckley

Introduction

In the UK, new religious movements (NRMs) are not restricted to centres of large populations such as London, but are widespread, being located everywhere from major cities through every size of town to tiny rural communities. In each of these settings, people seek advice from Church of England clergy about NRMs, ranging from other clergy wanting help on whether the parish hall should be rented to a certain group, to members of the public concerned about a particular movement in which a member of their family has become involved. Advice and counselling are sought on a whole variety of movements, problematic situations and individual responses.

More than 20 years ago, the Church of England established a network of advisers across the country in order to help answer queries around NRMs, and I am one such Diocesan Adviser.[1] The first part of this chapter offers some reflections on the establishment and the success of this network. Then I offer some reflections on the type of work involved through the use of some (anonymised) case studies, before concluding with some thoughts on the future of this work. It is important to realise that most Diocesan Advisers, including myself, are not professionally trained counsellors but are serving clergy who have an interest in this work and who use their general skills to offer advice and, where possible, some counselling.

Diocesan Advisers

From Inform's founding in 1988, it has received some funding from the main Church denominations in the UK. The Church of England has donated the largest amount of money with the Catholic Church and the Free Churches (mostly the Methodists) also making some contribution. Alongside the Church of England's financial contribution came the intention that there would be an Adviser in each diocese in the country (a total of 43) to advise the public on NRMs, with additional advisers serving the Catholic and Methodist Churches as well as a few others across the other denominations. The Adviser would be a member of the clergy who was, to some extent, knowledgeable and interested in the area of NRMs – although not necessarily an expert. The Adviser's knowledge and interest often came through personal experience through contact with a movement itself or with families affected by contact with a movement. In my case, I was appointed to the role in Sheffield as I had already had considerable contact with a number of NRMs including the Jesus People and The Unification Church (UC). The idea behind the network was that in each area there would be someone who could offer helpful, practical advice and possibly some counselling where appropriate. Each of these advisers could then access the resources of Inform for all of the enquiries that came to them where they had little or no knowledge. It was hoped that, over time, these Diocesan Advisers would come to build a network that could helpfully encourage and assist each other, where one person might have a special interest in one area or a particular NRM, and so become a resource to others.

Although this intention was good, it was never achieved. At the start of the new millennium, I conducted some brief research to ascertain how effective this system of Diocesan Advisers was in practice. Sadly I found that it was very patchy and often completely ineffective. Of the 43 dioceses across the Church of England, approximately one-third did not have an Adviser at all; one-third had an Adviser who did not really want to do the job; and only one-third of the dioceses had an Adviser who wanted to do the job, and was active in both offering advice and learning about the different NRMs, the changing environment of the world of NRMs and their study.

Quite a few dioceses had not attempted to find someone to occupy this position. Without an appointed Adviser, many difficulties and questions in those dioceses went unanswered or additional enquiries went to Inform as that was almost the only other place to which to turn for help. Some enquirers approached organisations such as FAIR (Family, Action, Information, Resource)[2] and others went to Church House.[3] I suspect that the majority of enquiries in these dioceses simply went unanswered. Even allowing for the possibility that when I did my research, the person who had acted as an Adviser had moved on and the place was temporarily vacant, the overall impression was that almost all of these dioceses never had an Adviser and had no intention of finding one.

In the one-third of the dioceses that had an Adviser who did not want the job, most had been asked to do the job alongside some other commitment such as being an inter-faith adviser and had felt unable to say 'no' to their Bishop. Others, it seemed, made the mistake of 'looking up' in a meeting when the Bishop was asking for someone to do this job and so, in the words of one such person, 'copped it'! This created the problem that such people did not know enough to be able to offer advice and were very largely unwilling, or unable due to time constraints, to learn about NRMs. People contacting these Advisers often found them unhelpful or were simply instructed to ring Inform – better than nothing of course, but totally lacking in local help or encouragement.

The one-third of the dioceses in which the Adviser actually wanted to fulfil the role have provided a useful resource over many years, and some Advisers have become very knowledgeable in certain areas, or with a particular NRM that has been of concern in their diocese or that has become of special interest to that Adviser (for whatever reason). Many Advisers have grown in the job, starting from a small knowledge base (perhaps only having experience of a handful of NRMs) and over the years have developed a wide range of knowledge and experience as they have responded to queries about many different movements by many individuals, churches, other organisations and the police. The effectiveness of these Advisers in their dioceses should not be underestimated for they provide local, personal and face-to-face assistance that in many cases is much more effective than advice given via the phone or email.

One of the difficulties in this area of work is the lack of knowledge or interest by Diocesan Bishops who have many calls on their time, limited resources and always need to allocate time and financial resources to those needs that are considered the higher priorities in a diocese. Sadly, this is not often an NRM Adviser. Since little emphasis is placed on this work in the diocese I have never had any supervision from the hierarchy for this work, and others like me would echo this. This has been a weakness in the structure of this work but perhaps is not surprising in the light of all that have I said about the low priority that it has in almost every diocese in the country. On a more humorous note, and being most careful not to reveal which diocese, I was once invited to consider a job which was part-time parish and part-time Adviser on NRMs in the diocese. Three days before an informal visit to consider the job, the Bishop's secretary rang to say that the job was no longer available as the Bishop had discovered someone was already doing the job in the diocese! I later discovered that this person fitted into the middle third of dioceses that have an Adviser who does not want to do the job. Sadly, following a recent conversation with Church House, I got the impression that this picture of 'thirds' has not changed much in the intervening years in terms of active Advisers – except that there are now less 'inactive' dioceses and more without an Adviser at all.

From this rather bleak picture, I turn to some specific cases that have come my way over the years and which, I feel, illustrate the need for Diocesan Advisers. My diocese is far from unique; and the following cases illustrate the range of enquiries with which a Diocesan Adviser might be presented, the problems and difficulties that arise and the often unsatisfactory conclusions to many of the discussions and, to some extent, the counselling that follow.

The Nine O'Clock Service

As the Adviser in Sheffield, I must mention the Nine O'Clock Service (NOS) that took place first at St. Thomas' Crookes[4] and then in the new Ponds Forge swimming complex. NOS was a radical approach to worship based around a rock group which encouraged a communal lifestyle. It appealed to students and other young people as it was immersed in their culture, but it also used the historic Church of England as a source for liturgy and spirituality. It became a media sensation in 1995 when allegations around the sexual behaviour of the leader, Chris Brain, came to light. This was the final in a series of revelations about the movement that very rapidly led to its demise, although earlier signs that all was not well with the movement had largely been ignored by those in the Church hierarchy. These signs included Brain's controlling behaviour towards members, his secrecy and his lack of accountability. Those who pointed out these earlier signs were shunned and informed that all was well because the then Archdeacon was attending and had the movement under control. The sexual impropriety allegations were not as extreme as the press tried to portray, but they were the tipping point that brought the whole enterprise down.

To my mind, there are two things which are particularly sad about this case. First, the extraordinarily creative and imaginative innovation of the new type of service that NOS created was something that the Church of England clearly needed in terms of relating the faith to modern culture. With the demise of NOS, much of that creative energy and inspiration was lost or treated with acute suspicion which still has an effect today.

Second, although warning signs about the 'cult like behaviour' of Chris Brain (such as his controlling behaviour towards members of the church) were pointed out by myself, other clergy and lay people to the Bishop, Archdeacon and the Diocesan Director of Ordinands, those concerns were not taken seriously, as a number of prominent theologians and church leaders gave NOS their enthusiastic support. It was as though they were so blinded by the stellar brilliance of the NOS innovation that they did not conceive of the possibility that they had a real problem in their midst. Most of these people seemed to find it very difficult, if not impossible, to conceive of such a controlling behaviour in the Church of England which has, generally speaking, systems in place to keep clergy in line with suitable accountability, not least in the selection of people for ordination.

In my role as Adviser, along with others, I tried to make the point to various senior people in the diocese that it was inappropriate that Chris Brain should be so 'fast-tracked' in his ordination, by-passing the usual assessments and careful observations that might pick up on character traits that could lead to problems in the future. By not serving a proper curacy in another parish after ordination, one complete layer of assessment was swept away. Such a mad rush to ordain a 'star' overlooked certain things that were often hard to identify with clarity because of the way in which Chris Brain controlled the whole of NOS, making it difficult to come up with hard evidence that could persuade the senior leadership that all was not well. Discovering that Brain had modelled the cassock in which he was to be ordained on the one in the film "The Mission" rang alarm bells amongst some clergy, including myself, that were simply ignored by those higher in the Church hierarchy, including the Diocesan Director of Ordinands, who assesses and makes recommendations for prospective ordination candidates. Later it turned out that theological students were writing Brain's ordination training essays for him, and this should have been spotted; but again the urgency to ordain such a creative and extraordinary man bypassed the usual checks.

When the debacle came out into the open, I found myself totally sidelined by the Archdeacon who did not want NOS to be seen as a 'cult' – even though it was so branded by the media. By keeping me away from all contact with NOS members, it was as though the Archdeacon was doing his utmost to make sure that the label was a media invention and was not something with which the Church of England agreed. The problem was that an Adviser like myself who could have helped (having had experience of strongly controlling movements) was denied the chance to do so. This was disgraceful and a failure by the diocese to offer a certain level of care that should have been given to individuals going through a very traumatic time. I did manage to give some advice to a couple of people who were designated as counsellors to those who were in need, even though they were not professionally trained counsellors, just clergy like myself. Later some people did find their way to some specialised help, but more could have been done from the start.

Roland Howard, in his book *The Rise and Fall of the Nine O'Clock Service*, writes, 'Others within the membership pleaded with Archdeacon to contact "cult experts", who would have the expertise to help people. Although there is a diocesan officer with responsibility for working with cult victims he was never contacted' (1996: 134).

Having an Adviser on NRMs is great – but only if they are used.

Necromancy – or not?

For the most part, Diocesan Advisers' work consists of routine matters such as responding to clergy, unfamiliar with a particular group, who anxiously enquire whether it should be permitted to meet in their church hall. Then there are the enquiries from families concerned about their (generally) young relatives joining an NRM. Do they need to be concerned? Will they ever see them again? Will they lose all their money? But every now and again something unexpected arises and receives some media attention as a result. Sometimes Advisers are as baffled as everyone else, and sometimes their knowledge can ease the situation and lead to reconciliation or some other benefit. The following case was certainly unexpected and to this day, in 2016, is at least partially unresolved. It illustrates the need for an Adviser who, even if they do not have all the answers, can give useful guidance to those involved.

In 1996 I was called to a shocking incident. Early one morning a man had been out walking his dog when the dog started playing with what turned out to be a human head. The owner of the dog thought it was a dummy and pulled the dog away but on closer inspection, realised that it was in fact a real human head. He immediately phoned the police. The police at first thought that a particularly gruesome murder had been committed but soon realised that the head showed signs of having been embalmed. They were therefore dealing with a grave robbery, not a murder.

The deceased man had been buried in a woodland burial site near Rotherham in an unmarked grave where, eventually, a tree was to be planted to mark the site. Sometime after the burial, the owner of the site noticed that the ground above the coffin had been disturbed but, as there were no obvious problems, did not take any action. It later became apparent that this was an initial investigation by the perpetrators to discover which was the 'head end' of the coffin. About a week later they returned, dug down and chopped through the coffin, severing the head and leaving behind various crudely drawn occult symbols. These symbols suggested that the perpetrators were almost certainly young and without any real knowledge of what they were doing – probably having read something in a book or magazine and copied it, badly. As mentioned above, the head was discovered twenty miles away, the following day, by the dog on its early morning walk.

The shock to the family and to the police should not be underestimated. I attended the exhumation of the rest of the body early on a very cold, snowy February morning and began to offer advice and help where I could. This involved dealing with both professionals and lay people.

First, there were the family members themselves, who were doubly upset and grieving. They had lost a loved member of the family whom they had laid to rest, only to discover that the body had been brutalised. They were in deep shock and traumatised. Later they had a very private cremation, after all had quietened down and the police had finished with their enquiries.

Second, I was dealing with police officers who were at first unsure about what, if any, crime had been committed. I spent a few hours with a number of officers trying to help them come to terms with what had happened and to shed some light on what I thought probably had been going on. This was partly to help them narrow down who they might be looking for in connection with the event. The police seemed to find it difficult to grasp the nature of the incident and to understand the possible explanation of an amateurish occult practice.

Third, the owners of the woodland burial site were also distraught about what had happened. They were worried that if it got into the press (which of course it did), they would have no more requests for burial at that site.

Fourth, I dealt with the media. I was interviewed by print journalists and on the radio, both local and national, and found it rather an odd experience as, for once, many of the journalists did not really know what questions to ask. For them, as for everyone else, this was so out of the ordinary that the usual frame of reference for a story for their paper or radio station was thrown.

In this particular case the counselling and help that was given was only partially successful, and there were loose ends that to my knowledge have never been tidied up. No one was arrested for the events that took place and for many of those involved there has never been a satisfactory closure and full explanation. Over time, and seemingly quite rapidly for the media and police, things move on and other events take over. However, the lasting damage remains with the relatives who understandably did not want any more press involvement and wanted to put things behind them as quickly as possible.

In a way this event does not fit into the ordinary work of a Diocesan Adviser as no known NRM was involved. The religious aspect was tenuous and crude, almost experimental and, it seems, without real understanding of what was being done. But, without an Adviser being available, the situation would have been harder to handle and cope with. Unintentionally, the police and media might have put more pressure on the grieving relatives. Not all situations result in completely satisfactory outcomes, but Diocesan Advisers do what they can, and this case illustrates the value of their availability for circumstances when some help is better than none. My role in this case was not so much counselling as such, more helping different people to understand something about what had happened and to take some of the media burden away from the grieving relatives.

Leaving a South Asian-based group

My final case illustrates other aspects of Diocesan Advisers' work. The bulk of Advisers' work is answering basic queries about a group, and just occasionally advice and help is sought by the parents of those who have joined an NRM, seeking answers to a variety of questions concerning their child(ren). Relatively infrequently, Diocesan Advisers are contacted by individuals or couples that are part of an NRM who either want to leave or have already left and are concerned for their future. The following case concerns a couple who belonged to a South Asian-based group, but for reasons that will become obvious below, both the couple and the group itself will remain anonymous here.

I was contacted by a man who wanted to talk through his involvement in a South Asian NRM that he had been a part of for some years and who had married a woman he had met in this group. A talented musician and craftsman, he had been involved in both construction work at the guru's house and in organising many of the group's activities including pujas, both in India and in England. Like many who belong to religious movements, he gradually discovered that all was not perfect in the organisation or with the leader or guru. What an individual does with that realisation varies enormously, from leaving to trying to resolve difficulties or simply putting up with it and recognising that 'no one is perfect'.

In this case, the discrepancy between the ideals, beliefs and the practices of the organisation and, in particular, the conduct of the main leader and those immediately below the leader in the organisational hierarchy, led to this couple leaving the NRM. As they had given their whole lives to this movement, the couple struggled with many aspects of a return to a life outside the movement. They also had information that made their lives extremely difficult. Their knowledge included alleged criminal activity that they referred to police at an international level. The result of the police investigation was that the individuals felt the need to create entirely new identities for themselves in order not to be discovered by the group. New names and a new address were just part of the change that they felt was utterly essential for their future safety and well-being. As the couple felt that they could be attacked by current members, they, quite justifiably, went to great lengths to preserve their safety and security.

This couple was seeking a multilayered comprehensive breadth of help. There was the adjustment to a new life outside of a movement that had been central to their lives for years, to which they had given time, money, emotion and huge efforts – an adjustment that was complicated and lengthy. It involved gaining employment and re-engaging with family and friends (wherever that was still possible) and deciding where to live and where to send their children to school. On the positive side, they had acquired skills during their time in the movement and these skills were put to profitable use after leaving.

In addition, they felt the need to talk about the situation in which they had been involved and report all that they knew about the conduct of certain individuals in the movement which, in some cases, was of a criminal nature. This was both in order to help the police investigation but also to help others to either not join the movement or to leave. Telling others about what had gone on was a cathartic experience for the couple as their specific knowledge became for them a serious burden to carry. The sense that a great injustice was not being rectified and that the perpetrators were not being held accountable led to the divulgence of their information to the relevant authorities. The downside to this was a greatly increased sense of risk and fear for the couple due to the potential for a current member to seek revenge or retaliation for revealing this information. As one of the allegations against this group was that a member had murdered an individual, this was taken extremely seriously by the police.

In this case, there was greater tension than usual when people leave a movement. The more they talked about the activities that had gone on in the movement, the more they increased the risk to their personal safety. To have gone quietly and simply 'disappeared' from the movement would have had little impact on their sense of safety. But because they were courageous and chose to talk to the authorities, they increased their risk.

The help I offered in this case was limited as at that point I had only been an Adviser for a few years and was still learning a great deal about the work. I also had no professional counselling qualifications and therefore what I initially attempted to do was to assist the couple to pass on their information to the relevant people. Part of the help I offered was to attempt to assist them in coming to terms with leaving an organisation that had played such a major part in their lives for so many years. Picking up the pieces of a former life (where that is feasible or even desired) is never easy as people and situations have moved on and re-engagement can never consist of simply continuing where they left off some years before. In this couple's case, this was extremely complicated because of the need to change their identities, and therefore much of what might have been possible in re-engaging for others leaving a movement, was simply impossible. They subsequently struggled with having to change their names, moving to a new area where they did not know anyone, finding work and raising children – and raising children is another level of complication that poses its own set of difficulties.

Another aspect of coming out of a movement, which this case illustrates, is the sense of betrayal and disillusionment if/when it is discovered that the leader or guru, or those under them, are not themselves living a life consistent with the group's beliefs and practices. For some, there can be a feeling that they have been duped into believing something that they now think is false. For others, the belief remains and is seen as true and valuable while the teacher is seen as at fault. In such cases, there can therefore be considerable value left in the positive things gained in the movement, while setting aside the negative things. With this particular couple there were positive things gained from the movement. For example, the man had met and married a woman from the movement – though not the person that the guru had initially wanted him to marry. But the cumulative negative side led to more problems and a much longer period of time coming to terms with the experience.

A Diocesan Adviser can help an individual to separate the completely negative from the partially negative as well as to identify the positive. Working with the individual or couple, the Adviser can sometimes help them evaluate their experiences, including world travel and practical skills acquired and, through this, enable them to see what can be accepted as positive or beneficial for the future. Quite often such counsel evolves over time, as the individual comes to terms with different aspects of their involvement in an NRM, moving sometimes from viewing everything in a negative way, to understanding that there can be some positives that can then be used helpfully in the future. In the case discussed above, changing identity was both very helpful but also limiting, as one or two avenues that could have been open to someone else leaving a movement, were not options available to them. Due to the fact that they were moving on into their new life, counselling help in this case proved unsatisfactory as it had to be cut short or otherwise limited.

Some general reflections on religion in Sheffield

During my years as a Diocesan Adviser, the work has changed considerably as movements of concern have either ceased to be a problem or have moved away from Sheffield (of course the work will be different again somewhere as large and as cosmopolitan as London). Groups such as The Unification Church simply have no influence in Sheffield as they once did. One of the major causes of public worry some years ago was the Jesus Army, who would set up a huge tent in a local park and, by their marching in combat clothing, were perceived as a considerable threat. But they have changed: the camouflaged coloured clothing has been changed to bright rainbow coloured clothing, they have taken over an old church and have become synonymous not with strident evangelism, but with social action reaching the marginalised and poor in ways that many others simply do not. In other words, as time passed, they changed, and now the perceived threat or anxiety they used to cause has gone.

Some well-known movements that caused concern in other areas never had a base in Sheffield, such as the International Churches of Christ that targeted university cities but, for whatever reason, did not come to Sheffield and therefore produced only a minimal number of queries for my work. ISKCON (the International Society for Krishna Consciousness) have a presence in Sheffield but no temple. Similarly, Scientology have no base in Sheffield, although they occasionally hold events in the city (such as a concert held in 2008 which promoted their anti-drugs campaign) which are then used as a vehicle to publicise Dianetics and their other teachings. Few people seem to become interested and, therefore, from my perspective, little concern is raised and there are few enquiries.

People from Sheffield and the surrounding area have a low response to any religion, including 'familiar' churches such as the Church of England, the Methodists or Roman Catholics. Indeed, in the area, some of the lowest church attendances are recorded in the whole of the UK. This may go some way to explain why many NRMs have no base in Sheffield and have only a very small number of individuals interested in such movements. Neither of the two universities in Sheffield has had the sorts of major problems over the years which have occurred in some other parts of the country, such as NRMs recruiting on campus or attempting to hire rooms by not being fully transparent about their true identity.

In recent years the biggest change (in terms of newer religious movements) has been the arrival from various African states of individuals bringing their religions (mostly variants of Christianity) with them. African expressions of Christianity are often markedly different from forms more traditional to the UK, and I have received a number of enquiries on this. The Church of England has some quite specific rules about who or what organisations can use a church for services.[5] The advice given in relation to this is theological, concerning beliefs and whether, for example, a church is Trinitarian.

Concerns exist with some of these new groups – concerns over the protection and safety of children have been paramount in various cities in recent years. For some groups wishing to use church premises, having passed any test on orthodoxy, the only major concern is that they have sufficient child safety measures in place and that they adhere to them. This becomes the most important aspect of the advice given to those seeking information on such groups wishing to use premises.

As the sorts of NRMs that have concerned people have changed, so have the individuals that are a worry to parents. In recent years I have had almost no student-aged individuals who, either through their parents or by themselves, have made contact with me concerning an NRM. Compared to the 1960s and 1970s, students nowadays seem to me to be less motivated by those idealistic dreams that used to result in demonstrations against apartheid or 'ban the bomb' or some such passionate political or social action. Similarly, they are less attracted to world-changing movements with a religious content. Most students, under pressure to achieve a good degree to justify the high student fees, are more concerned with study and some socialising or, in many cases, balancing all that with the need to have a part-time job to make ends meet. There seems little time left for idealistic dreaming of changing the world. As a result, what used to take a considerable amount of my time in attempting to help either the parents of a young person attracted to an NRM or the young person themselves, has now dwindled to almost nothing and, when this has occurred in recent years, it has actually been a serious mental health problem that has resulted in either joining a group or expressing a religious conviction in a manner that is clearly the product of mental instability in one form or another.

What has changed (and in marked contrast to even just ten years ago) is that much more of my work comes under the umbrella of mental health than previously. Even as I write these words in 2016, a new case has just arrived where the individual has been sectioned[6] and which will undoubtedly result in a complicated relationship with family and mental health carers, where the input of a Diocesan Adviser may help just a little bit in the eventual outcome for this particular person. This illustrates the increasing relationship between mental health professionals and my work, where strange religiously motivated behaviour is expressed in a sometimes uncomprehending secular environment. In one or two cases this has, in part, been related to the upsurge in use of the internet, where individuals have become immersed in a religious ideology or system, but have done this entirely online and therefore without any social context that might have shaped or at least modified that behaviour.

Conclusions

The work of Diocesan Advisers in the Church of England in the area of NRMs is very varied. Regional differences mean that different movements are of concern in different areas. Perhaps only London will have almost everything to cope with, while in Sheffield there are certain notable absences even though, like in any area, it has its own unique concerns – in this case, the NOS. Over time the Adviser's work has changed considerably and not just in terms of which NRMs are dealt with, but the very type of work that is encountered, such as the growth of mental health issues.

NRM Advisers depend on Inform for their knowledgeable database and on staff that assist us when we come across something that we know little or nothing about. Occasionally we can contribute to that knowledge resource by adding something new that may be of use to others. It would have been nice in this somewhat personal reflection on the work to be able to say that it always works out satisfactorily in the end, but the very nature of the work means that this is often not the case as most advisory work is extremely complex and, where people and situations move on, there can be untidy loose ends.

Much of the work that we do is often advisory and not counselling. I have mentioned the sorts of questions that are asked by clergy and others concerning the use of premises and the suitability of sharing in some activity with a particular NRM. Other work is on the edge of counselling where an Adviser acts as a conduit that enables a person to obtain suitable medical help, particularly in the mental health area. Some of the work would be better described as being a media or communications officer. Part of the work is teaching others about NRMs so that they are aware of the variety of religious movements. A small part of the work is what one might call counselling, albeit without a formal counselling qualification, but is more in line with the pastoral care of individuals that clergy deal with on a day to day basis. The only difference is that it has as its focus a particular situation influenced by an NRM, but it will often resemble situations involving such circumstances as grief, parenting, relationships and so on. Much of the work, like a lot of pastoral care, consists of simply being a good listener. However, knowledge of a particular NRM can often help in identifying the particular needs of the individual seeking help and providing insights that may assist the situation. Sometimes this is to help the individual(s) to vocalise their jumbled thoughts and feelings into some sort of coherent whole that simply helps them to feel that by doing so, they have regained control of that aspect of their lives. I have sometimes found that by listening and almost saying nothing, the individual talks themselves into an understanding of the situation that enables them to see the way forward that is appropriate for them. In other cases, what is needed is being able to place their experience in a much wider context so that they can understand 'the bigger picture'. In one case I dealt with a man whose daughter had joined an NRM and had no intention of leaving, so help to him was about managing his feelings and emotions – in short his sense of loss or grief over his daughter that he might never (or very rarely) see again.

Diocesan Advisers have, in the opinion of this Adviser, advanced the understanding of NRMs across the country, and it is a cause for regret that duly appointed Diocesan Advisers are not found in every diocese.

Notes

1 The Church of England is divided up into administrative districts called Dioceses that are supervised by a Bishop.
2 FAIR is 'Family, Action, Information, Resource' and is a 'cult' watching group based in the UK that in 2007 became the 'Family Survival Trust' – current website at www.familysurvivaltrust.org/.
3 Church House is the headquarters of the Archbishops' Council, the Church Commissioners and all its Boards and Councils as well as of the Church of

England Pensions Board and the National Society. It is also one of the meeting-places of the General Synod of the Church of England, the other being York.

4 St. Thomas' Crookes Church is one of the parishes in Sheffield characterised by lively charismatic worship.

5 The rules for use of a church are governed by "The Canons of the Church of England" which are updated each year. Rule B43 "Of relations with other Churches" is one that applies in this case.

6 That is, admitted to and kept in hospital under the Mental Health Act 1983 for the individual's own health and safety and/or for the protection of others. Consent does not have to be obtained from the individual.

References

Nine O'Clock service: Howard, R. 1996. *The Rise and Fall of the Nine O'Clock Service: A Cult within the Church?* London: Mowbray.

Severed head case – one example of press coverage: The Independent (21 February 1996) 'Body Exhumed in Severed Head Case'. Available at www.independent.co.uk/news/body-exhumed-in-severed-head-case-1320078.html (Accessed 6 June 2017).

The Canons of the Church of England (last updated January 2017). Available at www.churchofengland.org/about-us/structure/churchlawlegis/canons.aspx (Accessed 6 June 2017).

3 Enlightened or insane? Insights and dilemmas of wearing a psychotherapist's hat and a sociological hat in the field of new religious movements

Silke Steidinger

Introduction

It's complicated.

Let's keep it like that.

I currently work at Inform as an assistant research officer with a Master's degree in sociology, as a UKCP[1] registered attachment-based psychoanalytic psychotherapist in private practice, and as a psychotherapist in a National Health Service (NHS) Personality Disorders (PD) service, which offers a specialised two-year treatment consisting of group and individual mentalisation-based therapy (MBT) and psychiatric services. This is a personal paper motivated by a desire to juggle, balance and get the most out of three different work perspectives with regards to new religious movements (NRMs) and counselling.

It cannot be said that sociology and psychotherapy started off on the right foot when it comes to NRMs. The so-called 'cult wars', 'cult deaths', the anti-cult movement (ACM), 'Satanic Panics', the 'brainwashing' or 'mind control' metaphors and 'deprogramming' practices – including kidnapping – have not been conducive to collaborative efforts between sociologists and psychotherapists, and might have contributed to suspicion on both sides. The result is that, on the one hand, many psychotherapists still have prejudices about minority religions, and on the other, organisations and researchers with objective expertise on NRMs often struggle when it comes to providing help or recommendations to those who need more support than factual information.

When Professor Eileen Barker founded Inform, an independent research and information centre focusing on minority religions, in order to reduce the unnecessary suffering that she had observed, she attributed much of the suffering to a lack of objective information about NRMs. Whilst Inform was founded specifically to bring some of the findings of academia down from the 'ivory towers', it does not offer or recommend any form of counselling.

Therefore some of the issues that Inform grapples with centre on how to deal with distressed individuals, who to refer them to, and questions about a whole sector within counselling that specialises in 'exit' or 'reform' counselling. Inform also focuses on the widespread assumption that seeing a specialist counsellor is best for those affected by a 'cult'.[2] Inform tries to perform a balancing act between *Verstehen* (empathic understanding) and methodological agnosticism, which is similar to contemporary psychotherapeutic approaches, and might indicate that the two fields are growing closer together again. NRMs are situated at an intense intersection between sociology and psychotherapy where lots of nerves intersect, creating sensitive areas, intense reactions and blind spots. Put your seatbelts on.

As psychotherapists, we usually encounter religion and NRMs as one of many issues, and tend to see them as one of many aspects of an individual that we try to treat holistically. The main issues I have encountered here are around practitioners' prejudices, agency, conflicting paradigms and concepts such as 'brainwashing' and 'mind control'.

As a therapist I offer a treatment which is a clinical intervention. Inform, on the other hand, has an explicit policy of not providing or recommending any particular kind of therapy. One of the reasons for this is to keep a distance from the object of research where there is an overlap between the field of NRMs and therapies. For example, Triratna runs Mindfulness-Based Cognitive Therapy courses, Scientology offers auditing, and AA Twelve Step programmes require a spiritual element, to name but a few which are further explored in this volume. Further, Inform follows this policy in order to maintain a non-interventionist stance (apart from a commitment to report seriously illegal matters to the police).

Additionally, Eileen[3] did not feel able to recommend one therapy over another – the field of counselling is a supermarket similar to the 'religious supermarket' (Beckford 2014). There are 'sectarian' splits, and the training organisations themselves have at times been compared to 'cults'. The PD service and Inform both have quite clearly defined foci and limitations; attachment-based psychoanalytic psychotherapy tries to combine psychoanalytic concepts and external social factors from the outset and, partly because of this, might have vulnerabilities when it comes to NRMs in clinical work.

This means I am trying to make sense of three different settings with the aid of three different perspectives that sometimes clash, and sometimes enrich each other. Working with the different epistemologies of Inform, a PD service and attachment-based psychoanalytic psychotherapy can be like looking through a kaleidoscope, separate microscopes or a blurred or sharp 3D image.[4] Bear with me.

'Cults'

My first experience with 'cults' consisted of my parents warning me about these 'dangerous groups' that were on the news because of involvement with brainwashing, murders, sex and suicides. My friend's mother told us that whilst shopping she was approached by a dangerous group – she told us they 'brainwash' you and said we should stay away from Scientology or Dianetics. And that we should avoid the Jehovah's Witnesses with their Watchtower magazines just the same. Another friend's boyfriend left for university and then joined the Hare Krishnas. Our parents said he had 'joined a cult', and this was bad news. He dressed differently, became vegetarian and stopped eating onions. We were annoyed (mainly because cooking with him became a pain) and suspicious. We looked down on him, but were probably also secretly curious and envious. We thought he was lost to this dangerous group and was wasting his life. Well, he eventually left, graduated from university and today works as a pharmacist. He still looks back on his International Society for Krishna Consciousness (ISKCON) time as an important part of his life and of who he is today.

These groups and movements brought the unknown to our small town in the 1990s, and often triggered strong reactions. They caused many people to 'split': to revert to a rigid, prejudiced and dualistic way of thinking. This is somewhat understandable, but often unhelpful and can become quite toxic very quickly and contagiously. These groups also, however, aroused curiosity in others, who welcomed the arrival of something different with a certain calmness, but without necessarily joining or demonising. I will try to shed some light on the processes involved here in this chapter.

A Bachelor of Arts in comparative Religious Studies later, I remember getting annoyed when some friends had gone to a Landmark Forum/est (Erhard Seminar Training) event and were enthusiastically trying to get me and other friends to transfer money to sign up to the next weekend seminar, partly because they were asked to do so by the group, but also because they thought the seminars were 'amazing' and 'life-changing'. I refused. Some friends signed up, but after some thought and discussion, they asked for a refund, and got it. Others went, and some found it annoying, some found it 'amazing'. There was definitely pressure, both passed down from the group and even from our friends' enthusiasm. But we all had a choice.

Agency

Or did we? One of the questions is whether in fact there always is a choice, especially when it comes to more vulnerable individuals – even though not all NRMs encourage suicide or murder, some can nevertheless cause harm to some people. The following is an example that is relatively benign but provided me with experiential insight: During field research for a Master of Social Science (MSc) in Religion in Contemporary Society taught by Professor Barker at The London School of Economics, I 'found' myself applauding a picture of L. Ron Hubbard, Scientology's founder, at a Scientology Sunday Service.

So you have probably realised that I am not so keen on peer pressure and that I pride myself on being able to resist it. Well, I really didn't want to clap to L. Ron, but I did. Why? It was a baffling experience for me.

On reflection, I did feel pressured by the Scientologist leading the service and by the environment and others present, but what also played a role were my own prejudices and projections driven by anti-cult and media reports warning about dangerous cults, and my upbringing. After the event I felt quite ashamed and angry about 'having been made' to do this. In fact nobody made me do anything: I was the one who decided to go to a Scientology Service, I stood up and clapped. Yes there was some pressure, mainly what felt like peer pressure or pressure to socially conform, but I was the one giving in to this pressure. Some cannot bear the feelings arising from such an experience, and this might contribute to 'scapegoating' a cult – for many the only option is to split this off from oneself and project onto the group, ridding oneself of responsibility. This tends to happen outside of the individual's awareness.

During a similar research trip to a meditation drop-in at the Friends of the Western Buddhist Order (FWBO) (now Triratna, offering Mindfulness Cognitive Behavioural Therapy), I enjoyed the meditation but felt wary yet curious about the Buddhist rituals and chanting in which it was embedded. More recently, in 2014, I went to the Annual Gala of the International Association of Scientologists on an Inform research trip and got mild flashbacks for several days after what felt like having been 'bombarded' by images and loud speeches by their leader, David Miscavige, giving data on Scientology's widespread aid programmes (nothing here is black and white).[5] I have experienced 'the pull' as well and am no longer 'allowed' to go to Jehovah's Witnesses events since I returned completely 'loved up' after their annual convention, jokingly wanting to join (Inform's policy is not to employ a members of NRMs). What I am trying to say is that I have experienced some of the dynamics exerted by some NRMs, and how they can influence us to behave 'out of character' or 'against one's will', even though the concepts of agency and integrity get quite complicated here. Arguably, the more secure an individual is, the less susceptible they are likely to be in relation to such dynamics. Even if influenced temporarily, having a degree of secure attachment should shorten the time it takes for someone to become aware of a shift and to adjust their behaviour and thinking to be more in line with their values, character and world-view.

People join and leave NRMs in many different ways and for many different reasons. Often people think someone must be 'insane' to join a cult. This is not so (even though any religious belief might seem 'insane' in a secular society). Research has shown that the majority of NRM members show no signs of mental illness (and interestingly an estimated 66 per cent of British society has a secure attachment style [Bowlby 1969] meaning that they have a positive view of others and themselves, expect a positive and attuned response from others to their own attachment behaviour and are able to form stable and meaningful relationships), and that membership of some groups can contribute to well-being. Often, however, a potential convert can be vulnerable or going through a difficult time, and stumble across an NRM, searching for help or not, and get involved.

This raises clinical issues regarding agency. Do individuals know what is best for them? Should friends and relatives take decisions behind their back supposedly for the convert's own benefit? Does the therapist know what the client *really* wants and needs?

Methodology as a 'secure base'

I should also say that the MSc course, Eileen's guidance and the methodology of methodological agnosticism, *Verstehen* and the social scientific method allowed me to feel safe and grounded enough to allow myself to fully experience the gatherings, without feeling harmed by any of them, or wanting to join any of them. This has similarities to my psychotherapy training – teachers and training organisations should provide a secure base from which a trainee can explore herself/himself, and allow oneself to experientially be pulled into the client's dynamics, whilst learning how to stay grounded and safe. It also reminds me of the concept of the internal and external 'secure base' termed by John Bowlby (1988), a British psychoanalyst who conceptualised and emphasised the importance of attachment in human development and well-being. Having a secure base enables exploration because one knows one has a place, person or group to return to should something go wrong. It is a different situation if an individual does not have a secure base but is searching for this in a group.

Splitting, the paranoid/schizoid position and the scientific study of religion

These research trips and the MSc course started giving me quite a different perspective on NRMs, mainly because of first-hand experience, and the social scientific method. One of the first things Eileen taught us was that you can only generalise one thing about NRMs – that you cannot generalise about them, and that people do tend to generalise about them.

Reflecting back on this now, having qualified as a psychotherapist, it is quite common when faced with a group that is unknown, different and having a strong effect on its environment, to react driven by a specific *modus operandi*. Typically this is characterised by broad brush strokes, suspicion, paranoia, projective identification (for example evacuating one's fear and anger into another person), splitting (for instance by seeing 'all of those groups' as 'cults that control, brainwash and harm'), and reverting to prejudiced and rigid thinking. This is part of what Melanie Klein (1946) termed the 'paranoid/schizoid position' which is the early binary psychological mode of an infant, followed by the 'depressive position' which is a more nuanced developmental achievement, involving more reality testing and being able to tolerate a range of challenging and conflicting emotions.

The paranoid/schizoid position is driven by the part of the brain called the amygdala and is useful in 'fight or flight' situations, but maladaptive otherwise. We revert to it when stressed or upset. Some of us never quite made this developmental quantum leap, for various reasons, which means that some people generally operate in the paranoid/schizoid mode. It involves what we call 'failures in mentalising' in the PD service which I will come back to later.

Uncertainty and anxiety can trigger this in some of us as well, and this might be related to sociologist Bryan Wilson's explanation of what can make NRMs so attractive: the fact that they offer 'a surer, shorter, swifter, clearer way to salvation' (Wilson 1990: 205).

I remember being anxious when we had to go to three NRMs by ourselves for our assignment, but Eileen encouraged us to experientially explore and observe with openness and curiosity, but equipped with guidelines to stay safe and ethical. She taught us to experience the dynamics and everything else and use them as data in the spirit of *Verstehen*, and then leave (and not join!), analyse, get further data and perspectives and write about it – as objectively and non-judgmentally as possible, in the spirit of methodological agnosticism. This continues to be the practice at Inform. We also advise seekers to be mindful of what they are getting into from the start. We listen to members, former members, academics, critics and the researcher's experiential data from *Verstehen*, and then apply the methods of social science and produce reports integrating all perspectives, in an attempt to get as close to reality as possible. This is similar to processes involved in the development of a healthy sense of self and integrity.

So one could say Inform operates in the 'depressive position', which was possibly named as such because it involves being able to see reality with all its nuances and paradoxes and which requires the ability to bear the frustration, pain and sadness that comes with that, rather than projecting unbearable feelings on to others. It is also fitting because it puts the 'depressing' into Inform's 'depressive position approach', considering that Inform and those remaining objective about NRMs have often been called 'cult apologists' and have been viciously attacked for not jumping on the ACM/mind-control bandwagon. This reaction itself could be categorised as splitting or a paranoid/schizoid way of operating, which often causes a very angry reaction when something cannot be fitted into one of the binary categories. Inform remains a secure, solid base and as such manages not to engage in 'deviance amplification' (Wilkins 1964) or enactments.

Conscious splitting at the methodological level, however, can, despite its limitations, create clarity. This is what I have observed in my work for Inform and in MBT. This kind of splitting limits the focus and therefore sharpens it, knows its limitations and is also more able to engage in a clear dialectical process with other disciplines. Attachment-based psychoanalytic psychotherapy seems more vulnerable to prejudice about NRMs and using the mind control paradigm. Perhaps trying to combine internal and external factors from the outset, as well as a strong focus on trauma, also plays a role in this. Its focus on relationships can, however, give a deeper insight into sociological concepts like *Verstehen* and charisma, which is partly why I decided to train as a psychotherapist.

Conceptual and methodological issues: sociology, psychoanalysis and psychotherapy

The mindset and techniques of a psychoanalytic psychotherapist are very different from the methodology of the social sciences. In the footsteps of Freud (he himself left neurology behind before founding psychoanalysis), psychotherapists work with the unconscious, with affect and emotions, within a therapeutic relationship, trying to understand someone else's mind, with the coming together of transference and countertransference.[6] In contrast to psychotherapeutic techniques based on empathy, sociological *Verstehen* is limited since sociologists usually have not gone through psychotherapy training which, among other things, focuses on the trainee learning to understand their emotional responses (countertransference). Psychoanalytic work is by its nature somewhat difficult to grasp and to measure because there is an element of speculation involved when working with the unconscious, and listening to one's intuition, thoughts and feelings. This was especially so in traditional psychoanalytic approaches which give more authority and interpretive power to the therapist and are obviously quite at odds with the early social scientific study of religion modelled on the natural sciences and empirical falsifiability (Popper 1963). Sociology has itself gone through change and the development of different strands, and the scientific study of religion itself is very complex (Barker 2003): Durkheim's positivism applied the natural sciences to human activity in order to establish causality,[7] which could be seen as an attempt to split off and carve out a new field, and seems incompatible with psychoanalytic thinking. This is probably what led Karl Popper (1963) to call psychoanalysis a 'pseudoscience'. Weber, on the other hand, introduced the concept of *Verstehen* and qualitative methods. These two strands might represent two sides of a dialectic process, and researchers nowadays mix and match quantitative and qualitative methods depending on what is best suited for the study and circumstances.

Contemporary psychotherapy, especially attachment-based and relational strands, has moved to a more egalitarian approach where the therapist is no longer seen as 'the healthy expert' administering the 'cure' to a sick patient. Instead, therapy is seen as a co-created relationship and journey of joint discovery with the focus on the client. Emphasis is put on learning to 'sit with uncertainty' and taking time to find out with and from the client, rather than falsely thinking one knows better. MBT, which is based on attachment-based theory, urges practitioners to take on a 'not-knowing stance' and to teach by example that it is better to 'check things out' with the other, rather than going on assumptions. Attachment theory is increasingly backed up by neuro-scientific research, indicating a further rapprochement. Moreover, present-day neuroscience also backs up some of Freud's thinking which many saw as 'insane' during his lifetime.

NRMs in clinical work

The therapeutic issues when dealing with NRMs, in my opinion, are not so much about practitioners not knowing the details about a specific group but more about prejudice and agenda. Attachment-based psychotherapy training points out that we all have prejudices and that for being a good and responsible psychotherapist the importance lies in knowing and acknowledging them. The idea is that the more we disallow prejudices, the more they unconsciously creep into our thinking and clinical work. In my opinion this is a good approach and an important point, but, considering my experience of others at training organisations, this process nevertheless revealed immense prejudice regarding NRMs and was not always identified as such. Psychotherapists are in a position of power and have to be very careful and responsible with that. Objective information and the social scientific method itself can contribute to minimising prejudiced practice.

My experience in the NHS PD service reassuringly shows some similarities to the approach at Inform. That is, on the occasions when spiritual (or hallucinatory?) experiences were brought into clinical work, they were approached with a level of methodological agnosticism, not interpreted or judged. When this arose, the decision was to actually not focus on them but to focus on the patient's main psychological work with emphasis on practising reflective functioning, which gets clearly set out at the assessment stage, as well as being reviewed regularly. Psychiatrists in the team conduct mental state examinations to rule out psychotic illnesses, but PDs typically include hallucinatory elements. The PD service also showed a surprising tolerance towards NRMs/religion – patients enjoying involvement in church, spiritual and meditation groups are encouraged to build on these attachments and the positive experience. The NHS does, however, get criticised for endorsing various meditation courses without having a grasp of, or stance on, the different Buddhist groups offering them. One example is referring patients to Triratna who, under the name of Breathing Space offer Mindfulness-Based Cognitive Therapy which combines cognitive therapy with meditative practices and attitudes based on the cultivation of mindfulness. Another example is NHS pointing to the New Kadampa Tradition's meditation classes. This gets further complicated when mental health professionals are also members of NRMs, especially with regards to implicit endorsement and credibility.

Charisma, narcissism and 'brainwashing'

According to Barker (1989: 13), many NRMs have leaders exhibiting 'charisma', which 'implies that the leader's followers believe that he or she possesses a very special (possibly divine) quality and that the followers are, as a consequence, willing to grant him or her a special kind of authority over them'.

Decades before Bowlby brought the relational to the forefront of psychoanalytic psychotherapy by focusing on attachment, Weber brought the relational to sociology by emphasising the relational aspect in his definition of charismatic authority. Charismatic relationships could be seen as a meeting of early attachment styles, as the leader's ability to exert something that reverberates in the convert, often happening at a deep unconscious level that might go back to the preverbal self of a child (therefore hard to grasp and express).

There is usually an illusive and elusive quality to the traits that set a charismatic person apart from others: powerful to those who are susceptible, and curiously impotent to those who 'don't get it'. Such leadership often comes with a level of unavailability, which connects with what charisma is about as well – power and control. Followers can get into a cycle of preoccupied attachment with a leader they are attracted to but who is sometimes very, sometimes not at all, but never consistently, available to them – leading to, for example, obsessive behaviour or 'trying harder' to be liked by the leader. It can lead to a cycle similar to addiction where group membership, and relationship to the leader, causes inflammation and distress itself, that can only be 'made better' by seeking out the leader even more. Members can find themselves caught in the vicious cycle typical of insecure attachment.

Barker states that

> almost by definition, charismatic leaders are unpredictable, for they are bound by neither tradition nor rules; they are not answerable to other human beings. Thus, in so far as the leaders of NRMs are endowed by their followers with a charismatic authority, the followers accept the legitimacy of their leader's right to pronounce on every aspect of their lives.
>
> (Barker 1989: 13)

Barker warns that in these cases the leader may lack any accountability, require unquestioning obedience, and encourage a dependency upon the movement for material, spiritual and social resources (Barker 1989: 13).

There are similarities between charisma and Personality Disorders, specifically with narcissistic traits. PDs are characterised by pervasive problems with mentalising (reflective functioning) and empathy, stormy relationships, cycles of idealisation and devaluation of self and other, chronic feelings of emptiness, an unstable sense of self, splitting, suicidal ideation and attempts, self-harm or harming others. Narcissistic traits specifically involve a pervasive pattern of grandiosity (in fantasy or actual behaviour), the need for admiration and lack of empathy, often being interpersonally exploitative and getting angry if their needs are not met. It also involves creating a world view or image of the person that others 'buy into'.

At the core of Narcissistic Personality Disorder (NPD) is an underlying chronic feeling of emptiness and both self-loathing and self-aggrandisement. One theory is that it is a developmental deficit – the caregivers have not facilitated the child to develop beyond the normal phase of feeling omnipotent and without a healthy sense of self. As adults, those with an NPD diagnosis tend to see other people as objects whose function is to make the person with NPD feel better. In the NRM scenario, a leader with NPD can 'love-bomb' (Barker 1984) followers or potential new recruits, they can be used and dropped and regularly replaced by newcomers as required, which obviously can cause a lot of pain to followers. This can also explain pressures on members to proselytise – this type of leader needs followers just as much as followers end up needing him/her. Of course there is an asymmetry here. These traits were evident in the group around Mohan Singh, aka Michael Lyons, whose conviction for one rape and one assault was facilitated to some degree by Inform.[8]

As a way of coping, individuals with NPD have developed techniques that keep the illusion of omnipotence alive – being able to make others do what they want them to do. Those susceptible find themselves under some sort of spell, assign charismatic authority and confirm the person's illusion of omnipotence, or even justify it. This frequently happens non-verbally and without any conscious awareness. No wonder this can seem like brainwashing and mind control, but I think these concepts are judgmental and a shortcut.

Relationships between such leaders and followers are co-created, insecure and volatile. No doubt encounters with such individuals can be very traumatising. However, this is similar to any abusive relationship and not, as often implied, specific to cults. One can encounter this with a boss at work, a politician, a teacher, a parent, a partner or an artist. The hidden emptiness of a narcissist is also very attractive to many because the illusive nature of their fuzzy self allows space for the others' projections.

There is often a coming together of 'charismatic' (or narcissistic) people with others struggling with dependency issues (Barker 1989). The psychoanalytic concept of projective identification (Klein 1946) can help explain psychologically what sociologists mean by coercion. This is a primitive defence mechanism typical of the paranoid/schizoid position where an intolerable affect is split off and projected in such a way that the other person unconsciously identifies with it to the point of taking that emotion on as their own, without being aware of this process. This is very powerful, can be disturbing and can lead to unconscious enactments, again making the concept of agency and responsibility very difficult. Inform does not subscribe to these ideas, but I think that the process of projective identification plays a big role in why many are so scared and/or hostile towards NRMs.

This might be precisely what makes the brainwashing, mind control and ritual abuse paradigms so powerful – by blaming the other and portraying the convert as a victim to whom something has been done against their will, they relieve the individual of responsibility for their own actions that are often uncomfortable to reconcile. Barker (1984) showed in her seminal study *The Making of a Moonie* that the Unification Church was in fact not (as accused by many) 'brainwashing' people. Instead, she showed that the dynamics at play were neither irresistible nor irreversible (Barker 1984).

Co-facilitating an MBT group gives me theoretical and experiential insight into these dynamics. MBT developers Fonagy and Bateman (2006) discovered that people with Borderline Personality Disorder are hypersensitive to attachment and have a vulnerability to losing their ability to mentalise – which is the ability to have an accurate idea of the other's thoughts, feelings and intentions, as well as one's own. This disorder is very difficult to treat one-to-one as opposed to within a group or with two therapists, since the failure in mentalising can impair a therapist's functioning without him or her realising it. Failures in mentalising can create a 'fog' in a group setting, can make all the members of a group lose their capacity for clear thinking, collude and act out difficult feelings instead of baring them (also relevant for dynamics among followers in NRMs), and can cause strong emotional reactions such as anger, despair and anxiety, to name but a few. Someone reverting to a non-mentalised state can make even experienced therapists lose their own thinking and make them prone to 'colluding' and acting out, which is why we have two therapists present. We help patients understand and improve this with empathy rather than blame, but also with strong boundary setting.

What remains are the difficult questions for society as to whether someone is doing this consciously, or if this is done unconsciously, part of so-called primitive defence mechanisms, which often is the case. I think the way forward is both to offer treatment for PDs/NPD and to strengthen individuals to protect themselves from abusive relationships as an ongoing part of life, rather than getting stuck in cycles of assigning blame. MBT's perspective on 'brainwashing' is also quite disarming: We all have our failures in mentalising, just some of us more than others.

I argue that maybe it is a more useful approach to not focus on the group so much because this brings with it dangers of splitting and projection, and also might take away agency from the client. I think that a practitioner who does not have experience of NRMs can allow space for the client to tell them about their experience. Rather than approaching the issue as wanting to dismantle something that a group has done to them, it could be an idea to focus on building up the person's sense of self, integrate difficult experiences, and help the person build up a healthier relationship to themselves, others and reality. Such an approach would focus on the person's struggles in a holistic way: struggles connected to the experience with the group, but also those not connected to the group, including everything before joining,[9] especially early years and early relationships.

Mind control / reform counselling 'specialists'

There is, however, a widespread assumption that when it comes to distress in relation to any contact with an NRM, one needs someone specialising in NRMs, reform counselling, mind control or ritual abuse, or someone who has been in a cult themselves. I intend to challenge this.

In line with terms like brainwashing, mind control and pre- and post-cult personality, there is often an implicit or explicit assumption that members or ex-members are victims to whom something has been 'done' by cults and that this something needs to be 'undone', 'deprogrammed', urgently. What often goes amiss is considering what came first: psychological problems or membership.[10] The fact that many people might have joined at a time when they were already vulnerable, or joined *because* of being vulnerable often gets 'forgotten'. Freedom of choice (including the choice to be different) and agency also get bypassed.

The 'reform' counselling approaches tend to blame the group for all existing difficulties, and that is part of why I don't think seeing a 'cult' specialist is always the best way forward. Yes, there is space for appropriate anger, which is important, but this is different from toxic anger that can be fanned and in which one can get stuck. This quickly turns into ACM attempts to ban 'cults'; and there are worrying tendencies to use work towards the prevention of radicalisation for this end.

Relying on assumptions rather than gaining objective information also conveniently makes the group a blank screen that one can project onto. Interestingly some counsellors tend to refer to and collaborate with anti-cult organisations rather than with Inform. Maybe offering a structured treatment and/or an 'anti-cult' perspective also makes a counsellor more attractive than an uncertain 'not knowing stance', because, similarly to NRMs, they offer surer and faster remedies. It allows the client to remain in the more comfortable paranoid/schizoid mode; probably stuck and bound to repeat.

There is also an idea that only a cult specialist could understand the patient, but I disagree. This often stems from the idea that the experiences individuals have with certain NRMs are very different from what they have ever experienced before. They might find it difficult to make sense of and explain these experiences to others. They might even find it difficult to relate to the state of mind they had at the time. Friends and family might feel alienated by how incomprehensibly the person has apparently changed. An entanglement with a charismatic person can feel like being 'under someone's spell'. For those who have never experienced this, its existence is hard to believe or to grasp. However, many therapists will understand this experience; and a client will gather whether this is the case or not in the consultation.

The wounding wounded healer

What is also worth raising as a potential clinical issue with NRM counselling specialists, including those who themselves identify as 'ex-members', centres on motivation and agenda. Clinically speaking, the danger is that this kind of specialism comes with a practitioner who has an agenda, and even more worryingly, an agenda of which he or she might not be fully conscious. Often this approach can be driven by prejudices, generalisations and assumptions about NRMs, possibly triggered by a difficult personal experience the practitioner had with one. It is possible for someone's practice to be contaminated by an acting out of a traumatic experience. Contemporary psychotherapy approaches have the concept of the wounded healer – that by choosing to be a psychotherapist we also try to heal our own wounds. The more someone is aware of this the better, and arguably it is our woundedness that can make our attempts to help so much more powerful.

But there is a fine line between a wounded healer and a wounding healer. This also links with false memory syndrome. According to Barker

> studies in ritual satanic abuse, for example, have revealed a considerable body of evidence showing that therapists may not only help clients to construct a secondary version of reality, some construct a version of reality themselves, then put considerable pressure on the client to accept it.
> (Barker 2003: 10)

In fact I have observed this in respected psychotherapists in my training. Critics who point out lack of evidence (e.g. for Satanists sacrificing and eating babies) are dismissed as being part of 'the conspiracy'.

Another factor worth considering is whether exit counselling and the mind control approach have similarities to 'The Story of Bottled Water', involving so-called manufactured demand, where a narrative and whole paradigm are created, often creating anxiety about NRMs or conventional, less directive therapies (i.e. tap water being contaminated) and claiming to offer something much better, (i.e. bottled water, which is itself often tap water). Mind control and ritual abuse tags sell books, and for reasons I have already discussed, may be more attractive to certain clients too, partly because by putting blame on the other, one does not have to own shame, pain and anger about one's actions. Astonishing how similar the anti-cult movement can be to what it is fighting against.

At the PD service we are consciously trying to change patients' ways of thinking by trying to help them understand their own internal states better, as well as trying to help them speculate and establish the motivations and internal states of others more accurately and relationally. Does this mean we 'deprogramme' in a way by trying to get patients away from splitting, denial and projective identification towards mentalising and being able to tolerate all that reality brings with it: joy, pain, anxiety, loneliness, relationships? I think this 'neutral' way of helping someone towards healthier psychological functioning is less problematic than an approach with a paradigm such as that of 'religious abuse syndrome' or 'mind control'.

In a way, all groups and institutions 'programme' and all therapists 'deprogramme' or 'reprogramme' – neuroscience has shown that when we talk and relate to each other, we make new synaptic connections in our brains. We constantly reprogramme each other, and our brains keep this neuroplasticity that enables learning and change, into old age. This is the power of human relationships, and it gives hope for healing and change, explains why talking therapies work, especially the relational, psychodynamic ones. It is what happens when children go to school and kindergarten. It is definitely not something that only 'these evil cults' do.

Attachment

A high proportion of the distress caused by cults in fact is relational in nature. According to attachment theory, we all have different attachment styles that get formed in the first two years of life, depending on how our caregivers relate to us. If our caregivers were 'good enough', providing attuned and swift emotional regulation and allowed us to 'emerge' in relationship to them without impinging, neglecting or imposing themselves, we are likely to have internalised a secure relationship to self and others. If this care is not good enough because the parent is, for example, angry, depressed, unavailable, abusive or unstable, a child needs to be very resourceful to adapt. This leads to insecure attachment styles like avoidant, ambivalent or preoccupied ones, which are maladaptive in later life. Tragically, we are then prone to seek out and co-create these kinds of insecure relationships in later life, in effect repeating the early relational trauma of childhood and leading to a cycle of retraumatising re-enactments.

Similarly to MBT focusing solely on improving a patient's mentalising skills, attachment-based psychotherapy can offer to heal someone affected by an NRM through changing their attachment style by experiencing a secure relationship facilitated by the therapist. This is useful because it avoids splitting – the 'blame' is not put on the cult or the client. In combination with looking at the client's early life and unconscious conflicts, one can examine what it is in the client's attachment system that might contribute to being attracted to, and joining a particular group, and what dynamics came from the group that played into this maladaptive cycle. When it comes to changing our psychological make-up, gathering theoretical knowledge and insight is not enough – what causes the real shift is when this occurs alongside living and experiencing a different, more secure relationship. This can be healing in itself. It builds up self-esteem and a strong sense of self with integrity, and most importantly, it leads to breaking the traumatic pattern of seeking out, or staying in, negative relationships.

I think this approach also works well because it does not bypass agency. It places agency with the individual, and puts responsibility for decision making with the individual albeit with empathy towards coercive pressures. It does this in an empathic, non-blaming way by explaining it in the context of early attachments. It is not about pre- and post-cult personalities. It is about a gradual move from an insecure attachment style towards 'earned security'. Working towards this is an inside-out approach that is a very good protection from getting caught up with the wrong crowd or an abusive person. First, because it leads to integrity that makes a person robust when faced with challenging situations and able to say no when she or he does not want to do something. Second, because it leads to a person seeking out secure relationships, which also helps when getting entangled in something negative. I think that attachment-based psychotherapy can, if it stays clear from the mind-control paradigms, offer a profound and long-lasting change in a person's life, rather than just applying a sticking plaster.

All of this is also highly relevant because the relational stress that can occur in relation to involvement with a cult is that pre-existing relationships with friends, family and colleagues can get challenged or can break down. This might be a symptom of what is going on rather than something 'caused' by the cult (I think that for many it might be the less painful option to just focus on the cult). Systemic approaches (discussed in the following chapter) can give further insight here. Those with secure attachment styles tend not to need therapy, and they tend not to get bruised by NRMs – they either do not seek them out in the first place, or they leave when they realise something isn't quite right for them, or they choose a group which is itself based on secure attachments.

I think this is where the psychological work lies – in trying to find more secure ways of relating, to others and to oneself. This also leaves space to blame, criticise and prosecute a group for its actual wrongdoings, while it works towards self-empowerment and self-agency. Often those in the exit counselling field campaign to prevent people from joining certain groups. I don't think this is an ethical or helpful therapy goal – if one has achieved a secure relationship with one's self and others, it is possible to explore safely, collect data, check this with one's values and sense of self, talk to good friends about it, and then take a decision in line with one's integrity. Curiosity and exploration are an important part of, and move towards, mental health and a strong sense of self.

Counselling and Inform

The idea for this chapter arose as part of a talk for Inform's 25th Anniversary Conference in 2014. This occasion made me reflect afresh on Inform, which made me truly reappreciate it from my new perspective as a trained psychotherapist. I had felt frustrated by Inform's policy of not offering counselling and not having counselling training, which contributed to my decision to train as a psychotherapist. I can now see that, paradoxically, by not offering counselling or recommending counsellors, Inform offers something therapeutically containing[11] and useful.

Inform has drawn up guidelines for people who are anxious about the involvement of a relative or friend who has joined a religious movement: Inform encourages them to get as much accurate, balanced and up-to-date information as possible about the movement and/or the leader concerned and to keep in touch with the convert. This emphasises the importance and protective factors of good attachments and also implicitly keeps mentalising and the exchange of different perspectives going. It also favours reality checking over relying on assumptions. Inform encourages family members to listen and try to understand instead of forcing their own opinion on the convert. Inform stresses the importance of the convert's right to choose. We suggest a non-judgmental attitude, letting the convert know that you as friend or family member are there for them. Inform also suggests that one can share concerns about the group in a factual, supportive and non-confrontational manner and that one can encourage the convert to consider these in light of their own experiences. Another idea is to encourage 'What if?' questions. If there are grounds for believing that there is actual danger or criminal activity, Inform's advice is to contact the police, social services or the relevant embassies in the case of foreign nationals. If Inform comes across serious criminal activities, it will contact the relevant agencies whilst preserving the confidentiality of the informant.

Some enquirers have been to other advice agencies prior to finding Inform and might have received a response based on a different perspective. Alternatively, they might have been met with an emotionally loaded response, which can feel validating for some, but for others it can mean further inflammation and re-traumatisation. For these individuals, Inform's very factual, calm, non-judgmental yet empathetic approach, led by what the enquirer brings, not by its own agenda, can actually feel very grounding. In fact, this approach is similar to non-impinging psychotherapeutic principles. From a psychotherapist's perspective, this is one of the unique and vitally important aspects of what Inform offers when it comes to NRM-related emotional difficulties.

I think that the way forward for Inform is, on the one hand, to refer those enquirers who want more help than that available at Inform to relatively 'neutral' places such as a GP or mental health charities with a neutral stance on NRMs, that can assess and refer to mental health services within the National Health Service or charities. This is important because frequently the most seemingly obvious cause of distress, e.g. involvement with a 'cult', might not be the root of the problem; there might have been long-standing problems prior to involvement with the group. There might be underlying attachment issues, a PD, or a psychotic illness that are the problem. Or the problem might be that it is only the friends and family who have the problem, and not the individual in question.

On the other hand, I think that Inform can play a vital part in supporting and educating mental health practitioners, organisations and training organisations. Inform can do this by giving objective information about specific groups, and, maybe more importantly, it can give insight into the methodology it uses, which can act as a powerful protection against prejudice, which is bad news for anyone's clinical practice.

I would like to end by mentioning the fact that for a very troubled former patient of ours at the Personality Disorders service Catholicism (in the eyes of many the most 'dangerous cult' of them all) was one of the main protective factors in a long battle with serious suicide attempts.

Confused? Good.

Notes

1 UK Council for Psychotherapy
2 At Inform we do not use the word cult because of its negative popular use. I will use it in this chapter when referring to others who use it.
3 Maybe I should refer to Eileen as Professor Barker, but I think referring to her as 'Eileen' reflects one of the strengths of Inform (similarly set up as the PD service) – we are a long-standing team with strong attachments and a large network of

former staff and academics, resembling The Hotel California ('you can check out but you can never leave').

4 I do not practise as a psychotherapist at Inform.

5 This time my colleague felt obliged to clap. Repeatedly, for two hours (sigh).

6 According to Lemma, transference is 'as a process in which current emotions, phantasies and parts of the self are externalised in the relationship with the therapist. This allows the therapist to experience the relational implications of internalised early developmental models that are to some degree modified through projective processes. Nowadays most therapists view their reactions and feelings towards the patient as countertransference, which allows for an understanding of the patient's as-yet unverbalised, and times, pre-verbal, experience. When the patient projects unwanted feeling into us, we understand this, in our countertransference, as an opportunity to feel and experience for ourselves what the patient may be feeling' (Lemma 2016: 254).

7 Interestingly, he chose to compare rates of suicide among different religious denominations for this, and struggled with the psychology of the former.

8 BBC News 27 July 2010. www.bbc.co.uk/news/uk-10770395.

9 This is somewhat different for second generation members born into a movement.

10 It should be pointed out that many members and followers do not encounter psychological problems.

11 A container being understood as an 'auxiliary digestive tract for emotional events, a human mind (i.e. a container) with the capability to accept, absorb and transform these experiences into meaning' (Lemma 2016: 44).

References

Barker, E. 1984. *The Making of a Moonie: Brainwashing or Choice?* Oxford: Basil Blackwell.

Barker, E. 1989. *New Religious Movements: A Practical Introduction*. London: HMSO.

Barker, E. 2003. The scientific study of religion? You must be joking!, in: L. L. Dawson (ed.) *Cults and New Religious Movements. A Reader*. London: Blackwell Publishing, pp. 7–25.

Beckford, J. 2004. Why Britain doesn't go to church. *BBC News*. Online article Available at: http://news.bbc.co.uk/2/hi/programmes/wtwtgod/3475483.stm (Accessed 12 June 2017).

Bowlby, J. 1969. *Attachment. Attachment and Loss: Vol. 1. Loss*. New York: Basic Books.

Bowlby, J. 1988. *A Secure Base: Parent-Child Attachment and Healthy Human Development*. Tavistock professional book. London: Routledge.

Fonagy, P. and A. Bateman. 2006. *Mentalization-based Treatment for Borderline Personality Disorder: A Practical Guide*. Oxford: Oxford University Press.

Klein, M. 1946. Notes on some schizoid mechanisms. *International Journal of Psycho-Analysis*, 27, 99–110.

Lemma, A. 2016. *Introduction to the Practice of Psychoanalytic Psychotherapy*. Malden, MA: Wiley Blackwell.

Popper, K. 1963. *Conjectures and Refutations: The Growth of Scientific Knowledge*. New York: Basic Books.

Wilkins, L.T. 1964. *Social Deviance*. London: Tavistock.

Wilson, B. 1990. *The Social Dimensions of Sectarianism: Sects and New Religious Movements in Contemporary Society*. Oxford: Claredon.

4 New religious movements and systemic/family psychotherapy

Alastair Pearson

Introduction

In this chapter I describe how systemic ideas and practices are used in therapy to help people experiencing religious and spiritual distress.[1] I begin with a retelling of episodes in my own life to illustrate the importance attached in systemic practice to the therapist's ability to consider their own history and social identities, and how this relates to the conduct of therapy. I will outline the key features of systemic practice, and demonstrate their application in clinical practice. Readers will be invited to consider for themselves questions that may be included in the practice of spiritual assessment. The chapter will conclude with discussion of some of the challenges for practice in this area, and reflections on links between my own experience of being part of an NRM and how this has shaped my development as a therapist.

The family therapist

We sat in a semicircle, somewhere in 'posh' London. A 12-year-old me, my younger brother and sister, mum and dad, facing a middle-aged man who asked us questions about our family. I hardly remember a word he said, it was a long time ago. But what does stick in my memory is what it felt like, what it did to me. It *hurt* me. Outwardly I giggled, inside I was contorted, in turmoil, as the therapist invited me to participate in a conversation that I was nowhere near ready to have. The sessions had been arranged as a way of helping our family cope with parental separation. However, I was in a state of denial, unable to accept that the separation was anything other than a passing phase. My own story, my own experience, my own voice, were never heard, never even invited. Nothing that was said connected with my unspeakable reality. The prescription from the therapist consisted of proposals for a housework rota and discipline from my mother. I left the sessions with my heart pounding, not wanting to return and be made to suffer like this again.

The Elder

Three years later and I am sitting in the house of an Elder. He is part of the leadership team of the Evangelical Free Church I attended with my mother. It was the church of her childhood, traditionally conservative in theology but now part of the Charismatic movement that developed in the 1970s. I spoke to him about my struggles with my parents' separation, of the anger and hatred that had been stirred up in me. I told him that I had experienced a conviction that these feelings went against my Christian beliefs, and I wanted help with this. I was nervous. He began to pray for me, but as he did so my anxiety grew. I began to cry, sliding down the sofa onto the floor. He began to speak to demons, joined by his wife, speaking in tongues. I howled and wailed and writhed, screaming 'No' again and again. All the while they shouted at the demons to leave me. It went on and on, pain and bewilderment coursing through me, all my pent-up feelings of rejection and loss pouring out. My demons, it turned out, were stubborn and unwilling to leave, so the Elder told them to be still, and eventually I calmed. I went home to my mother, and explained what had happened. I now believed that my extreme emotions were caused by Satanic demons living inside me. My mind racing, I took it upon myself to try and cast them down the toilet, without success.

The following day my mother called the Elder and said I needed help. She arranged for me to return to the house, where the Elders were meeting with the Pastor. I was scared, thinking that I was going to vomit as I'd heard this happened when demons were cast out. But this time it was different. There was no talk of demons, instead I was invited to seek and offer forgiveness. One of the Elders asked me what I saw in my mind, I told him I was having a vision of Jesus with his arms around my family. As we prayed I felt the pain, the rejection, the anger that had dominated my life for five years melt away, to be replaced by a profound sense of peace, of oneness with God. In the year that followed, the house in which I had writhed became a place of dancing, of prayer, prophecy and singing in the spirit in tongues of men and angels. In that place the End Times were upon us, miracles were expected and Jesus would be returning soon. In that place 'the mind' within each of us was the enemy of the Holy Spirit; we were to be led by the God who spoke directly to us, as we went out into the world, Satan's domain, to proclaim the Kingdom of God. There was no place for doubt in this world.

The psychiatrist

But my doubt was not to be denied, finding its way in unexpectedly via an article describing the near-death experiences of people going to hell and coming back, of non-Christians visiting heaven and returning to life. This contradicted what I had been taught, namely that only true believers would be saved. I felt confused and over the months that followed I questioned everything I had believed and experienced in the movement. I couldn't concentrate, I felt deep distress and had panic attacks as I thought for the first time about suffering, about hell, about how I could know anything at all. This time I went to the GP, who prescribed anti-depressants and sent me to a psychiatrist. I made every effort not to tell the psychiatrist what was going on because I didn't think he would understand and that he might think I was mad. He ended his involvement with the observation 'what strikes me is how little you've actually told me'. He had failed to find a way to enable me to open up, to allow me to take a risk, and trust him sufficiently to invite him into my world of spiritual distress.

Thirty years later and I have become the middle-aged 'man in the chair', a systemic/family psychotherapist offering therapy to people with problems arising from involvement with a new religious movement (NRM). Groups I have encountered in the course of my therapy practice include the Exclusive Brethren, New Kadampa Tradition, Divine Light Mission, Subud and World of Yaad. My practice is also informed by experience of working in multi-cultural and Muslim communities as a systemic/family psychotherapist in a Child and Adolescent Mental Health Service (CAMHS).

The term 'new religious movement' (NRM) is used with considerable caution and is by no means unproblematic. Its primary value to me as a therapist is that it serves as a less pejorative term than the label of 'cult' (Barker 1989). The designation NRM does not imply that the group is of necessity 'bad', nor does it resolve debate as to how 'new' or 'religious' a particular group may be, but an NRM will be seen, by some at least, as unconventional and controversial. A comparison with the Christian charismatic movement that I was part of in the 1980s illustrates such definitional difficulties: for some it represented a return to Biblical truth, for others it was religion 'gone wrong' (Howard 1997). Neither is it a simple matter to define what is meant by 'systemic psychotherapy', however I offer the following summary of a few key features:

- 'Systemic' refers to the body of theory and practice that believes human behaviour can only be understood properly when seen within its social context.
- Systemic/Family Psychotherapists use systemic theory when working with families, and are sometimes referred to as 'family therapists'. They may also be known as systemic psychotherapists when providing organisational consultation or individual therapy.
- Systemic psychotherapy originated in the 1960s and 1970s. It evolved from the diagnostic and individual focus of the psychoanalytic tradition to a more relational and interpersonal approach to therapy (Dallos and Draper 2000). Systemic therapy focuses on understanding the client's belief system and identifying ways in which therapy can bring about better relationships and the realization of hopes and goals. It has been influenced by feminism and 'post-modern' theories and sees itself as the most radical and innovative of the mainstream psychotherapies (Rivett and Street 2009).

- Whilst there are various systemic models, all seek to help clients overcome problems through drawing on strengths, resources and a collaborative relationship. Systemic therapists have developed a wide range of practices to facilitate this. These include working with distress using an intergenerational framework and tools like the genogram;[2] working with a team who offer the benefit of multiple perspectives; working intensively with interactions that take place in the session; limiting 'problem talk' while emphasising solutions for the here and now; and the use of therapeutic letters to support change outside of sessions.

Systemic psychotherapy: a case study

To illustrate how systemic thinking and practice can be used to help clients experiencing distress related to involvement in an NRM, I will present a composite case study (Duffy 2010), an amalgamation of work with different clients illustrating 'real life' practice. Names, identifying features and aspects of the therapy have been changed to protect confidentiality. I use the word 'systemic' in the same way as 'Christian' might be used to describe a broad framework of belief without reference to denominational sub-groups. The practice outlined represents my own ecumenical blending of a range of systemic models, organised by the conviction that theory and practice should be adapted to the needs of the client. Readers interested in finding out more about the systemic approach may refer to introductory texts (Dallos and Draper 2000; Rivett and Street 2009; Hills 2013).

Sharon is a woman in her late twenties, identifying as mixed English/Caribbean heritage. She wanted therapy to help cope with the depression she suffered after she left a radical Christian community, within which she had resided for five years. In childhood, she attended a Church of England congregation with her parents, but became disillusioned with its 'deadness'. When she read about the 'Toronto Blessing', a movement in which the Holy Spirit is evidenced by a dramatic bodily experience, she felt led to attend a church where this was happening. She experienced the Blessing, and formed relationships that would lead her to the community. The community required all money and possessions to be shared, and was run by a leadership team that initially seemed nurturing and encouraging but had become increasingly authoritarian, claiming knowledge of God's will for community members. Whilst this made sense to her at first, one of the leaders began to suggest that God wanted them to have a sexual relationship, and from this point onwards she became increasingly disorientated and anxious, not knowing whom to trust or how she could leave a community on which she was completely dependent. After a sexual assault, her survival instincts kicked in, and she returned to her parents who, despite being estranged from her, allowed her to stay with them whilst she decided what to do next.

First session

When people arrive for their first session, they have already been on a journey with the idea of therapy. They may come well informed about the kind of therapy on offer, or know very little. They may be feeling ready to take the risk of trusting a stranger, or they may be terrified of making themselves vulnerable to being misunderstood or let down. As a registered therapist, I am required by my professional Code of Ethics (AFT 2011) to negotiate a clear therapeutic contract with the client addressing the nature of the therapy, the aims, risks, limitations, alternatives and fees. Whilst rules of ethical conduct are important, ethical practice also needs to incorporate relational or 'process ethics' (Swim, St. George and Wulff 2001). To be ethical from a relational perspective requires a 'therapeutic relationship' (Flaskas 1996) in which the therapist is experienced as connected and able to communicate in a way that fits with the client's own way of thinking, speaking and relating. I therefore asked Sharon questions like 'what would I have to do to somehow "get it wrong" with you?' or 'what would need to have happened for you to leave the session today feeling confident that we can do business together?' What emerged was that Sharon was so distressed by the abuse, loss of friends, confusion about her relationship with God and hopelessness for the future that she was unable to specify any particular goal for therapy. In addition, she was experiencing suicidal thoughts, although not to the point of planning to act on them. This led to a discussion of the circumstances in which I might need to break her entitlement to confidentiality and contact community mental health services. We agreed that my role as therapist, at least initially, would be to function as an outsider witness (Carey and Russell 2003), able to provide her with a safe space in which to articulate and express her pain and dilemmas with someone who could listen without expressing anxiety or judgement. We considered how the therapy would approach the sexual abuse she had reported, including the implications of me being a male therapist. We agreed that we would focus on the effects on her spiritual and social life, and that she would see a female therapist if she wished to address sexual abuse as the primary issue.

Throughout the session I tracked not only what Sharon was saying, but also the thoughts and feelings that I was experiencing in response. Self-reflexivity (Burnham 1993) is a key idea in systemic psychotherapy, and refers to the capacity of the therapist to be aware of how their experiences and social identities are connected to those of the client and how they are shaping the therapy. In a context of societal inequality, self-reflexivity also serves as a tool to limit the scope for therapy to be experienced as oppressive. These identities are categorised as gender, geography, race, religion, age, ability, appearance, class, culture, ethnicity, education, employment, sexuality, sexual orientation and spirituality, known collectively as the GGRRAAACCEEESSS (Burnham 1993; Totsuka 2014). Memories of my religious and spiritual experience were triggered by similarities with Sharon's account of spiritual abuse, but professional development meant that I was not re-traumatised or distracted from focussing on my client's story and needs. However, I was knowingly influenced by my experience of therapeutic and religious power when I said to Sharon, 'if you choose to work with me I will do all I can to support you as you try to make sense of what you've been through' and 'it's ok to take your time and only share what you feel ready to'. My systemic training helped me understand the ideas and social context that had shaped my own disastrous experience of family therapy as a 12-year-old. I now appreciate how much more child-friendly and aware of power family therapy has become.

Opinions on the appropriateness of self-disclosure by the therapist vary in the systemic field (Roberts 2005), but, as with any intervention, sharing aspects of your personal life should only be done if it will benefit the therapy. What is less contentious is the therapist drawing on personal experience as a resource to generate questions that connect with their client's experience, thereby opening up new areas for exploration. Drawing on my own experience of post-NRM distress, I understood Sharon to be in a state of unsafe uncertainty (Mason 1993). My own experience of therapy made me cautious about taking strong positions, and I realised that placing too much responsibility on Sharon to shape the session could have been overwhelming for her. My task was to convey to her authority and expertise, helping her feel calm and focussed enough to think about her life without undermining her own capacity for responsibility and growth. I did this by observing that it was not uncommon for those leaving hierarchical communities to have conflicting feelings about assuming more responsibility for their lives and that adjusting could take time. We agreed that I would initially take an active role in leading the sessions, but she had the option to redirect the focus at any point and she increasingly did so as the work progressed.

Parent session

A few weeks after my first meeting with Sharon I had a call from her mother, Jocelyn, asking if she and her husband John could meet with me, as they were very worried about Sharon. They had found my details on an appointment letter, but had not asked her permission to call as they were afraid she would refuse. Having established that the concerns did not warrant an assessment by mental health services, I advised there was no alternative to gaining Sharon's consent to speak with me. In her next session Sharon said that things felt unbearable at home and I had her permission to see her parents provided I did not share anything about our work. She did not feel strong enough to be part of the meeting. When I met Sharon's parents, Jocelyn described angrily and at length how Sharon's presence and unreasonable behaviour were intolerable, and that their capacity and willingness to continue to 'walk on eggshells' around her was being sorely tested. Jocelyn questioned the effectiveness of my therapy with Sharon, as it didn't seem to be helping, and she asked if I was sure I was the best person for the job.

I was unprepared for Jocelyn's comments and experienced a momentary loss of confidence in the face of such a critical monologue. The thought 'no wonder Sharon was attracted to the idea of an alternative family if this is what she had to put up with' entered my mind. Jocelyn of course had no idea that my background might make it hard for me to tolerate strongly expressed emotion or criticism. Within my inner conversation (Rober 1999), I challenged myself to focus on the needs of Sharon and positively reframed Jocelyn's comments as her expressions of care and love for her daughter.

Having established an appreciative frame for the discussion, we mapped ways in which the parents' lives were being impacted by Sharon, drawing on an idea known as 'in the corner' lifestyle (White 1987). This explores how family life changes when it becomes organised around a diagnosis of mental illness in the adult child. We discussed sleep patterns, mood, socialisation, patterns of communication, with the parents' divergent views elaborated upon and framed as a rich, resourceful conversation rather than as problems to be resolved. The aim was to assist the parents to consider how, despite their worries, they could enjoy and shape their relationship in accordance with their beliefs and values, reimagining what a parental role might look like in their circumstances. What emerged was that, unknown to Sharon, her father had been diagnosed with a serious heart condition and, from Jocelyn's point of view, stress caused by Sharon could literally be the death of him. Furthermore, Jocelyn had experienced her own mother as extremely critical, leaving her with a deep sense of inadequacy. Every night, as she listened to Sharon crying herself to sleep, Jocelyn felt such an overwhelming sense of failure and helplessness as a mother that her own relationship with God was in crisis. She felt unable to share this with her husband because she was afraid of the consequences. Once Jocelyn and John had acknowledged the significance of John's illness on their relationship, they were able to think very differently about how they could best respond to the needs of their daughter. Throughout the session there had been an empty chair to represent Sharon. Inviting family members to see things from the point of view of others and notice interactional patterns is a priority in systemic therapy. Having methods with which to do this, even where key people are not present, creates greater intensity and possibilities for healing. Having asked questions such as 'what do you think Sharon would say if she was to comment on what has just been said?' and 'what difference would it make to Sharon to know that the two of you are strong enough to work out your difficulties?' I invited Jocelyn and John to rehearse a conversation they would like to have with Sharon, building on their learning from the session.

Final session

The final session took place 18 months after Sharon and I began working together. We had met ten times, increasing the length between sessions as Sharon's distress lessened and strategies for progressing had been worked out.

She had reported the sexual assault to the police, and was about to start psychotherapy with her local NHS service.

We began by reviewing what had been helpful about the therapy. Seeking and learning from client feedback is an integral part of systemic practice, and also serves the purpose of reinforcing and sustaining changes for the client. It transpired that the session with Jocelyn and John had the desired effect of helping Sharon and her parents to reconnect as a family. It wasn't easy, but they had established a more open and adult dialogue with each other in which some of the unspoken problems from Sharon's childhood were acknowledged. This enabled Sharon to feel safe enough to agree to a family session in which we mapped out the family religious genogram (O'Hanlon 2006), exploring her family's history of religion and spirituality through several generations. This helped Sharon realise that her decision to join the community was driven by a desire for acceptance and close relationship that she felt was lacking in her family. Discussing this with her parents and addressing unresolved family issues and their connections with her spirituality had been crucial to the healing process. She had appreciated the initial approach of acknowledging her distress without rushing to 'fix it'. After a while, however, she had started to feel anxious at the lack of progress, so had been glad that I was able to take risks and challenge her when needed. As developing my confidence to take relational risks (Mason 2005) has been an important part of my development as a therapist, I appreciated this feedback. Sharon also noted that linking her to the local MIND[3] provision and volunteering opportunities had been helpful. This reflects the systemic belief in the importance of accessing resources in clients' social not just family contexts (Boyd-Franklin and Bry 2000). The fact that I advertise as a therapist specialising in problems relating to religious experience was important, as for Sharon it meant that she could come to therapy with confidence that the therapist would be open to working with her religious experience and spirituality.

Whilst a traditional model of psychotherapy might focus on how the client has benefited from therapy, a systemic approach acknowledges ways in which the therapist also benefits. I never forget that my livelihood and sense of personal and social worth are intimately connected with the distress of others. I grow through the relationships I develop in my work, and the understanding of human experience that comes with it. So when I say goodbye to clients I also convey my appreciation of the qualities that I have witnessed and the way in which our work has provided me with learning that I can take into my life. Sharon told me that her ability to accept the positive things I had to say was a sign of how much she had changed from when we first met.

Reflecting team comments

To qualify as a systemic/family therapist takes four years, including two years seeing clients as part of a team. Training involves learning how to work as a reflecting team (Andersen 1992), where team members discuss hypotheses and reactions to a session in front of the therapist and client. The idea is to ensure the client gets the benefit of multiple perspectives to help clarify their own dilemmas and resources. The dialogue must be appreciative and tentative because, generally speaking, people are less likely to listen to feedback if they are feeling criticised or instructed. To illustrate this, a colleague offers a reflection on his experience of reading the case study:

> I was moved by your account Alastair of your troubled times as an adolescent and of your various attempts to find help at that time. I felt confident from your account that Sharon and other clients like her have benefited hugely from your learning from these experiences, and your ability to be carefully self-reflexive about the use that you make of these experiences in your work.
>
> What I especially got from your account of the work was the importance of taking things slowly and at the client's pace early in such work, when they are coming to you in a state of considerable distress. It is tempting I find to move quickly into making suggestions about ways forward and Sharon clearly gives you the feedback that this would not have been as helpful as the approach that you took. More generally I feel that you provide a helpful guide for therapists like myself who do not have your direct experience of NRMs, about issues likely to arise in work with clients such as Sharon, who have had some involvement, and are uncertain about their way forward.
>
> I felt pleased as a systemic therapist that you had been able to include some direct work with the wider family and wanted to know more about how often this proves possible in your experience? So much of therapeutic practice is based on the idea of change coming from individuals making new sense of their experiences, and this seemed to me to be a good example of how attending to relationship issues is crucial for individuals to find new ways to go on together.

Questions for the reader

Systemic practice uses reflexive questions (Tomm 1987) to trigger new ideas and possibilities for the client. In order to demonstrate these in a practical way here are a few such questions you may wish to consider:

> What aspects of Sharon's experience could you connect with? Did anything surprise you, bemuse you, help you? Would it be easy or difficult for you to change your views on NRMs? When did you last significantly change your opinion about anything? What accounts for this? Who in your family knows most about your relationship with spirituality? Who would you be most and least likely to discuss it with and why? Does this matter to you? What connections do you make between your cultural

identity and views on religion? Has your interest in systemic psychotherapy increased or lessened? What did these questions do to you?

Discussion

My desire to offer counselling to people harmed as a result of involvement with an NRM predates my training as a systemic psychotherapist and arose from a personal experience of an NRM. It was based on what I now see as a misplaced idea that shared experience makes it easier to understand and be helpful. I now take the position that shared experience can constrain as well as be useful, but more importantly, the meanings attached to experience are always complex and unique to the individual so what matters most is the therapeutic skill that any qualified therapist should possess. It is crucial that people experiencing distress in relation to an NRM have access to therapists who are competent to respond to the range of complex mental health, family and social problems that may need addressing. Membership of the United Kingdom Council for Psychotherapy (UKCP) or British Association for Counselling and Psychotherapy (BACP) requires that psychotherapists are bound by a code of ethics, undertake ongoing training and are properly supervised. The difficulty though is that western psychotherapeutic models (including psychology and psychiatry) have struggled to embrace positively the spiritual lives of clients. This has been linked to Freud's hostility to religion, the influence of behaviourism, the general concern of therapists not to impose personal beliefs on clients, a lack of confidence in entering the domain of theology or an association between religion and oppression (O'Hanlon 2006). Therefore training may neglect the development of the skills required to work confidently with the religious identities, problems and resources of clients. As this chapter illustrates, fear of religious experience being misunderstood is a major disincentive to accessing mainstream therapeutic support. So long as this is the case specialist services will continue to exist.

As a systemic therapist who was hurt by involvement in an NRM, I have had to work hard to avoid the prejudice that NRMs are inherently harmful. It is worth remembering that many of the problems associated with NRMs are common features of groups in general. Furthermore, Pilgrim (1997) points to connections between the processes of psychotherapy and those of religion, commenting that 'When we think about psychotherapy as a peculiar setting with unexpected rules (compared to everyday life), an alternative construction can be put forward of its being a secular extension of religious rituals'. In addition I am interested in the positive contributions made to individual and social life by NRMs. Walsh (1999) argues that increasing relativism, globalisation and social instability have led to many seeking peace and a sense of belonging in 'fundamentalist' and other sources of spiritual resilience. Griffith and Griffith (2002) see both the established religions and 'many of the newer spiritualities' as calling their followers to compassion and justice. With this in mind, I seek to privilege the client's preferences for their spiritual life. This may include helping them strengthen rather than end their involvement with an NRM.

This is not to suggest that an appreciative approach renders religious abuse any more acceptable than abuse in other contexts, but therapists do face complex dilemmas when deciding how to approach destructive religious experience. Melissa and James Griffith (2002) summed up this tension; 'How to honor a personal narrative is confusing when the stories, beliefs, and traditions that are the core of a person's spiritual life are ones that seem intrinsically destructive'. Such personal narratives and traditions may include belief in direct communication with God and strong respect for leadership. In order to work with spiritual abuse, it may be necessary to include God, family or group leaders as conversation partners.

Returning to personal context, there are a number of ways in which systemic ideas have helped me make sense of my religious experience. Whilst cited in systemic circles for his contributions to social constructionist thinking (Berger and Luckmann 1966), I was helped by the analysis of religious experience offered by Peter Berger in *A Rumour of Angels* (1969). Berger points to the importance of plausibility structures, the network of relationships and organization that give rise to and sustain belief. Intense relationships with friends and authority figures helped to legitimize and maintain my extreme version of faith.

However, social support for my beliefs cannot fully account for their intensity. It is important to remember that human experience is embodied as well as embedded in social networks (Hardham 1996). Out of my mouth had come other languages, my mind saw visions and at times I was so overcome with emotion and a sense of God's presence that I had no choice but to fall to my knees in worship. Whilst being embedded in a supportive social network was a factor in sustaining my faith it was this array of intense embodied experience that made doubting the reality of what I believed nonsensical.

So what brought about the collapse of my belief system that had been 'beyond doubt'? Here I turn to the idea of scripts (Byng-Hall 1995). Byng-Hall suggests that when the stories we tell ourselves are 'coherent', regardless of how 'dysfunctional' they may seem from the outside, life will make sense to us. After a while my own healing and gifts became less important to me as I became troubled that I never saw the spectacular healings I was told to expect. I became increasingly disappointed that the people around me continued to be pretty 'ordinary' human beings, not the spirit-filled warriors they should have been. Incoherent scripts were emerging at social and theological levels with sufficient force to bring down the foundations of belief and self.

Conclusion

In this chapter I have outlined some of the key assumptions and practices of systemic psychotherapy, and shown how they can be used in therapy in work with clients who have experienced psychological difficulties as a result of involvement with a new religious movement. I have shared aspects of my own NRM experience in order to demonstrate the importance of self-reflexivity on the part of the therapist and I have invited readers to consider their own positioning through consideration of therapeutic reflexive questions. I have also suggested that therapy in this area needs to hold in mind the possibility that NRMs as social phenomena, and involvement at individual level, can in some contexts be positive. Such an appreciative approach should not be misinterpreted as a denial of problems, but understood as part of the process of establishing a genuine dialogue and relationship with clients and the groups to which they belong.

Reflecting on the effects of my charismatic experiences, I wrote in 2009 'I continue to mourn the loss of the comfort and thrill of certain knowledge and meaning, and often feel somehow less than real or substantial as a person' (Pearson 2009). I am pleased to say that this is no longer true, but I am struck that it has taken 30 years for the harmful aftershocks of my teenage spiritual crisis to subside and for a confident new story to emerge, which in no small measure is supported by systemic ideas. Indeed, there is an argument that the systemic thinking, with its emphasis on 'the interconnection of everything', is inherently spiritual. This is not to say there are no continuities with my charismatic self. I have a concern for consistency between my professed values and actual behaviour, high expectations of those in authority and a capacity for public performance. Neither can I forget that it was through the ritual of prayer that I was dramatically healed of deep emotional wounds. However, challenging the thought may be for psychotherapists, my experience points to the importance of exploring client religious and spiritual beliefs, problems and resources as a routine aspect of assessment and therapeutic relationship, regardless of the type and service location of the therapy being provided. My experience of powerful, non-negotiated spiritual and therapeutic interventions has encouraged my embrace of a highly collaborative and non-diagnostic form of psychotherapy in order to help others. This is something I see as a vocation and expression of spirituality that I can dare to call my own.

Notes

1 Thanks to Philip Messent, Reenee Singh and Mark Rivett for their contributions and support in the writing of this chapter.
2 A multi-generational family tree mapping relationships and patterns over time.
3 A charity (www.mind.org.uk) providing advice and support for anyone experiencing a mental health problem.

References

AFT (Association for Family Therapy & Systemic Practice). 2011. *Code of Ethics and Practice*. Warrington: AFT.

Andersen, T. 1992. Reflections on reflecting with families, in: S. McNamee and K. Gergen (eds) *Therapy as Social Construction*. London: Sage, pp. 54–68.

Barker, E. 1989. *New Religious Movements: A Practical Introduction*. London: HMSO.

Berger, P. 1969. *A Rumor of Angels*. Garden City, NY: Doubleday Anchor Books.

Berger, P. and T. Luckmann. 1966. *The Social Construction of Reality*. Garden City, NY: Doubleday.

Boyd-Franklin, N. and B. Bry. 2000. *Reaching Out in Family Therapy*. New York: The Guilford Press.

Burnham, J. 1993. Systemic supervision: the evolution of reflexivity in the context of the supervisory relationship. *Human Systems*, 4(19), 349–81.

Byng-Hall, J. 1995. *Rewriting Family Scripts*. New York: The Guilford Press.

Carey, M. and S. Russell. 2003. Outsider-witness practices: some answers to commonly asked questions. *International Journal of Narrative Therapy & Community Work*, 1(2013), 3–16.

Dallos, R. and R. Draper. 2000. *An Introduction to Family Therapy*. Buckingham: Open University Press.

Duffy, M. 2010. Writing about clients: developing composite case material and its rationale. *Counselling and Values*, 54, 135–53.

Flaskas, C. 1996. Understanding the therapeutic relationship: using psychoanalytic ideas in the systemic context, in C. Flaskas, A. Perlesz and E.S. Wertheim (eds) *The Therapeutic Relationship in Systemic Therapy*. London: Karnac Books.

Griffith, J. and M. Griffith 2002. *Encountering the Sacred in Psychotherapy*. New York: The Guilford Press.

Hardham, V. 1996. Embedded and embodied in the therapeutic relationship: understanding the therapist's use of self systemically, in C. Flaskas, A. Perlesz and E.S. Wertheim (eds) *The Therapeutic Relationship in Systemic Therapy*. London: Karnac Books.

Hills, J. 2013. *Introduction to Family Therapy: A User's Guide*. Basingstoke: Palgrave Macmillan.

Howard, R. 1997. *Charismania*. Woonsocket, RI: Mowbray.

Mason, B. 1993. Towards positions of safe uncertainty. *Human Systems: The Journal of Systemic Consultation and Management*, 4, 189–200.

Mason, B. 2005. Risk taking and training. *Journal of Family Therapy*, 27(3), 298–301.

O'Hanlon, B. 2006. *Pathways to Spirituality*. New York: W.W. Norton and Company.

Pearson, A. 2009. Let's Talk: the application of systemic theory and practice to new religious movements and their past and current adherents. *Context*, 104, 26–28.

Pilgrim, D. 1997. *Psychotherapy and Society*. London: Sage.

Rivett, R. and E. Street 2009. *Family Therapy: 100 Key Points & Techniques*. London: Routledge.

Rober, P. 1999. The therapist's inner conversation in family therapy practice. *Family Process*, 38, 209–28.

Roberts, J. 2005. Transparency and self-disclosure in family therapy: dangers and possibilities. *Family Process* 44(1), 45–63.

Swim, S., S.A. St. George and D. Wulff. 2001. Process ethics: a collaborative partnership. *Journal of Systemic Therapies*, 20(4), 14–24.

Tomm, K. 1987. Interventive interviewing: part II. Reflexive questioning as a means to enable self-healing. *Family Process*, 26, 167–83.

Totsuka, Y. 2014. 'Which aspects of the social GGRRAAACCEEESSSS grab you most?' The social GGRRAAACCEEESSSS exercise for a supervision group to promote therapists' self reflexivity. *Journal of Family Therapy*, 3, 86–106.

Walsh, F. (ed.). 1999. *Spiritual Resources in Family Therapy*. New York: The Guilford Press.

White, M. 1987. Family therapy and schizophrenia: addressing 'the in-the-corner' lifestyle. *Dulwich Centre Newsletter*, Spring, 47–57.

Part II

Practitioners' approaches

5 Therapy with former members of destructive cults

Lorna Goldberg

Introduction

This chapter highlights considerations for professionals who provide therapy for first- generation and second-generation former cult members. Some individuals who believe they have been harmed by their involvement in a destructive cult[1] and who are experiencing difficulties in their post-cult lives seek therapy with me. In order to help them, I employ an integrated approach that utilizes both psycho-education and psychodynamic psychotherapy.[2] In this therapeutic method, instead of focusing on whether or not a group is a cult *per se*, I focus upon the specific manner in which the group's use of influence interacted with and affected the personality dynamics of each of my clients. Psycho-education focuses on the outside processes of the group while psychodynamic psychotherapy focuses on how those group dynamics affect the inner personality features, conflicts and emotional life of each of my clients.

Differences and commonalities in the treatment approach for first-generation and second-generation former cult members

For first-generation former cult members (those who joined in adulthood), I recommend a treatment approach that focuses on exploration of the cult experience prior to exploration of childhood. Most first-generation former cult members seek therapy because of troubling after-effects that they believe are related to their cult involvement. Many wish to understand how and why they became involved in a group that resulted in disrupting their life. They wish to comprehend why their behaviour changed so radically within the cult; that is, how they came to give up pre-cult relationships, beliefs, interests and their moral code. Cult education, which begins with deconstructing the recruitment process, can clarify what has often been a mystifying, overwhelming, self-defeating and often traumatic experience (Lifton 1961). Therefore, the therapist utilises an approach where the goal initially centers on helping clients distinguish between dynamics of cult-induced personality change that originates from undue influence in cult recruitment from personality characteristics, interests and beliefs derived from pre-cult family development (Goldberg 1993).

With second-generation former cult members (those who were born and raised in cults, also referred to as second-generation adults or SGAs), the early childhood experience and the cult experience are one and the same. The cult structure is often authoritarian in style with a single worldview and with decision making imposed from above. The therapist needs to appreciate that the cult past is integral to the person's sense of self and it will be expressed in character traits (Goldberg 2006) and psychological conflicts and defences. These clients often need help in making the transition to the wider culture. The therapist is aided by the perspective that second-generation former members can be considered as being similar to refugees who have departed from countries in which an authoritarian leader demands total obedience. In this alternative culture, some cult leaders establish the childrearing rules that parents are expected to follow without question. As a result, empathy between parents and children is undermined, and children are at risk of abuse or neglect (Stein 1997; Goldberg 2003).

While second-generation former cult members might feel relief and newfound freedom on leaving a cult, there might also be loneliness and a sense of otherness. As with immigrants, many second-generation former cult members leave their group without family and friends. They may discover that social interactions in the cult contrast with the mainstream world and, often, there are gaps in their academic education and knowledge of popular culture. Therefore, psycho-education includes providing second-generation former cult members with practical information about the mainstream world and, also, providing help in accessing basic resources. Referrals to other professionals and organisations are part of the therapy process (Bardin 2013).

Initial engagement in therapy

In the first session with all former cult members, I address the mechanics of the therapy process and describe how this will unfold in the future. I address potential transference issues, common post-cult problems, and focus upon the individual's strengths. Former cult members who come for therapy often are filled with shame; they tend to be self-blaming. In many cases, this appears to be an outgrowth of a cult experience that kept them shamed and blamed.

It is crucial for all clients, but particularly for former cult members, that therapy becomes a collaborative process and that clients feel free to have different beliefs than the beliefs of their therapist. For example, a client expressed a desire to see a so-called 'intuitive' and was fearful that I might not approve. In contrast to the cult's demand that she align with them to prove her loyalty, I pointed out that there would be many times in therapy when we might not agree, but this is part of many healthy relationships.

The therapist pays attention not only to words, but also to character style (including body language) as well as transference[3] and countertransference[4] reactions. Observation of these factors can provide the therapist and the client with insight into the client's emotions and, sometimes, uncovers erroneous thoughts. Former cult members maintain self-defeating assumptions or beliefs that are accepted as true and that generally are not expressed to others. Clients are helped to gain better insight into distorted beliefs that may lead to self-defeating behaviours. For example, a depressed client who felt guilty about having left her group was spending an inordinate amount of time cleaning her apartment rather than socialising with friends and family. Her sister was puzzled by this behaviour, because this individual always enjoyed socialising prior to the cult. I explored this woman's need to constantly clean. Upon reflection, she was able to voice her belief that she was 'dirty', because she secretly wanted to do 'indulgent' things, such as going to a movie or a dance club. The cult message was the need to resist indulgent pleasures and this dictum continued to control her life after she left. My client appeared to be holding onto this particular cult dictum as an unconscious way to avoid dating and, potentially, engaging in a sexual relationship. Therapy allowed her to better understand her own unconscious reasons for her avoidance and, thus, work them through so she could begin to engage in social activities again. I began to notice that my previously depressed client began to appear more animated and the feeling in the room started to become lighter.

A respectful collaborative therapy approach serves to increase development of cognitive abilities, reality testing and clients' assertion on their own behalf. This includes allowing clients to set the pace of therapy. For example, a client with whom I worked had spent her childhood in a cult that was physically abusive. Although I was aware of published reports of severe corporal punishment, the client initially avoided exploration of childhood physical abuse. Although my client might have been subjected to this abuse, I felt that it was important to allow this aspect of her life to unfold only when she was ready to explore it with me. This therapeutic experience contrasted with her cult childhood where, she later explained to me, she was verbally or physically assaulted.

It is my contention that without an understanding of the cult's deceptive and exploitative techniques, those who leave cults tend to be plagued by doubts and symptoms longer than those who gain such an understanding. The process of working side by side with former cult members to identify the deceptions, manipulations and the shaming of a destructive cult allows both first-generation and second-generation former cult members to see how they were harmed. This focus shifts them away from seeing themselves as flawed or 'stupid'. I generally have found that those first-generation former cult members who come for therapy with me over the last 40 years appear to have similar pre-existing psychological factors or family backgrounds to those who do not join cults. The factor that appears to be the most salient is that the group captures recruits' interest at times of transition, uncertainty, or dissatisfaction (Goldberg and Goldberg 1982) with a message that resonates. Some of them might be defined as 'spiritual seekers', but many simply were approached by a group with a hidden agenda that offered them the possibility of comfort and affiliation at a time that they were vulnerable. In contrast to this, more fortunate individuals at vulnerable times might gain a sense of affiliation from a group that operates in a straightforward and open manner.

Excluding feelings about having 'joined' a cult, second-generation former cult members have many of the same after-effects as those experienced by first-generation former members. However, in contrast to first-generation former cult members, the cult identity of second-generation members is integral to their present personality (Goldberg 2006).

Example of first-generation former cult member

In order to highlight post-cult problems that former cult members typically experience, I will provide a case study to illustrate how these difficulties can emerge within the therapy process.

Self-blame and confusion

Gayle (a pseudonym) had left a Bible-based group after five years of involvement. A friend, who departed before her, had referred Gayle to me. Gayle was a conservatively dressed young woman with a serious demeanor. In her first session, Gayle focused on her sadness that a group that she initially believed to be holy had ultimately exploited her. She blamed herself for being 'stupid' and felt depressed about loss of money, time and confidence. She was confused about how this could have happened. Prior to joining, she had viewed herself as an intelligent person. She wondered whether she would ever trust her own judgment again.

Suppression of negative thoughts

I told Gayle that in our work together we would pay careful attention to thoughts that might be influencing her present behaviour, as these thoughts may be preventing her from moving forward. I wondered how she had dealt with her thoughts in the cult? Gayle responded that she generally tried to not pay attention to her thoughts. She feared that negative thoughts would undermine her true purpose to live a holy life. She added that when she had negative thoughts, she would dismiss them. Negative thoughts were seen as 'Satanic'. After some initial difficulty, Gayle connected negative thoughts with feelings of shame. I suggested that labelling negative thoughts or doubts as 'Satanic' and, therefore, shameful, appeared to be a vehicle used by the group to undermine her critical thinking. Since everyone has negative as well as positive thoughts, these doubts indicated healthy reality testing. I added that, after years of being told how to handle her thoughts, she might experience my suggestion to share her thoughts with me as a requirement of therapy. However, I reassured her that ultimately, it would be her choice to determine what to speak about in her sessions.

Difficulty making decisions

After years of looking to her pastor for direction, Gayle described feeling stuck and unable to make decisions. Gayle wanted a new job and to live on her own (she had returned to living with her parents), but she was unable to take any steps towards looking for a job or a new apartment. Whenever she thought about taking action, she feared that she would make a terrible mistake. She added: 'It took me two months to be able to call you'. I told her that she was describing a common after-effect of cult involvement. Gayle recalled that decision making had not been difficult prior to joining the cult. However, now, when thinking about different job possibilities, she also felt unable to justify her five years working for the cult. We explored different options to describe her cult activities. Additionally, we explored Gayle's fear of taking the wrong job. Gayle smiled and acknowledged that she always can leave.

Potential transference feelings

I told Gayle that I did not expect her to always agree with me and I might make mistakes. She had uncomfortable feelings in the church, but had disregarded them, so it would be valuable to explore if she felt she must disregard uncomfortable feelings with me. Her group did not tolerate differences of opinion or allow discussion of disappointment with her pastor. However, I explained, in relationships there are always differences and disappointments. If Gayle tried to pay attention to her feelings, even her negative ones, and talked with me about them, we would be able to discern whether there was something that I had said or done in a session to make her uncomfortable or whether the source of these feelings came from other places. Transference feelings from the cult as well as from her family life would be re-experienced in therapy. Some potential transference feelings that former cult members can experience towards therapists include fear of being exploited, anxiety about being controlled and fear of criticism.

Dealing with a harsh conscience stemming from the cult

Gayle initially thought that I would be angry with her if she missed a session, came late, or disagreed with me. She was trying too hard to please me and become the 'perfect' client. I was feeling uncomfortable about her anxiety regarding my potential negative reactions. I pointed out this tendency one day when she apologised for a 'forgotten' session. I shared with her my thought that, sometimes, people 'forget' sessions when they don't feel like coming for various reasons. Gayle smiled sheepishly and said, 'That might be true'. I told her that, perhaps, there would come a time when she would be free to let herself and me know about her negative feelings directly, because she would see that I could accept hearing about them.

Gayle's expectation that I would have harsh attitudes towards her helped her understand the nature of her relationship with her cult leader and her readiness to expect those in her present life to be critical. (In her pre-cult life, her parents had not been particularly harsh with her.) She came to see how this assumption also was a projection of her own self-critical attitude; that is, her expectation that her behaviour should be perfect.

Cult induced passivity and reliance on others

Gayle's passivity and reliance on others was, in part, an after-effect of cult involvement. Gayle had become used to relying on her leader, who purported to have all the answers for life. However, I made it clear that therapy was a place for her to discover her own wishes and goals. At times, Gayle struggled with uncertainty. However, her executive functions and self-confidence grew as she began relying on her own viewpoint.

Gaining an understanding of cult control

Gayle felt she was 'stupid' for joining the cult in the first place. However, we agreed that at that time she believed the cult would be beneficial for her and no one indicated the underlying nature of the group. Therefore, I expressed doubt that she became involved because she was 'stupid'; it was more likely that she was uninformed about the true nature of the group. I emphasised that it was my impression that she was attracted to her group because of a healthy human desire for a sense of community or a better world, particularly at a vulnerable time. As she better understood all the factors and pressures underlying her participation in the church, she might begin to feel less stupid, confused and stuck. She might also begin to gain clarity regarding the process that led to her disregarding negative feelings about her experience.

Cult vulnerability

Gayle and I began to focus on her life at the point of joining the cult, particularly focusing upon her emotional vulnerability. Our step-by-step analysis of her experience shifted her from the overwhelming emotion of shame that was prevalent in the beginning of therapy. Shameful feelings that derived from her participation in a cult decreased as she began to gain an understanding of the manipulations used by her group. Gayle came to understand that it would make sense for naïve and/or idealistic people to be dazzled by the group's indoctrination tactics. For example, Gayle initially believed that her cult was a Christian church and this was comforting to her. At the outset, she had no idea about all that would be required of her. However, over time, Gayle began to see how the inspiring, 'spontaneous' services of young people were actually carefully staged. In fact, through a variety of fear tactics ('You must do this to be saved…'), individuals were pressured to attend church each day and to serve the cult leaders in numerous other ways, such as by tithing, and babysitting for the minister's wife.

Finding a community to escape from loneliness

In continuing our exploration of the factors that led to Gayle joining the group, Gayle expressed that she had been feeling lonely and uncertain about her future after college. Although she was working as an office manager, she found work to be uninspiring. It was difficult to connect with friends or meet young men. While shopping at a local mall, Gayle was approached by two young women, who were friendly and appeared to be 'just like me'. They encouraged her to join them for a service at their church. Gayle, who felt disconnected from her Roman Catholic faith, decided that this was worth a try. She found the service exciting and, after a year of feeling disheartened about returning home and feeling isolated from college friends, it was comforting to have young people all around her. Everyone was friendly and the service had stirring songs and an enthusiastic sermon led by a handsome pastor. Gail agreed that the pastor was like a motivational speaker whose style contrasted with her local priest, who led the service with little emotion. In time, Gayle realised that she had escaped loneliness and uncertainty about her future by joining the church and placing herself under the protection of an idealised figure.

Cult ecstasy, dissociation and interference with critical thinking

Gayle began to understand how the church induced her to experience ecstatic emotion[5] and suppress critical thought processes. The pastor was a charismatic leader who led his congregation in passionate songs, delivered stirring sermons and demanded frequent group activities. Gayle believed that she was in the midst of a world of true believers and she was experiencing the excitement of feeling total unity with others. A powerful emotional feeling of ecstasy swept over her, and her pastor credited himself with providing her with this emotional reaction.

At the same time, every moment was filled with work, church services, Bible study or recruiting. The amplified emotion and exhaustion from emotional church services and constant activity resulted in loss of sleep, privacy and space to think. She reported that she often felt 'spaced out'.

All of this served to increase her state of suggestibility. Furthermore, Gayle was encouraged to suppress normal emotional responses by relabelling them as 'negative' or 'selfish'. For example, when Gayle wanted to spend time with her family, she was admonished, 'Is it more important to spend time with your family or to spend time serving God?'. This type of scolding from her pastor or other members induced guilty feelings in Gayle for her 'selfish' needs, which not only included time spent with family, but also time spent with friends in 'fun' activities, such as going to movies or to clubs. She eventually began to accept the attitude that fun activities with family and friends were trivial compared with her higher mission to save the world.

Gayle's sense of a higher mission initially increased her self-esteem after college when she was adrift. However, eventually, her self-esteem plummeted, that is, when she was unable to live up to the impossibly high demands that were placed on her. Over time, she saw less of her mother. She dropped old friends completely. This drove Gayle to spend more time in the cult working harder to prove her devotion and loyalty. Her cult became her new family and their message became her own (Lifton 1961).

The pastor interpreted Gayle's altered state of devotion as God's intervention. Her pastor had provided her with a new beginning and a new pseudo-identity was formed above her original personality (West and Martin 1994), a personality that was re-socialised into accepting the attitudes of the group.

Creation of distance between Gayle and family, friends and the outside world

Gayle's mother voiced concern about the group and how time-consuming it had become. As she had been instructed, Gayle shared her mother's concerns with the pastor. Before the cult, Gayle had been missing her father and entering into the cult soon after his death made her particularly vulnerable to the pastor, her new father figure, when he criticised her mother's 'selfish' attitudes as harmful to Gayle's spiritual growth. In time, as a result of the pastor's influence, Gayle began to see her mother negatively. She left her home, moving into an apartment with other female members of the church. After several months, again, as a result of the pastor's influence, Gayle left her employment to work for the group full-time. At that point, her involvement with outsiders became minimal.

Doubts are suppressed by shaming

Gayle described how, after some time in the group, she began to have concerns about the pastor's lavish lifestyle. This was in stark contrast to the members who lived a simple lifestyle. Another member reported Gayle's concerns to the pastor, who reproached her for 'simplistic thinking' and 'material concerns'. He declared that in order to do his good work in the world he had to be respected by other leaders and needed to show that he was a leader among leaders. Gayle recalled that the pastor made her feel 'small' and 'ashamed' for questioning him. She learned from this incident that it was dangerous to express doubts to other members, because she could not trust them to keep confidentiality. Gayle learned that she would be shamed and belittled if she questioned the pastor's behaviour. The pastor had turned the tables and made Gayle believe that she was the materialistic one. As a result of this experience, when Gayle had concerns about some of the unethical proselytising and fundraising, she kept her feelings to herself and rationalised this by reminding herself that the ends justified the means.

Sacrificing for the Cult

After the incident with the pastor, Gayle felt more determined to show her loyalty to the church and prove herself as a true believer. She gave the pastor her inheritance from her grandmother. Letting go of her own emotional and material needs gave Gayle some sense of relief. She did this because she believed she was on a holy path.[6] I asked Gayle about her thinking at the time. She indicated that she was influenced by church doctrine; that is, personal finances were not important and giving her inheritance to the church and jewellery to the pastor's wife was a way of displaying love for God. She recalled that members were held in a positive light if they donated money and services to the group. Members were told that they were showing true commitment and they would be rewarded both with special praise by the pastor and in Heaven. In contrast, those who chose to keep their finances and pre-cult jobs were seen in a negative light; they were made to feel selfish and greedy.

Fear of the outside world

The pastor created a black and white vision of the world; outsiders were selfish and indulgent while church members were kind and self-sacrificing. As in a number of cults, Gayle had been filled with phobias about leaving (Hassan 1988). The pastor predicted terrible consequences for those who left, including that all 'outsiders' were going to Hell.

After a few years in the cult, Gayle had a chance meeting with a friend who had left the group. Prior to meeting her, Gayle had imagined that leaving had destroyed her friend's life. Gayle's friend appeared to be living a good life; she was happily married and had fulfilling work. After the meeting, Gayle's friend began to send her emails that cited the corruption in the cult. Simultaneously, Gayle had been having doubts about some of the pastor's actions. Now the emails were confirming her doubts. Through these emails, Gayle discovered that the pastor had been involved in scandals in another country and had whitewashed his past. She discovered that the pastor was exploiting members to line his own pockets and that he was buying properties in his home country. Gayle eventually doubted the group enough to consider leaving. With some trepidation, Gayle secretly arranged to speak with her friend. This meeting further confirmed her doubts and Gayle decided to leave. She indicated that, in the beginning stage of her involvement, she probably would have dismissed this negative information. However, after more time, the emails confirmed some of the hypocrisy that she previously had rationalised.

Gayle left with ambivalent feelings. Although she felt some relief and was able to see the exploitative behaviour, she also was fearful of going to Hell.

She feared she was no longer a good person and believed that God would punish her, by making her gravely ill or fail at life. Gayle began to see how these thoughts were connected to suggestions from the cult leader. Simultaneously, reading of cult-related literature allowed Gayle to see how phobia induction was a controlling process in many cults. Gayle began to see how the leader induced unfounded fears in her. She spoke about this when she attended a support group and she discovered that others had similar reactions upon leaving their groups.

Induced paranoia

As Gayle became more aware of the cult's deception, she experienced a period of mild paranoia and began to see deception everywhere. She talked about the motivational speakers on television that acted as if they had all the answers. She analysed politicians and pointed out their evasions. She wanted to date, but feared she might get involved with a manipulative man. I explored Gayle's untrusting behaviour first as an after-effect of cult deception. However, we also looked to her experiences with boyfriends prior to joining the cult and focused upon family experiences. It was important for Gayle to see that, although she had been somewhat naive, she didn't have these fears in her life prior to the cult. Therefore, understanding that her paranoia was cult-induced allowed Gayle to begin to become less fearful.

Difficulty in taking pleasure in life

Gayle was reluctant to return to her pre-cult interests – dancing, music and photography. Noting this hesitancy, I questioned Gayle about what thoughts might prevent her from participating in these areas. Gayle laughed and said, 'I can't believe that I still feel those interests are frivolous. It is just fun, but I feel I should live a more serious life. It's as if I feel guilty about this'. Gayle recognised that these were not her thoughts prior to joining; she was made to feel this way in her church.

Childhood identity is submerged under new cult identity

Gayle described how unnerving it was for her to realise that she had submerged so much of her core identity within the cult. She wondered who she actually was after having experienced this drastic personality change. Therapy would help her deconstruct and begin to understand how she had been induced to change her beliefs and do things that she would never have done prior to her church involvement.

In reflecting on the consequences of her self-renunciation and personality change in the cult (Lalich 2004), Gayle began to focus upon her difficult present circumstances. She had neither money nor a job. Her grandmother had left her money and jewellery, intending for Gayle to have financial security. It now was gone.

Positive experiences in the cult and a desire for a meaningful life

Gayle was feeling lonely, especially compared to the intensity of the group experience. Gayle missed her cult friends and the feeling that they were involved in a common goal. It made her feel sad that her cult friendships were conditional, based upon her group loyalty. Now she was shunned. Gayle was mourning the loss of a valuable part of her cult life.

Gayle showed concern about having a life 'without meaning'. She had a high standard for herself and she believed that she was not living up to this standard. Although she considered that this attitude was, in part, cult-induced, she also believed that she wanted to keep this aspect of her identity. Now Gayle would be in charge of providing her life with meaning.

Once Gayle had more clarity about why she participated in the group, and learned about some of the typical after effects, we started to discuss her pre-cult life and how some of her pre-cult beliefs and vulnerabilities had been reflected in her post-cult behaviour. In order to gain an understanding of her early life, we spent time exploring her life with her parents and friends. In time, she chose to end therapy. However, it was understood that if she felt that she needed to return in the future she always would be welcome.

Benefit of a support group

A support group for former cult members that I co-lead initially supplemented Gayle's individual therapy. In the support group, Gayle was able to recognise the commonalities of cult coercive behaviour (Goldberg and Goldberg 1982). After Gayle ended individual therapy, she periodically attended the support group. At times she brought along former members of her cult who were engaged in the beginning stage of their recovery. Gayle continued to help former cult members by easing their transition to the world outside of the cult. This was one of Gayle's contributions to a meaningful life.

Goals of therapy

The aim of psychotherapy with former cult members is to help clients live more productively in the present. In order to do this, clients need to be able to become consciously aware of how the cult past as well as life prior to the cult is constantly affecting them and shaping their present life.

Most first-generation former cult members seek therapy because of troubling after effects related to their cult experience. They primarily wish to explore the radical changes in behaviour that occurred; that is, how they were induced to give up pre-cult relationships, beliefs, interests and their pre-cult moral code. Therefore, in the beginning of therapy, I recommend a treatment approach that initially examines the influence of cult dynamics before early childhood experiences are explored. It is crucial to understand how cult reshaping occurs.

Those who enter cults in adulthood begin reshaping their original character structure after recruitment into the cult environment. Recruits change because the cult deceptively gives them false explanations for what they are experiencing. Their time in the cult results in superimposing a new cult personality on top of the cult member's original character, as described by West and Martin (1998) and Jenkinson (2008). This change occurs, because, over time, recruits unconsciously need to find adaptive solutions to fit in as loyal members of the cult. Therefore, cult members are placed into a suggestible state by the combination of powerful emotion that is reinterpreted as coming from some kind of higher power as well as constant activity and lack of sleep that serves to suppress both their critical thinking and, ultimately, aspects of their personalities. This is reinforced by how the cult leader labels the cult members' critical thinking and idiosyncratic personality traits as negative or disloyal if they don't support cult leaders' goals. These attempts to suppress lead to cult created beliefs and character traits that become undermining when former cult members leave for the wider world. Some examples of these beliefs include the belief that once they leave the cult, they will die, become gravely ill, or have a major accident, because they no longer are under the cult leaders' protective powers. Some examples of cult induced character traits can include passivity, a proclivity to experience shame and guilt and a black and white view of the world that is reflected in suspiciousness towards outsiders or those who have a different view.

Cult education first deconstructs the recruitment process to clarify what usually has been a mystifying, overwhelming, self-defeating and often traumatic experience for the recruit. Utilisation of an approach where the goal is to help clients gain a better grasp first on their cult recruitment experience and, later, on their early family development provides clients with a contrast between behaviour change from undue influence and behaviour that was developed over time in their pre-cult life.

Without an understanding of the cult's deceptive and coercive techniques, those who leave destructive cults tend to be plagued by doubts and symptoms for longer than those who gain such an understanding. The process of learning about the methods of a destructive cult allows clients to see how they were purposely deceived. This focus shifts them away from blaming themselves as flawed or 'stupid' individuals.

The factor that appears to be the most salient is that the cult captures the recruit's interest at a time of transition, uncertainty, or dissatisfaction, often in early adulthood, employing a message that resonates for that particular individual (Goldberg and Goldberg 1982).

Excluding feelings about having 'joined' a cult, second-generation former cult members struggle with some of the same aftereffects experienced by first-generation former cult members. That includes feelings of guilt, shame, paranoia that result from living in a black and white world and developing a harsh conscience after living with a punishing leader. However, in contrast to first-generation cult members, the early childhood experience and the cult experience of second-generation adults (SGAs) are one and the same and will be preserved in specific character traits and defences (Goldberg 2006). Therapists working with SGAs often are seeing individuals who experienced a childhood of neglect and/or abuse, because their parents are pressured to serve the needs of the cult leader prior to serving their children's needs. Similar to refugees from an authoritarian culture, they have been raised in a culture defined by the predilections and abusive practices of the cult leader. SGAs respond best to therapy that addresses these aspects of their past and helps them gain an understanding of and resources from mainstream culture.

Departing cult members bring cult-related attitudes into the mainstream culture after they have left. Cult leaders tend to keep their members from exiting by instilling them with fears of the outside world. They also demand perfection from their followers and use the fact that members have failed to reach perfection as an excuse to abuse and to keep them striving and feeling small. Both first and second-generation former cult members enter into mainstream culture with cult-induced paranoia and a grandiose wish to attain perfection. Goals include the need to lessen anxiety about the mainstream world and the people in it and to lessen depression, which often is attached to feelings of self-reproach and loss.

Lalich (2004) describes the process of cult commitment as 'bounded choice'. There is a fusion between the ideal of personal freedom, which was promised in the ideology, and the demands for self-renunciation, which are prescribed by the rules and norms. Responding to the demands of the cult leader requires repeated acts of self-renunciation; but, at the same time, the cultist is experiencing relief at having found the answer, which is experienced as a personal relief (2004: 14–16).

After seeing the cult leader as the sole arbiter of reality and perfection, there is a tendency to transfer those feelings on to a therapist. It is important for the therapist to help former cult members understand the limitations of, and mistakes made by, all human beings, including the therapist, and to help clients think critically, articulate their own point of view and begin to appreciate their unique identity.

During difficult times and periods of uncertainty, many experience relief by identifying with idealised figures (Spruiell 1979). Cult leaders can appear to relieve loneliness, pain, anxieties and uncertainties with proclamations of certainty and righteousness. At a time of crisis or of experiencing some degree of distress, it is common, under the influence of a protective, reassuring and charismatic leader, to regress and defend against the more unacceptable or confusing emotions within and to project them onto the wider world (Goldberg 2012). Therefore, a goal of therapy is to help former cult members become more able to tolerate their uncomfortable human feelings and to feel more confident about their potential ability to successfully manage their life.

Notes

1 I use the definition adopted by the Wingspread Conference where experts in the field agreed upon the following definition of a destructive cult:

> a group or movement exhibiting a great or excessive devotion or dedication to some person, idea, or thing and employing unethically manipulative techniques of persuasion and control … to advance the goals of the group's leaders to the actual or possible detriment of members, their families, or the community.
>
> (West and Langone 1985: 119–120)

I do not use the term 'New Religious Movement' as many cults are not religious.

2 Psychodynamic therapy focuses on unconscious processes as they are manifested in the client's present behaviour. The goals of psychodynamic therapy are client self-awareness and understanding of the influence of the past on present. (www.ncbi.nlm.nih.gov/books/NBK64952) (National Center for Biotechnology Information). Last accessed 13/2/2017.

3 Freud defined transference as the displacement of feelings, originating with important figures from early life, onto the analyst (Freud 1940). Transference also occurs in present life with friends, family members and work colleagues.

4 Countertransference originally was defined as a situation in which a therapist's feelings and attitudes toward a client stem from feelings derived from situations in the past that have been displaced onto the patient (Moore and Fine 1990). Heiman expanded this definition to focus upon how the

> analyst's immediate emotional response to his patient is a significant pointer to the patient's unconscious processes and guides him towards fuller understanding.… The emotions aroused in the analyst will be of value to his patient, if used as one more source of insight into the patient's unconscious conflicts and defenses; and when these are interpreted and worked through, the ensuing changes in the patient's ego include the strengthening of his reality sense so that he sees his analyst as a human being not a god or demon, and the "human" relationship in the analytic situation follows.
>
> (Heiman 1950)

Therefore, instead of something the analyst must overcome, Heiman viewed countertransference as a tool to better understand the patient. A more contemporary approach suggests that transference and countertransference should be analyzed as a mutual interactional process instead of becoming artificially split off from one another as if they each occur in isolation. This is the relational perspective (Aron 1991).

5 Farber writes about the ecstasy that can be found in cults. She cites Melanie Klein, who originated the term 'manic defense', to refer to a mental operation that provides protection from depressive as well as paranoid anxieties. This defense aids in coping with painful affects. It plays a central role for those who need to defend against feeling grief and sadness and those who are unable to mourn. It creates the illusion that we are omnipotent, standing above our vulnerable self (Farber 2013).

6 Lalich describes how resocialisation in the cult is a two-person process and there is personal relief for the cult member in renunciation of the self (Lalich 2004: 14–16).

References

Aron, L. 1991. The patient's experience of the analyst's subjectivity. *Psychoanalytic Dialogues*, 1, 29–51.

Bardin, L. 2013. *Starting Out: To Find Your Way in Mainstream America*. E-Book published by the International Cultic Studies Association.

Farber, S.K. 2013. *Hungry for Ecstasy*. Lanhan, MD: Jason Aronson (subsidiary of Rowman & Littlefield Publishing Group, Inc.).

Freud, S. 1940. *An Outline of Psychoanalysis*. *S.E.*, 23, 141–207. London: Hogarth Press.

Goldberg, L. 1993. Guidelines for therapists, in M. Langone (ed.) *Recovery from Cults*. New York: Norton Press.

Goldberg, L. 2003. Reflections on marriage after the cult. *Cultic Studies Review*, 2(1), 9–29.

Goldberg, L. 2006. Raised in cultic groups: the impact on the development of certain aspects of character. *Cultic Studies Review*, 5(1), 1–28.

Goldberg, L. 2012. Influence of a charismatic antisocial cult leader: psychotherapy with an ex-cultist prosecuted for criminal behavior. *International Journal of Cultic Studies*, 3, 15–24.

Goldberg, L. and W. Goldberg. 1982. Group work with former cultists. *Social Work*, 27(2): 165–70.

Hassan, S. 1988. *Combatting Cult Mind Control*. Randolph, VT: Park Street Press.

Heiman, P. 1950. On counter-transference. *International Journal of Psycho-Analysis*, 31, 81–84.

Jenkinson, G. 2008. An investigation into cult pseudo-personality: what is it and how does it form? *Cultic Studies Review*, 7(3), 199–224.

Lalich, J. 2004. *Bounded Choice*. Berkeley: University of California Press.

Lifton, R. 1961. *Thought Reform and the Psychology of Totalism*. New York: The Norton Press.

Moore, B. and B. Fine (eds.) 1990. *Psychoanalytic Terms and Concepts*. Binghamton, NY: Val-Ballou Press.

Spruiell, V. 1979. Freud's concept of idealization. *Journal of the American Psychoanalytic Association*, 27, 777–91.

Stein, A. 1997. Mothers in cults: the influence of cults on the relationship of mothers to their children. *Cultic Studies Journal*, 14(1), 40–57.

West, L.J. and M.D. Langone. 1985. *Cultism: A Conference for Scholars and Policy Makers*. Summary of proceedings of the Wingspread conference on cultism, September 9–11. Weston, MA: American Family Foundation.

West, L.J. and P. Martin. 1994. Pseudo-identity and the treatment of personality change in victims of captivity and cults, in S. J. Lynn and J. Rhue (eds) *Dissociation*. New York: Guilford Press, pp. 268–88.

6 The psychological development and consequences of involvement with new religious movements

Counselling issues for members, former members and families

Linda Dubrow-Marshall and Roderick Dubrow-Marshall

Introduction

The psychological effects of belonging to and leaving new religious movements and other new social movements or minority belief groups or organisations (sometimes also referred to as extremist groups, cults, sects or high demand groups or coercive environments),[1] have been extensively researched and documented (Langone 1995; Aronoff, Lynn and Malinoski 2000; Dubrow-Marshall 2010; Almendros et al. 2011; Dubrow-Marshall and Dubrow-Marshall 2015). There has also been a related increase over several decades in helping approaches and counselling for current and former members of cultic groups and their families, which offer additional data and insights (Martin et al. 1992; Jenkinson 2013).

Research and practice in this area have therefore begun to indicate distinct group-related patterns of psychological involvement in new religious or other social movements which has allowed for specific counselling responses. These can be tailored to the needs of clients in particular contexts with an approach taking into account the complexity of the psychological journey into, within and out of high-demand and extremist environments (Giambalvo and Henry 2010). The development and consequences of such involvement are described extensively elsewhere (Lifton 1961, 2000; Dubrow-Marshall and Dubrow-Marshall 2015) and here the focus will be on how such patterns and trends (including, for example, length of involvement, level of commitment or isolation) inform counselling approaches as forms of evidence-based and efficacious counselling practice (Dubrow-Marshall 2013).

In particular, we attempt to show how the psychological contract (as defined, for example, by Thomas et al. [2016] as the perceived reciprocal relationship between individuals and groups or organisations) and the commitment which members of minority belief systems make, fundamentally define self-identity in ways which render other aspects of identity temporarily or sometimes permanently redundant or submerged (Dubrow-Marshall 2010). As such we will argue that membership of new religious movements or cult-like groups offers members a huge psychological gain in terms of identity and self-esteem which fills a common existential gap present in most psychologically healthy people, and which is hard if not impossible to replace upon disengaging and leaving. It follows that the duty of care of such groups should extend to ensuring that members do not overly identify or involve themselves in their organisation to the potential detriment of their mental health, even if that appears to be against the belief system of the group and its overall *raison d'être*.

It is this area of care and self-care, where it often appears (particularly to outsiders) that the mental well-being of members is considered to be of lesser importance than the beliefs and practice of the group. It is this imbalance of priorities that presents one of the greatest challenges to members, families, former members and counsellors and psychologists working with them in the quest to create healthy and functional relationships and environments which are compatible with minority or extremist beliefs and ideas in liberal and democratic societies where pluralism and healthiness are equally valued and cherished tenets. It is to be noted that these challenges also abound for 'mainstream' organisations (including companies, hospitals and universities) that appear to require excessive devotion of time, energy and identity from their members or employees (Tourish 2013).

This chapter will describe a specialist model of counselling for members, former members and families who have been involved with new religious movements or cults (also referred to as minority belief groups or organisations, cultic groups, high demand groups, extremist groups and abusive groups and relationships) which feature undue influence, defined by Peisah et al. (2009: 9) as 'overpowering or overbearing of the testator's volition, judgment or wishes by substitution of one mind for another', and coercive persuasion, defined by Schein (1961) as including the psychological processes of compliance, confession and indoctrination. The model has been adapted broadly by practitioners working with RETIRN (the Re-entry Therapy, Information and Referral Network), which was founded in 1983 in the USA by Linda Dubrow-Marshall, Steve Eichel, Roberta and Steven Eisenberg and Gary Schoenberg, and founded in 2004 in the United Kingdom by Linda and Roderick Dubrow-Marshall (authors of this chapter). While the various practitioners have different ways of working with clients, they share a core system of beliefs about how to approach working with members, former members and families which acknowledges their particular needs and separates them from counselling issues in general.

The chapter will also describe how the RETIRN model of intervening in cult-related cases emphasises the commonly observed and measured psychological processes and suffering experienced by individuals and families who have been affected by new religious movements and other relationships and groups where undue influence is evident rather than focusing on the specific ideologies of the group (Langone 1995). The model also emphasises the importance of unconditional positive regard in families, supportive and respectful interventions and a non-judgemental psycho-educational model. This approach can be compared to other approaches which have focused on this population (Martin 1993; Giambalvo and Henry 2010; Jenkinson 2013). The development and consequences of involvement with new religious movements and cults will be shown to inform how these counselling models can be appropriate for working with individuals adversely affected by their involvement with these groups or relationships.

Psychological aetiology – factors contributing to involvement with new religious movements or cults

There has been much debate and research about which, if any, psychological factors may lead to a person's vulnerability to recruitment into a new religious movement or cult, and whether those factors may also contribute to post-exit psychopathology (as well as, or instead of, the group dynamics or influence). Some have argued for a focus on preexisting individual and family psychodynamics and psychopathology as reasons for people joining or staying in extremist groups (such as Namini and Murken 2009). Others have indicated that involvement with cult helping groups as important factors in the mental health issues reported after people leave such groups compared to those that remain inside (Galanter 1988). It is also posited that more benign contextual factors and fate, 'being in the wrong place at the wrong time', are key factors in people becoming members (Hassan 1990; Singer 2003) rather than a specific psychological predisposition and pathology (for a balanced review of these debates see Langone, 2000, 2005).[2]

It has been shown (Hassan 1990; Singer 2003) that a broad range of individuals coming from a variety of family, religious, educational and socioeconomic backgrounds have been recruited into cults or high pressure groups, which therefore indicates against a specific 'type' of person who might be susceptible to undue influence and thought reform (Lifton 1961, 2000), and more importantly indicates that there is not a common preexisting psychopathology (beyond the normal variation in such symptomology in the general population) (Langone 1995). Indeed, it has also been demonstrated that recruitment to new religious movements or to cults often requires attraction to a leader, group, idea, mission or purpose, and this requires some 'normal' responsiveness to social influence (Hassan 2000). It follows that people who are (already) psychotic or psychopathic may be less vulnerable to undue group influence as they are more attuned to their internal needs than to other people or to wider causes or missions.

One aspect of recruitment to new religious movements or cults which has often been reported is that people were in a period of transition when they were drawn into the group, which indicates that vulnerability to group pressure may be intensified when people are going through a period of change of lifestyle, change of identity/sense of self, a geographical move or moving into a different stage of life. At these times, people may be more open to new ideas, people and ways of living as they are moving forward and they may indeed be confused about who they are or the meaning of their lives (Singer 2003). Furthermore, people who are recruited may not have full information about the group they are joining, and deceptive practices, including withholding of information about the group, have been widely reported (Hassan 1990; Atack 2016). The accountability of group members may be of a lower standard than in other groups, so abusive groups may not be transparent about their structure or purpose (Hassan 1990). Health and safety standards that would be legally upheld in other organisations may not be applied, and this can make people more vulnerable to undue influence as their personal needs may be compromised in order to meet group needs (Singer 2003). Once they have joined, they may be deprived of contact with people outside the group with differing opinions, or even adequate rest, sleep, food, exercise and other basic needs in a way that has been defined by Lifton (1961) as 'milieu control'.

In addition to people who are recruited (often referred to as 'first-generation' members), other people are born or raised in new religious movements or cults and are now commonly referred to as 'second-generation' members. In their cases, there is no possibility of a preexisting pre-group psychopathology, although if someone has emotional difficulties after having left, it can be hard to distinguish between the group and familial factors which might be responsible/contributing factors. Dubrow-Marshall and Martin (2005) have reported that group induced psychopathology nevertheless exists in both first- and second-generation former members as distinct from family-induced harm. Additionally, some groups separate children from their families to varying degrees, so this can create psychological issues including a feeling of abandonment. Many former second-generation members report conflicts around feelings of loyalty to their families and feeling angry at their parents for raising them in a restrictive environment, sometimes one in which they were abused physically, emotionally or sexually. There may have been deficits in their education or training for a career which might make it very difficult for them to survive and thrive outside of the group.

There are implications for counselling related to these issues of the psychological development of involvement in high demand or cultic group environments. The RETIRN (Re-entry Therapy, Information and Referral Network) model of intervention, while eclectic in practice, is person-centred and phenomenological in its core beliefs. It has stressed the importance of keeping an open mind to the client's experience and not pre-judging them as possessing any particular psychological features because of their involvement. Assessment of psychological issues to be addressed in therapy is therefore more challenging when working with former members of new religious movements or cults compared to other client groups. It may not be possible to accurately assess what 'symptoms' the person has which are related to group involvement versus what difficulties may reflect pre-cult personality or the experience of growing up in the group until adequate time has passed since the person's exit of the group. This may happen in stages, as even after physically leaving the group they may still feel allegiance to it and hold onto beliefs and practices, and even language which is idiosyncratic to the group. This can be analogous to working with former addicts, where it is impossible to fully evaluate the person's mental state until they are free from their addiction and have completed the withdrawal process. Some difficulties related to coercive environments will abate naturally as people move away from the group, so it is arguable that counselling can most usefully focus on the psychological issues that remain unresolved.

The psychological sequelae for second-generation families are distinctive (Goldberg 2006 and Chapter 5; Kendall 2009) because the child or 'adult child' did not have a pre-group identity, and may have missed out on many culturally shared experiences resulting in difficulties fitting in when they leave the group. As the child grows up, they may question their family's involvement, creating family conflict. Of course it is a normal developmental stage for children to question their family values or way of life, but for second-generation children, their family ties usually were profoundly affected by the group involvement and there may be attachment issues. If the child leaves the group as an adolescent or adult, they may be shunned by their families and group and their loyalties are questioned. The individual is uprooted and does not fit in with peers outside of the group. Sometimes families leave because of child abuse by the leader or group members, but sometimes the child is not believed.

First-generation former members who were frequently subjected to high-pressure techniques to join a group may be very sensitive to the slightest pressure in the psychotherapeutic relationship, while second-generation former members may be very sensitive to getting close to the counsellor/psychotherapist or trusting ideas which they put forward, including the challenging of irrational ideas in the group, which might be done in a cognitive-behavioural approach. The RETIRN model has emphasised a gentle, sensitive and permissive approach that is tolerant of non-traditional forms of entry into psychotherapy, and that respects the client's pacing, before focusing more on a psycho-educational approach which challenges the client's cult-influenced perception of the group experience. While many prospective clients may ask numerous questions before making initial or subsequent appointments for counselling, former members may tend to be more cautious and inquisitive, which may make counsellors feel uncomfortable, but needs to be tolerated so that the client can feel emotionally safe. A good strategy for counsellors is to ask former members to wait until after the initial session to schedule another appointment, effectively role modelling how to make post-cult decisions, where the ability to take one's time, consult with others, 'sleep on it' and access information are suddenly options which were previously restricted.

However, for some people, it is a very abrupt change to make their own decisions outside the group, and they may feel incapable of making even simple decisions, such as what to eat or wear (especially if these were once prescribed behaviours), and support by the therapist to explore various options is helpful. In practice, this may mean that a person will explore counselling in a non-traditional way, such as coming for a session or two and then waiting some considerable time before returning. In one case, a former member called off and on for a year asking various questions about the therapist's psychotherapeutic approach before making even the first appointment, and this was not negatively judged.

As the groups vary in their recruitment practices, it is important, where possible, to gain information about how the group operates so that the counsellor can assist the individual to process this information and to examine more closely their experience of joining the group. This can be analogous to some of the issues in helping victims of abuse and trafficking to understand how they were 'groomed' before a particular experience, as there is sometimes a prolonged period of grooming which may include acts which appear to be caring but are actually manipulative. Understandably, people who have had such experiences will have a harder time establishing trust in a psychotherapeutic relationship, despite the necessity for trust as a cornerstone of the therapeutic relationship.

For current members that seek psychotherapy, it is important to assess what issues have motivated them to seek help. Because RETIRN associates are known as specialists in the area of cults or new religious movements, it has been typical for current members who have contacted us to be considering exit, and it has been our strategy to listen carefully to their ambivalence and help them to consider their options, similarly to how we would help anyone who was considering leaving a relationship. An exception to being non-judgmental would be if there was evidence of current abuse, health and safety issues or criminal activity, which would need to be addressed. Generally, therapists can explore both overt and covert client agendas and supportively explore if discomfort might be related to conditions in the group.

Family members who are concerned about a loved one's involvement in what might be a cultic group will typically benefit from a psycho-educational and supportive approach that allows them to understand cultic recruitment with greater compassion and to appreciate how important it is for the member to exit of their own volition and not under family pressure. Education about the dynamics of undue influence tends to mitigate feelings of anger and abandonment, and helps to promote a positive relationship with the family member.

Additionally, family members of second-generation members who have left their group can be helped in counselling to understand the complex feelings that their children may have towards them. If they understand their own recruitment, they will be better able to 'forgive' themselves for getting their families involved and to be able to explain to their children (including adult children) the nature of their involvement and any pressure they may have been placed under to involve their entire families. Sometimes family members have helped their children to leave the group, and sometimes they have not been able to, and have faced the terrible pain of being shunned and not having any contact with their children who are still in the group. Where possible, it is helpful for these families to meet other families in the same situation as it may be difficult for others to be empathetic to the complicated situation and feelings that they are facing.

Psychological sequelae of involvement with new religious movements or cults – implications for counselling and support[3]

When looking at the psychological consequences of involvement in new religious movements or cults, the RETIRN model has adopted a holistic view to fully appreciate the impact of the experience upon the person. This is pictured in Figure 6.1, which illustrates the interaction of the effect upon body, mind and spirit.

Although there is an interaction between these various domains of existence, it is also worth examining them separately within the counselling relationship. First, the physical body may have been negatively impacted in the group experience and sometimes in an extreme way, such as physical and/or sexual abuse. There may have been physical neglect such as inattention to medical conditions, or a lack of adequate sleep, rest and food as sacrificing one's personal needs for the sake of the group/leader/mission was actively encouraged, or due to unorthodox beliefs about bodily needs, disease or medication/medical treatment. Sexuality can be over-emphasised or under-emphasised with extremes of permissiveness or restrictiveness being advocated, or power being abused to coerce sexual relationships or prohibit couples from being sexual with each other. Non-heterosexual feelings are also sometimes dealt with harshly and judgmentally, and gender identification issues may have been ignored. Physical appearance, including clothing and hair, may have been closely controlled, and body and self-image altered. Therapeutic interventions for the body may

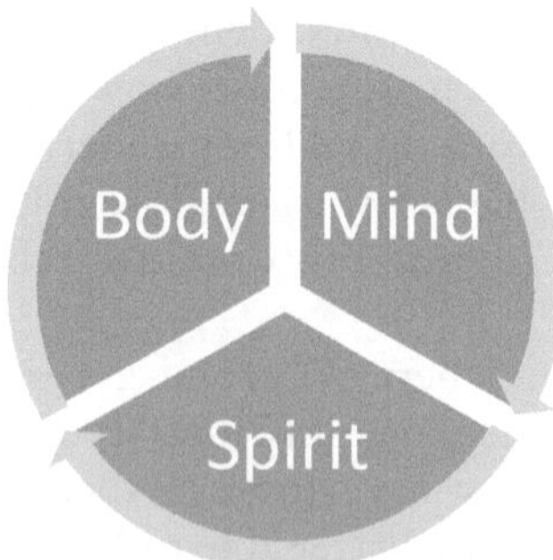

Figure 6.1 A holistic view.

include rest, healthy nutrition, modifying appearance and, where necessary, a referral for specialist medical treatment is also made.

Turning to the 'mind', the psychological consequences of high demand group membership, including the effect of sexual and physical abuse, can frequently include post-traumatic stress disorder, depression, anxiety and dissociative disorders, which are the psychological symptoms typically presented by clients who have exited groups and who have requested help (Dubrow-Marshall 2010). Related disorders may include addictive behaviours, eating disorders, mood disorders, self-harming behaviours, suicidal tendencies and personality disorders. Self-esteem, personal integrity and body image have often been deleteriously affected. Counselling or psychotherapy have the potential to address all these psychological issues and others that may be presented by the client.

The spiritual impact of membership and leaving new religious movements or cults is also important to consider, as clients who have been traumatised by abuse may find it nearly impossible to 'have faith' in a variety of arenas – trust of people, belief in a just world, faith in a higher power. Confidence in their own judgment or ability to take care of themselves can be tarnished and diminished, sometimes permanently (Langone 1995; Aronoff, Malinoski and Lynn 2000). A referral to a religious or spiritual leader will be appreciated by some clients.[4]

Former members also report how they initially or for some time gained a huge amount through their group beliefs and devotion and how the 'rollercoaster effect' of leaving is traumatic both spiritually and existentially. This can involve feelings of depression and dissociation that are consequences of both the extreme devotion to the group and its leader which is never completely fulfilled and hence creates existential distress and emptiness in and of itself, as well as further emptiness and distress that is created when that devotion ends. This points to the need for a healthy level of devotion and critical thinking in religious or other groups that is based on authentic relationships and which does not engender over-dependency on the group and leader and the discarding of other beliefs and passions that is both psychologically detrimental *sui generis* but is also additionally harmful if the devotion to the group and leader diminishes or ceases. Research indicating an explanatory theory of Totalistic Identity (Dubrow-Marshall and Martin 2008; Dubrow-Marshall 2010) evidences how a group-based psychopathology (including depression and dissociation) emerges through excessive or total identification with a group to the exclusion of other identifications and interests and where there is a lack of authenticity to relationships in the group, including between members and with the leader(s).

An initial challenge to helping former members is in establishing an authentic therapeutic relationship and in being able to gain the person's trust. It is common for former members to feel a sense of betrayal emanating from their relationships within the group, particularly with the leader, but also with other members. They may have been recruited under false pretences and sometimes without knowing the name of the group that they were joining. Transparency on the part of the psychotherapist is therefore essential in providing a restorative relationship, as well as the core conditions advocated within client-centred therapy (Rogers 2004) of empathy, congruence, genuineness and unconditional positive regard and respect. However, it can be difficult to be person-centred and transparent when the therapist is in possession of more information than the client about some of the harmful practices of the group. Clients need to proceed at their own pace in evaluating the abusive aspects of their involvement. Practitioners face similar dilemmas when working with survivors of domestic violence who may decide to re-enter the abusive relationship upon promises from their partner that the violence will not reoccur, working with addicts who may lose their sobriety or working with people who self-harm – in other words, anytime when there may be a conflict between promoting client autonomy and psychotherapeutic values of 'non-maleficence' (doing no harm) and 'respect for people's rights and dignity'(APA 2010), and the professional role of promoting psychological health. Abusive relationships have been likened to cults and have sometimes been referred to as 'one on one cults' (Herman 1992).

Psychological consequences, as previously noted, have included post-traumatic stress and related symptoms, such as depression, anxiety and dissociation. The late Dr Paul Martin and his co-workers gave a battery of psychological tests to clients who came to the Wellspring Retreat and Resource Center pre- and post-treatment, over many years, where they participated in a specialised two-week residential treatment programme including psychotherapy and psycho-education.[5] Research has shown (e.g. Martin et al. 1992; Dubrow-Marshall and Martin 2005) that a number of psychological problems were presented at the beginning and ameliorated by the treatment at Wellspring. They include depression, anxiety, dissociation, identity issues, dependency issues, ruptured family relationships and delayed developmental issues (as people may have missed developmental milestones because their cultic involvement prevented them from proceeding with various life tasks). The Wellspring findings also resonate with wider assessments and research of this population that has consistently shown psychological harm consistent with and related to group membership (e.g. Aronoff, Lynn and Malinoski 2000; Almendros et al. 2011; Dubrow-Marshall and Dubrow-Marshall 2015).

While practitioners should not assume that any of these reported difficulties will necessarily be present with former members, it is wise to assess for them because they have been commonly observed as the research cited above demonstrates. Integrative approaches can be useful in designing sensitive and appropriate psychological interventions, mindful of the impact of abuse and undue influence and with the client potentially learning from their experiences and changing their environment and relationships in order to enhance their psychological well-being. Helping people to understand where their cognitions may have become irrational based on group beliefs and challenging these beliefs and considering alternatives, helps them to consider a broader range of experiences and a more accurate sense of self and potentialities. Psycho-education about what occurs in highly manipulative environments is key to fostering recovery for members and former members, and is also very important for family members. Meeting others who have been through similar situations enables them to de-stigmatise their experience and reduce feelings of shame.

The 'Re-Entry Therapy' part of the RETIRN name refers to helping the person to readjust to life outside of the new religious movement or cult, or in the case of second generation members, to adjust and experience some things for the first time, which might include full access to information through the media and internet. Two critical areas of the RETIRN model are cognitive functioning and affective functioning. People's critical thinking and decision-making skills were typically compromised in the group as the group and/or its leader manipulated and controlled their belief system and behaviours, and individual dissent was discouraged or punished in an attempt to promote the group's needs over individual needs, and to maintain group coherence and loyalty. It is sometimes the individuals' families who bring former members to psychotherapy, so therefore the first step might be to help the client to decide for themselves if they want to participate and to engage their interest and motivation to examine their experience. Psychotherapists can also help clients to consider options and make decisions, ranging from minor ones to significant ones, while being mindful not to overwhelm the client with choices. Clients can be helped to experiment with decisions, along the lines of behavioural experiments in cognitive behaviour therapy (Westbrook, Kennerley and Kirk 2011), and therapists can normalise the experience of making the 'wrong' decision and lessening shame while fostering experimentation and openness to experience. This process can also help former clients to feel less ashamed of choices they may have made during their group involvement, as they learn about the difference between coercive decisions or bounded choice decisions (Lalich 2001) and more freely chosen decisions.

In relation to affective functioning, former members may present with restricted affect, flattened affect or inappropriate affect as their abusive experience may have included coercion not to express their emotions and not to even be aware of their own emotional state, as group needs superseded those of the individual. The cult members' sense of identity, of what they prefer, personal values and expression of anger may all have been deeply compromised while in the group. Psychotherapists can create a safe environment within which they can validate clients' feelings rather than suppressing them. Former members typically have feelings of ambivalence towards their former group, leader, members and ideology; and therapists can help them to tolerate ambiguity and ambivalence (Dubrow-Marshall 2013). Giambalvo and Henry (2010) have incorporated work on grief into the Colorado Model, a weekend workshop for former members of cultic groups, sponsored by the International Cultic Studies Association. Former members experience grief in a number of areas including grief related to loss of time, opportunities and friends in the group, guilt over people whom they recruited or important events they missed while devoted to the group (e.g. funerals or care-taking of loved ones), and an existential void where previously the group had provided a sense of meaning and purpose and a world-view where now there is a loss.

Other key aspects of psychological functioning which are often impacted by undue influence and coercive persuasion include the effects of having gone against personal values as encouraged by the group (which may include illegal behaviours) or being confused about what their personal values are; an interruption of education and career plans and perhaps diminished career prospects as it is difficult to explain a gap in work history where the person may only have participated in fundraising and recruitment activities; confusion about sexuality or sexual preferences; and spiritual confusion where some former members will try out different religious or spiritually based activities or groups as part of their recovery.

The psychological damage to interpersonal relationships has often been profound, especially if one person is involved with the group and not their families, but also in cases where children are raised in the group, or where family relationships are disrupted by the group. Figure 6.2 illustrates how the individual's needs can be 'funnelled' into the group, potentially alongside family relations, work and social life.

Families who have turned to RETIRN for help have endured much suffering and greatly miss being close to their loved ones, fear for their safety, are isolated from others who either do not understand what is meant by a coercive, cultic group or blame the family for the person's involvement, and are angry and frustrated by their unsuccessful efforts to have an impact. They may feel as though they do not recognise their loved one, who now views their group as their new family, as illustrated in Figure 6.3.

Conclusions – lessons for counselling approaches with members, former members and families affected by new religious movements or cults.

The RETIRN model of counselling – as with other approaches reviewed in this chapter (e.g. Giambalvo and Henry 2010) grew out of a passionate interest in the phenomena involved in undue influence and high-pressure

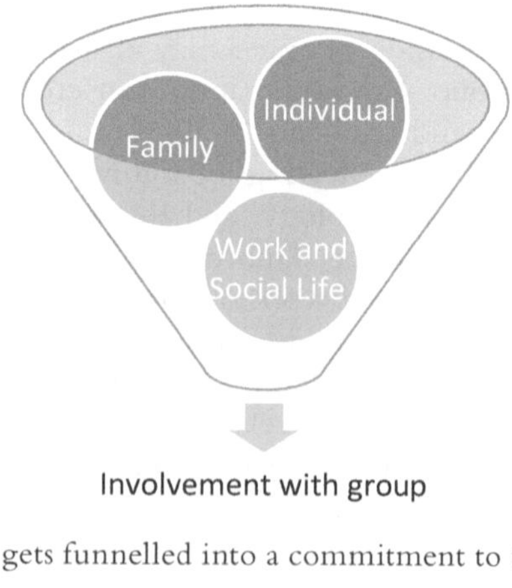

Figure 6.2 Former life gets funnelled into a commitment to the group.

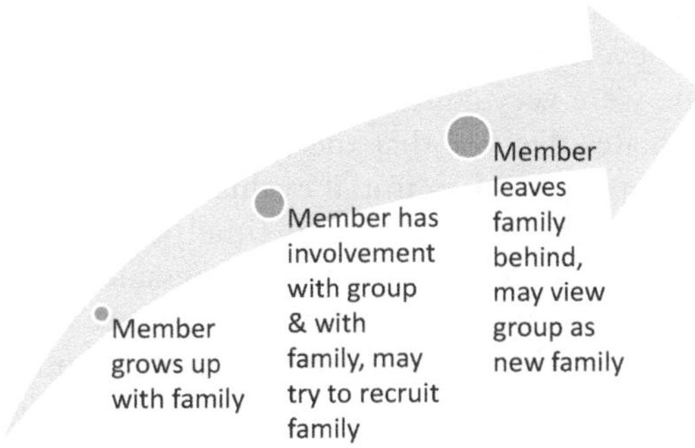

Figure 6.3 Transformation of familial ties related to group involvement – this pictures the journey of a first generation cult member away from their family, which is illustrative of many, but not all, cases.

environments or groups, a deeply felt empathy for individuals who had been harmed by their involvement, an appreciation of the complexity of the cases and a belief that a unique approach needed to evolve for this work as the needs were different to those relating to common mental health problems, even when some of the symptoms were the same (e.g. depression and anxiety). RETIRN has worked with people who have experienced a broad range of high-pressure and coercive groups and relationships, including for example 'psychotherapy cults' (Temerlin and Temerlin 1982), which is where the psychotherapist conducts an unethical practice resembling cultic leaders, often involving group therapy where confidentiality is typically violated and members are exploited. Clients presenting with such experiences provide unique challenges to therapists in gaining trust and in nurturing authentic psychotherapeutic relationships.

The founders of RETIRN (as well as other specialist counsellors in this field) were all concerned about the negative consequences of involvement with high-pressure groups and relationships although they came from a number of different perspectives – direct experience, research and clinical experience. They recognised an unmet need for mental health professionals to offer services to individuals and families, and they were eager to make an impact in this field. However, they felt challenged when working with this population who presented differently to other clients and who presented very complex histories and relationships. The value of a team approach was soon appreciated as dialogue about how to proceed in helping clients created a better consideration of how to proceed. The options of how to approach individuals and families seemed to require a great flexibility as every case was unique. For example, some families asked for help and all felt unified in being concerned about the involvement of a loved one, whereas in others there was great conflict about these issues with one parent being very concerned and the other parent disagreeing. Members who asked for help were in various stages of awareness: some were eager to leave and needed support whereas others felt coerced to consult and really did not want to leave at all, and some were very conflicted and ambivalent about their involvement. Former members sometimes still believed in the ideology of their group, some were very angry and hurt and some were very confused and felt unable to make any decisions.

RETIRN associates decided that their preferred way to work would be to have at least two people do an initial evaluation session and then plan any future interventions. After trying various time periods for this, they found that two hours was the preferred time for an assessment which allowed time to cover the complicated histories and details and yet not too long so as to be exhausting and overwhelming – both for client(s) and practitioner alike. After the original RETIRN associates had been meeting for a year, they presented a symposium at the annual convention of the Pennsylvania Psychological Association in June 1983 titled 'Psychotherapy for ex-cultists: a new specialty?' acknowledging the need for a specialist approach to working with this client group which valued team working and consultation. The rationale for needing a specialist approach was based on some fundamental differences which emerged as RETIRN mental health professionals considered the tasks of working with former cult members. While client autonomy is a key principle of professional ethical codes of practice (BACP 2016; APA 2010), it is important to consider the harm that might be caused by involvement in abusive groups and relationships and to express concern for clients' physical, emotional and spiritual safety. Working with people whose ability to think critically might have been compromised also presents specific challenges.

The often huge gain in belief and self-identity that comes with a group and its leader, which is nevertheless also often unfulfilled, unrequited and unreciprocated both while inside, and after leaving the group, represents a fundamentally unhealthy psychological position existentially which leaves former members asking critical questions about who they are and the purpose of their lives which the group did not and could not answer. As well as clearly pointing to a duty of care on all groups and organisations towards their members, whether new or mainstream religions, political groups or parties, or businesses and charities, to look after their members and to keep the group/life balance in check with a healthy level of identification and reliance on the group, such experiences also present uniquely experiential and life-questioning challenges in clients to which counsellors, therapists and psychologists need to be attuned and ready to appropriately respond. The painstaking and efficacious work of numerous mental health professionals over many years with such clients (Langone 1995; Giambalvo and Henry 2010) only goes to show the need for more sensitivity and understanding in counselling for people whose search for meaning and freedom feels irredeemable, hopeless and never-ending (Fromm 2001). For some former group members, shorn of the ultimately false promises and nirvana of their group and guru, and where the sacred now appears profane, the road to psychological health and fulfilment can be a long one and the importance of well-informed and tailored counselling approaches for such survivors cannot be underestimated.

Notes

1 Such terms are often used inter-changeably as they refer to different examples of a broad set of phenomena which have similar characteristics (Langone 1995; Singer 2003; Dubrow-Marshall and Dubrow-Marshall 2015). In this chapter the term 'new religious movements' or 'cults' will typically be used, even though it is acknowledged that no single term accurately encapsulates the variety and diversity of the social groups that are the subject of this chapter and the research and writing that is cited (for example 'new religious movement', while used widely here in common with other chapters in this volume, explicitly ignores groups or social movements with a non-religious ideology e.g. political groups).

2 Langone (2000, 2005) sets out in detail how positions and arguments amongst academics became polarised in what has been referred to as the 'cult wars' and how a process of increased dialogue amongst scholars, practitioners and researchers subsequently led to an increased understanding across divergent areas of focus and concern and a gradual depolarisation in the debate over these phenomena.

3 This section will focus further on the psychological sequelae and consequences of involvement with new religious movements or cult like groups that have been presented when people have sought professional help (with RETIRN and other helping organisations). It is acknowledged that these may not reflect the experiences of all people who have been involved with these types of groups and as such these are cited as commonly reported psychological consequences of involvement rather than as uniform experiences or effects.

4 The 'referral network' part of the RETIRN name acknowledges the importance of recognising the principle of 'working within our competence' as advocated by the professional organisations (BPS 2009; APA 2010; BACP 2016; HCPC 2016), so an essential part of the assessment is to refer to other professionals as needed. This may include medical and legal referrals, as well as referrals to support groups, addictions professionals, trauma experts, or pastoral counselling.

5 The Wellspring Retreat and Resource Center for many years operated the only residential treatment programme in the world that was tailored to the needs of survivors of abusive groups and relationships including through a specific psycho-education programme and therapeutic interventions which related to the harm that resulted from exposure to the high demand or coercive group or relationship. The Wellspring Retreat continues to operate a tailored day treatment programme of this nature at its facility in southern Ohio in the USA (www.wellspringretreat.org).

References

Almendros, C., M. Gamez-Guadix, A. Rodriguez-Carballeira and J. Carrobles. 2011. Assessment of psychological abuse in manipulative groups. *International Journal of Cultic Studies*, 2, 61–76.

American Psychological Association. 2010. *Ethical Principles of Psychologists and Code of Conduct*. Washington, DC: American Psychological Association.

Aronoff, J., S. Lynn and P. Malinoski. 2000. Are cultic environments psychologically harmful? *Clinical Psychology Review*, 20(1), 91–111.

Atack, J. 2016. *Opening Minds: The Secret World of Manipulation, Undue Influence and Brainwashing*. London: Open Minds Foundation.

Banisadr, M. 2009. Terrorist organizations are cults. *Cultic Studies Review*, 8(2), 154–84.

British Association for Counselling and Psychotherapy. 2016. *Ethical Framework for the Counselling Professions*. Lutterworth: British Association for Counselling and Psychotherapy.

British Psychological Society. 2009. *Code of Ethics and Conduct*. Leicester: British Psychological Society.

Dubrow-Marshall, L. 2013. Curiosity and willingness to learn: Linda Dubrow-Marshall offers advice for counsellors on working with former cult members. *Therapy Today*, May, 22.

Dubrow-Marshall, R.P. 2010. The influence continuum – the good, the dubious and the harmful – evidence and implications for policy and practice in the 21st century. *International Journal of Cultic Studies*, 1(1), 1–13.

Dubrow-Marshall, R.P. and L. Dubrow-Marshall. 2015. Cults and mental health, in: H.S. Friedman (ed.) *The Encyclopaedia of Mental Health*. New York: Academic Press, pp. 393–401.

Dubrow-Marshall, R. and P. Martin. 2005. Building a model of post-group pathology in ex-members of cultic groups. Unpublished manuscript presented at the *Annual Conference of the International Cultic Studies Association*, Universidad Autonoma de Madrid.

Dubrow-Marshall, R. and P. Martin. 2008. Exploring and developing a model and theory of totalistic identity in ex-cult members. Unpublished manuscript presented to the *Annual Conference of the International Cultic Studies Association*, University of Pennsylvania.

Fromm, E. 2001. *The Fear of Freedom*. New York: Routledge.

Galanter, M. 1988. Zealous self-help groups as adjuncts to psychiatric treatment: a study of Recovery, Inc. *American Journal of Psychiatry*, 145(10), 1248–53.

Giambalvo, C. and R. Henry. 2010. ICSA recovery workshops: the Colorado model. *ICSA Today*, 10(1), 3–9, 21.

Goldberg, L. 2006. Raised in cultic groups: the impact on the development of certain aspects of character. *Cultic Studies Review*, 5(1), 1–26.

Hassan, S. 1990. *Combating Cult Mind Control*. Rochester, VT: Park Street Press.

Hassan, S. 2000. *Releasing the Bonds: Empowering People to Think for Themselves*. Newton, MA: Freedom of Mind Press.

Health and Care Professions Council. 2016. *Standards of Conduct, Performance and Ethics*. London: Health and Care Professions Council.

Herman, J. 1992. *Trauma and Recovery*. New York: Basic Books.

Jenkinson, G. 2013. Working with cult survivors. *Therapy Today*, May, 18–21.

Kendall, L. 2009. The value of counselling for second-generation former sect members. Unpublished manuscript presented at the *Annual Conference of the International Cultic Studies Association*, Geneva.

Lalich, J. 2001. *Bounded Choice: True Believers and Charismatic Cults*. Oakland: University of California Press.

Langone, M. 1995. *Recovery from Cults: Help for Victims of Psychological and Spiritual Abuse*. New York: W.W. Norton.

Langone, M. 2000. The two 'camps' of cultic studies: time for a dialogue. *Cultic Studies Journal*, 17, 55–68.

Langone, M. 2005. Cult Awareness Groups and NRM Scholars: Toward Depolarization of Key Issues. *Cultic Studies Review*, 4(2), 146–68.

Lifton, R. 1961. *Thought Reform and the Psychology of Totalism*. New York: W.W. Norton.

Lifton, R. 2000. *Destroying the World to Save It: Aum Shinrikyo, Apocalyptic Violence, and the New Global Terrorism*. New York: Henry Holt.

Martin, P. 1993. *Cult-Proofing Your Kids*. Grand Rapids, MI: Zondervan.

Martin, P., M. Langone, A. Dole and J. Wiltrout. 1992. Post-cult symptoms as measured by the MCMI before and after residential treatment. *Cultic Studies Journal*, 9, 219–49.

Namini, S. and S. Murken. 2009. Self-chosen involvement in new religious movements (NRMs): well-being and mental health from a longitudinal perspective. *Mental Health, Religion and Culture*, 12(6), 561–85.

Pesiah, C., S. Finkel, K. Shulman, P. Melding, J. Luxenberg, J. Heinik, R. Jacoby, B. Reisberg, G. Stoppe, A. Barker, H. Firmino and H. Bennett 2009. The wills of older people: risk factors for undue influence. *International Psychogeriatrics*, 21(1), 7–15.

Rogers, C. 2004. *On Becoming a Person*. London: Robinson Publishing.

Schein, E. with I. Schneier and C. Barker. 1961. *Coercive Persuasion: A Socio-Psychological Analysis of the "Brainwashing" of American Civilian Prisoners by the Chinese Communists*. New York: W.W. Norton.

Singer, M. 2003. *Cults in Our Midst*. San Francisco, CA: Jossey Bass.

Temerlin, M. K. and J.W. Temerlin 1982. Psychotherapy cults: an iatrogenic perversion. *Psychotherapy: Theory, Research, and Practice*, 19(2), 131–41.

Thomas, D.C., E.C. Ravlin, Y. Liao, D.L. Morrell and K. Au. 2016. Collectivist values, exchange ideology and psychological contract preference. *Management International Review*, 56(2), 255–81.

Tourish, D. 2013. *The Dark Side of Transformational Leadership: A Critical Perspective*. East Sussex: Routledge.

Westbrook, D., H. Kennerley and Kirk, J. 2011. *An Introduction to Cognitive Behaviour Therapy: Skills and Applications*. 2nd ed. London: Sage Publications.

7 Show the fly the way out of the fly bottle

Using art and philosophy to counsel those impacted by controversial new social movements

Joseph Szimhart

To avoid the risk of repeating too much of what other cult intervention specialists or exit coaches[1] might cover in this volume, this chapter is focused on how I apply a four-aspect model to potentially harmful new social movements or relationships variously labelled closed social systems, cults or new religious movements. After decades of working with people impacted by controversial minority groups including people who were members or related to members, I came to view cults in a more nuanced way, not necessarily good or bad. I could argue that cult activity, in its proper meaning, has been necessary for human social evolution. As an artist, I look through aesthetics at religious movements, at how they are framed and how well the movement expresses and develops its foundation story. One of the core problems with new movements beyond their immaturity in style and governance is the tendency to *freeze* in a narrative with behaviours that invite ridicule from outsiders while creating an elitist defence response from within. New movements with grandiose agendas tend to overlook refinements in language and idea, resist social adaptation and decry common rules of law. In a word, they are immature in the sense that the kids marooned on an island in William Golding's 1954 novel *Lord of the Flies* were immature. This us-versus-them posturing creates and invites social and intellectual problems. I address these problems through the following four-part *orbiting* model when I work with clients: *Transcendent Attraction, Exclusive Authority, Circular Tension and Exit Perils.*[2]

Transcendent attraction is a common doorway into any new religion or self-improvement venture that offers a deeper knowing of self, being, purpose or relationship. The experience of transcendence, often exhilarating, can bond one to the group in which it occurs. Transcendence can be viewed cynically as bait to bring one closer to the source of the experience, namely an exclusive authority figure around whom group activities revolve. The new member goes into a psychological orbit resulting in a circular tension conditioned by what is better or worse, good or evil and pure or contaminated. Following rituals, rules and avoiding doubt prevent falling back into a perilous, non-group environment that includes fall from grace, loss of investment and, most importantly, the daunting renewal of identification and socialization.

I unpack that model while addressing certain philosophical notions that help my clients come to grips with those perennial questions that cult leaders tend to focus on: Why are we here? Who am I? Where am I going? What is my purpose? What is the way to realise the truth? In assessing people harmed by cult activity, I concentrate more on *circular tension* that represents the activity of devotion to a central theme and authority while orbiting something not well grounded in social reality and applicable science. In other words, people can get in a rut or bottled up within high demand relationships and minority religions, yet claim to feel free within a social and psychological bottle as long as what is outside appears perilous – they feel safe until what is inside begins to feel too stifling and until what is outside appears far less perilous.

Der Fliege den Ausweg aus dem Fliegenglas zeigen – Ludwig Wittgenstein[3]

Ludwig Wittgenstein (1889–1951) famously stated that the only purpose left for philosophy was to 'show the fly the way out of the fly bottle'. He had his critics – Karl Popper being one – but he also argued for a return to 'ordinary language' as a pragmatic way to avoid highly specialised philosophical jargon. But Wittgenstein denied being a pragmatist because he wanted to avoid another *Weltanschauung* or world view. In concert with this pragmatic idea, neither do I propose another world view to my clients coming out of cults. When someone asks me what I intend to replace the cult ideas with, I answer, 'bad question'. I am not interested in replacing a world view – I am interested in good approaches to a better view. Along with Wittgenstein's critique of high-brow philosophical language, one could say the same about the specialised jargon inherent in many new movements.

Without daring to emulate Wittgenstein as a philosopher, I am mimicking his idea in *Philosophical Investigations*, article 107.[4] In that passage, Wittgenstein is saying that philosophical language needs to enter the ordinary *muddy* world where there is *friction* for it to have any practical value at all. Self-sealing cults often have this same unmuddy claim, to create a totalistic or absolute *language game* or milieu that is unlike the ordinary life, full of norms, surrounding it. Insular language might avoid contradiction but it can only work inside its own system. Cult language can be self-serving, often slick with internal jargon, and airtight with a kind of circular logic peculiar to the cult. Cult language does not work easily, if at all, in the ordinary, muddy world but cult language does manage to separate insiders from outsiders: *If he speaks like us, he is one of us.* Insular movements are often elite enterprises that are condescending towards the ignorant, the unsaved or unenlightened outsider. In this essay, I call that elite psychosocial environment the *fly bottle* and the cult members the *flies* inside it. The exit coach's job in counselling is to show the fly the limits of living in the bottle while revealing that the environment outside is quite good. The way out is apparent if the fly inside sees the way out and feels safe choosing to exit.

Allow me to address one professional problem regarding the topic of this volume: I am not licensed or formally certified to counsel, teach or testify as a court witness regarding minority religions or social relationships (although I have testified in several court cases). I have an undergraduate degree in arts and sciences with a post-graduate Certificate in Fine Arts. Yet, for decades I have had a relatively good reputation for helping persons to emerge from what subsequently appears to them as an ill-advised, if not harmful, experience in a self-sealing social arrangement. My supervisors at the behavioural health hospital where I have worked since 1998 have been satisfied with my performance as a crisis caseworker. Beyond my formal studies in fine arts, one might describe me as someone who learns and trains on the job. Cult intervention specialists or deprogrammers by any other name have mostly learned on the job – there was no other way, practically speaking.

Another significant matter has to do with art. I do not do art therapy with clients, nor do I discuss art as such, as fine arts and art history. My way in to the cult experience and out again had a lot to do with aesthetics, and my approach to studying the problem has been through aesthetics. Does a new group pass the smell test? How does it look? What does it sound like? Is it a good design? How original is it? What are its influences? Is it a fake? (Asking that last question begs a lot of questions in art as in religion). In other words, I look at a problematic group as I might a painting by assessing its elegance and context, its lucidity and intent. Because I have a long history in art studies and production, I can apply that skill with some proficiency when I view and assess unfamiliar artwork. I think that anyone who has spent decades studying new religious movements does the same – there is an immediate recognition of what might be going on through an aesthetic response. We can turn to a judicial adage: When trying to explain how we recognise pornography, Supreme Court justice Potter Stewart stated, 'I know it when I see it' (Jacobellis v. Ohio, 1964). Aesthetic skill may not produce a final interpretation, but it can provide good leads to an accurate assessment.

Biographic background

My cult specialist career began shortly after I emerged from what I now see as a weird and wayward rite of passage through a comparatively large New Age religion. Three to five thousand 'Keepers of the Flame' or 'chelas' might attend quarterly conferences in California at the time I was involved. I attended three conferences from 1979 to 1980. I was formally initiated as a Keeper of the Flame at a 1979 conference. This New Age religion, the Summit Lighthouse (also known as Church Universal and Triumphant or CUT) was based primarily on the 'I AM' Activity founded by Guy Ballard and Edna Ballard in the early 1930s. CUT also absorbed Agni Yoga teachings founded by Nicholas Roerich and Helena Roerich in the early 1920s. I began Agni Yoga and Theosophy readings in 1975, and that primed my attraction to CUT several years later. All these groups borrowed heavily from the Theosophical Society co-founded in 1875 by H. P. Blavatsky. CUT, like the 'I AM' Activity, combined aspects of American patriotism, Mahayana Buddhism, New Thought religion, Indian Sant Mat and fundamentalist Christianity. When I was attracted to Nicholas Roerich's paintings in 1975, I quickly discovered that Roerich and many of his contemporary artists including Wassily Kandinsky and Piet Mondrian were devoted to Blavatsky's Theosophy. I already had a deep attraction to the work and ideas of Mondrian and Kandinsky since the late 1960s. The pieces of this puzzle as a picture of deep knowledge with practical application all seemed to come together for me in CUT.

The central focus of all these groups was devotion to a channel, amanuensis or Messenger through whom discarnate Ascended Masters, adepts, angels and gods (collectively known as the Great White Brotherhood) communicated to mankind. The goal was to end reincarnation or to 'ascend' and attain nirvana or moksha in this lifetime. The premise was that the Masters embody and reveal a perennial wisdom or gnosis from which all religions and sciences emerge. The primary ritual of CUT was *decreeing*, which is a form of rapid mantra chanting for hours a day, preferably in group formation to maximize the vibratory power. Decreeing was also called the *Power of the Spoken Word*, purportedly the most powerful alchemical force in the universe. A key exit peril, if a believer dared to defect, was that one could be hurled into 10,000 lifetimes of suffering before another opportunity to ascend arrived.

I struggled with the many internal conflicts among Theosophy groups, yet I found the attraction of a living Messenger in CUT compelling. My first wife divorced me in 1979 over my new behaviours related to diet, sex, colours, music and time spent listening to tapes of teachings. After I sufficiently recovered from my desperate, anxiety-ridden defection toward the end of 1980, I helped several friends to emerge from CUT. Two of those members had recruited me and wondered why I defected. They wanted to talk with me. My reasons, experience and evidence after several hours of conversation were apparently convincing enough for all three of them to quit the group too. But the incident that sparked my career as a cult intervention specialist occurred during that pre-Christmas season in 1980.

Coincidental intervention: Four Square with ugly gospel

At the time, I lived in Santa Fe, New Mexico, where I was working as a portrait sketch artist in a shopping mall. Linda, age nineteen, worked there at a retail store. She approached me to do a pastel study of her for her fiancé as a surprise gift. She asked me to copy her high school graduation photo. I worked on her image off and on as a shill for two weeks during which time Linda would stop by to chat during her breaks. Religion came up in our conversation almost immediately when she asked if I was Christian. I learned that

Linda was a member of a local, Four Square Gospel church led by a dynamic preacher who had 'prophesied' that God wanted her to marry a fellow parishioner. Initially, she attempted to recruit me. In sharing my cult story with her we were surprised that my New Age guru and her Christian preacher not only used the same Old King James translation, but they also quoted the same passages to reinforce man's right to command God as well as to separate from antagonistic friends and family. My former guru also approved of and suggested marriages among her staff – suggestions amounted to commands. I pointed out that many passages in the Old King James were poorly translated – not elegant. We examined how to read them properly in context. We talked about a lot more. Linda finally admitted that she was struggling with her church and marriage commitments. By the time I finished the portrait just before Christmas, she decided to end her engagement, quit the 'cult' church and send her portrait to her parents. She had not spoken to them in over six months. They lived in Texas and had no idea where she had moved to after she dropped out of college in Albuquerque. Her parents had expressed some concern over her new church affiliation before she cut them off. Her preacher convinced her that her parents were apostate as Baptists.

Now, that was interesting enough for me to see the life-changing effect of sharing my humble research and experience. But one month later, the day before I was to leave town for India, I was pumping petrol into my pick-up truck when I heard a strange man call my name. That man was Linda's father. Her parents had come to pick her up at the end of January and they were on their way home to Texas. Her father ran up to me, shook my hand effusively saying, 'You're the guy! My daughter was looking for you!' Linda could not get hold of me after Christmas because I ended my phone service after having moved out of my apartment. As we chatted, the parents said they wanted to do something for me to thank me. I did not want anything, but did agree to share a meal. So, we went to a nearby diner. We ate after praying together. We discussed what occurred between Linda and me at the mall. Linda was clearly grateful and happy to be back with her folks again.

That family experience struck a chord in me about how otherwise 'normal' relationships can be deeply harmed by manipulative preachers with overvalued beliefs. I wanted to know more about the cult problem. Five years later, I was chairman of a local cult information group and I began working with established cult interventionists. In hindsight, after perhaps five hundred or more formal interventions, my approach has been through ordinary communication, albeit about extraordinary situations. One early cult interventionist I saw on a 1980 television report said that *deprogramming was mostly talk.*

By *formal intervention* I mean an arranged meeting with a cult member who in most cases had no idea I would be present. Some person or persons that I had coached well ahead of time would introduce me. That person could be a relative, friend or possibly a trusted therapist. My job, whether I worked alone or with a colleague, would be to gain rapport with the cult member, then invite them to talk things out in present company. The average intervention meeting lasted several days and more if the cult member decided to engage. The counselling relationship might extend if the member chose to emerge from the group or relationship. I am not including involuntary interventions in this model, but I should disclose that from 1986 through 1992 I participated in dramatic situations wherein cult members were initially held against their will. In any case, gaining rapport with an upset or surprised group member was necessary. Convincing a person to trust in me and in the sources of information being offered was and is key in all cases. In surprise interventions, I always gave the cult member power over my presence immediately, stating that if they wanted me to leave, I would. The prepared family would remain to try to have me invited back. If I could not gain rapport, the intervention attempt would fall apart in a day or two on average.

I will describe two cases using my four-aspect, orbiting model to explore what I offer to clients. I have extensive files and notes that I referenced for these case examples. One caution: There is no order to how I approach these themes with anyone, nor do I necessarily mention the themes by name. Client and group member names are altered to protect identities. Group and leader names are accurate.

Case one: *Ancient Dance and Music* or dancing with Gurdjieff

This first case did not involve a formal intervention with me engaging the cult members. My client was Alan, the father of two young adult daughters who were members of a relatively new group outside Santa Fe, NM where I lived at the time. Alan called me from New Jersey in 1987. He got my name from a cult clinic in New York. His concern was to reconnect with his two daughters who had cut off all means of contact with their family. Alan was not inclined to try to attempt exit counselling, but he wanted to speak with them again. Alan and his wife were liberal Jewish parents who did not impose religion on their daughters. As Alan described his daughters and what little he knew of the group – he did not know the group name or exact location – I realized that I knew the group and had hired his younger daughter several times to model for my life drawing class at a local college. I had lived in Santa Fe for 11 years and encountered and researched several dozen new movements, most quite small, in the region. Alan's daughters had taken on new, *sacred* names unknown to their parents when Alan called me.

Ancient Dance and Music or ADAM was a 'household cult' with five to six core members, several of whom lived with the leader, his wife and two children in a rural area southeast of Santa Fe.[5] ADAM offered classes that included drumming circles, art production, chanting, movements and esoteric lectures by Drew K. the leader. ADAM was incorporated in 1984 and inspired by a *Fourth Way* enterprise led by E.J. Gold (b. 1941) out of Nevada City, CA. Fourth Way cults, also known as *The Work*, stem from the teachings of G. I. Gurdjieff (1877?–1949).[6] Gold's father, Horace Gold, worked for a major magazine and mixed with famous artists in New York City. Horace was a Gurdjieff student. E. J. Gold in his youth claimed to meet Gurdjieff in person.[7] Gurdjieff employed theatre, dance, esoteric therapy, guru submission and hard physical labour to bring his students to self-transformation.

The coincidence that I actually knew his daughters and the group was uncanny for Alan. We arranged for him to fly out to meet me in Santa Fe. We met for a full day at his hotel before attempting to reach out to his daughters. Alan needed an education about ADAM and what his daughters were actually doing. Why were his daughters attracted?

Transcendent Attraction

Since I was keenly aware of ADAM for several years – I had spent a day at the cult house interviewing Drew K., the leader, for example, and my wife had worked with the leader's wife at a local restaurant for a year – I could give Alan a deep appreciation for what attracted and retained his daughters. ADAM advertised its services and classes in Santa Fe and was peripherally active in the vibrant local art scene. They held private art auctions at local hotels that included original work by E. J. Gold and famous artist prints by Miro, Chagall and others. Most items for sale listed around four or five hundred dollars. The leader, Drew, advertised some of his native Indian-looking art under the name *Martin Silverwolf.* Jennifer, Alan's other daughter, moved to town first, soon joined the group around 1983, and then recruited her sister. Marta got deeply involved and signed as the 'agent' for ADAM's incorporation as a 'non-profit' in New Mexico in 1984. The group also operated the small, short-lived *Thunderbear Gallery* in downtown Santa Fe. Alan's daughters were mixing with important people in the art and spiritual milieus of a special art and seeker town.

The premise of Fourth Way cults is that an eternal gnosis could be transmitted from an adept to worthy students through various transformational techniques and 'shocks' to the student's ego. All ADAM activities were the means to this end and not ends in themselves.

Exclusive Authority

Gurdjieff called this spiritual awakening process Self-Remembering. Gurdjieff claimed to have been initiated into his gnosis by a secret Sufi sect called the Sarmoun Brotherhood, thus empowering him to initiate others by direct transmission. Research exposes that Gurdjieff was a clever liar or, perhaps, that he devised what Plato called a pious fraud. His secret brotherhood was most likely a reinvention of the imaginary White Brotherhood of secret masters introduced by H. P. Blavatsky in her Theosophy movement. In any case, I wanted to impress on Alan that the Gurdjieff style by way of the *Sly Man* (the fourth way) gave his daughters and ADAM a sacred excuse for all the secrecy, cover names, faux Native American agenda, and front groups.

Drew K. had the power and authority, transmitted to him by E. J. Gold to initiate Alan's daughters. Drew told me that Gurdjieff sometimes transmitted this power to someone through an 'enabling substance' inserted in a piece of candy called *kefa*. Drew also claimed that initiation to wake up the human 'machine' or robotic self could come through his sperm during 'Tantric' sex, ritual dancing, using certain psychedelic drugs (entheogens) under his guidance and sacred drumming. Drew taught that commitment to *The Work* must be total, yet when I confronted him about the danger of dropping out, he merely answered: Why would you want to leave? Drew claimed there was no difference between *The Work* and the world – it was a matter of awareness.

Circular Tension

Once the transcendent awareness was absorbed through ritual, ecstasy, instruction and submission to the authority figure, Alan's daughters assumed a special posture to life that centred on ADAM activities. This new psychosocial orientation moved them from a wider frame of reference into a tighter one. ADAM was like a new moon orbiting Earth with Alan's daughters now in orbit around that new *moon*. This special posture offered them the means of escaping the limitations of the body 'machine'. They viewed themselves as on the cutting edge of spiritual evolution. Tension arose in all of ADAM's members, and perhaps in the leader as well, over who could claim to be enlightened or close to the goal and who was not. Struggle or 'work' indicated progress while continuous projects offered a sense of movement around the ultimate mission: to 'create' an eternal soul. Proofs of enlightenment, like a successful auction, were indications of shamanic powers. One story about Gurdjieff reiterated by Drew held that Gurdjieff through concentration alone could kill a yak at some distance – one thousand meters in one story. Psychic power, though eschewed by most Fourth Way enthusiasts, yet remains the proof that *The Work* works. ADAM members were also always in tension not to claim more powers than the leader, yet they had to behave as more enlightened than outsiders.

Exit Perils

Defection, as stated above, was not a viable option as re-entry to the unenlightened world *below* could be disastrous to the now refined mind, body and spirit. One young man I knew who was devoted to Drew and ADAM for eight years, finally broke away in 1994 after several years of struggle with the mission. He came to realize it was all a sham, he confronted the leader, left the household and moved in with an artist friend of mine for a month. My artist friend, who was well-acquainted with ADAM and had participated in group drum circles, related to me how much effort he spent just talking with the ex-member about confusion, anxious sleepless nights, fears of spiritual repercussion and deep anger over wasted time, effort and money. My artist friend said he now understood what I meant by recovery. He had a bona fide cult client sleeping on his couch!

As mentioned above, Alan was not inclined to hire me to help engage his daughters directly. A formal intervention was a huge leap for him and his wife with their tolerant values. While Alan was in Santa Fe, he did wish to visit his daughters. From past experience, he was certain that if he announced his coming, they would refuse him or group members would say they were unavailable. So I coached him on what to expect if he showed up unannounced. One key warning: *Do not stare at the leader's gauze-stuffed nose.* Drew K., a thin, white fellow of less than average height, had a cancer, a sarcoma, up his right nostril. He avoided standard medical treatment for spiritual reasons. His nostril bled slightly but continuously, so he packed it heavily with gauze that was generally blood coloured. Early in the morning, I drove twenty miles south of Santa Fe with Alan following to show him the cult house. I directed him to just show up at the front door. My source told me all core members, including both his daughters, would be there. I coached Alan to describe how he intuited where they lived after having a powerful dream to come visit them. He told them he had a vision where the house might be. The ruse worked well enough. I also coached Alan how to approach the leader with group language. Alan told him he felt like he was *remembering* something deep inside.

Alan managed to spend an hour with the leader and his two daughters at first, then only with the leader for the final two hours. When Alan first arrived and knocked, he could see inside through a screen door. He noticed a shocked Marta holding a baby that she quickly passed to the leader's wife who took the baby to a back room. Although Alan noted some initial shock to other occupants, the leader casually invited him inside. Alan stayed until he felt uncomfortable, as there was an obvious wall of secrecy that no one would breach. No one questioned Alan further after he explained that a vision compelled him to visit and guided him there. He thanked them for their hospitality, then drove away after a vague indication that he could visit again.

I met with Alan at his hotel as soon as he returned from the visit. During our debriefing session, I revealed that the baby he saw was his grandson. I explained that I did not want him to have that emotional burden on the first visit unless his daughter told him. I knew that her baby was due months before. Alan was tearful. My suspicion was that the leader was the father. I took Alan to the county office where we viewed the birth record. Indeed, the baby's parents were listed as his daughter and the leader under their official birth names. We returned to his hotel's tavern where I bought two whiskeys. I toasted Alan and his first grandchild, wishing them the best in the future.

Alan's mother-in-law and sister-in-law had a two-day visit with the girls in Santa Fe the following year in 1988, so his daring appearance did bear some fruit. I lost contact with Alan by 1990 and the group when I moved to Pennsylvania two years later.

As an aside, my artist friend told me that Alan's daughter Marta died later in the 1990s. The circumstances are unknown to me. The leader passed away also around that time. ADAM no longer exists.

Case two: A *Miracle of Love*

With this case, my four-part orbiting model will be implied, not specified with the headings *Transcendent Attraction, Exclusive Authority, Circular Tension, and Exit Perils.*

Miracle of Love (MoL) was formed by an eccentric *International Society for Krishna Consciousness* (ISKCON) devotee in 1988 in San Diego, California. David Swanson, who joined ISKCON at age seventeen in 1967, had a radical mental status change in 1987 when he became withdrawn, purportedly in a meditative state. He announced that a deity named Gourasana had taken over his body and mind. Significantly, the ISKCON founder Swami Prabhupada died in 1987 as did Rajneesh/Osho in 1990, both of whom garnered heavy criticism as major cult leaders. Rajneesh *sannyasins* (devotees) were among many 'career truth seekers' attracted to MoL.[8]

Swanson in his Gourasana persona, 'The Golden One', claimed to be 'more powerful' in God energy than Krishna, Buddha and Jesus as 'the first modern-day Incarnation of God'.[9] As Gourasana, Swanson spouted platitudes but became less functional, allowed a pinkie fingernail to grow very long and dressed in white, silky pyjamas while two members attended to his every need. Swanson's wife Carole Seidman (later named *Kalindi*) and another known as 'Gayle' or *The Lady* were the early lead players. In 1993, the group established the *Church of the Exodus*. Swanson died in 1995 leaving Kalindi to claim that Lord Gourasana now worked exclusively through her. In 1994, Kalindi and The Lady developed week-long intensives modelled on the popular mass trainings for consciousness-raising. Participants were instructed to not reveal MoL intensive details to anyone. In 1998, a nine-day MoL intensive cost over $2000. Intensives were gruelling psychosocial encounters designed to break down old personal patterns while infusing trust in the promises of MoL. Intensives ended with hug fests, endorphins flying around in brains (so to speak) and the announcement that the joy they were experiencing was God's love and energy.[10] Support staff served for little or no pay although some received regular wages. Many staff abandoned families and partners while moving around to serve at intensives.

Thousands, including celebrities and upper middle-class seekers, have paid for MoL intensives. The transcendent goal of MoL was to accelerate *moksha* or union with God and freedom from rebirth. MoL designed a Hinduised version of a mass training cult: 'MoL philosophy is a loose mix of teachings of Sri Rajneesh, Gurdjieff, EST (sic) and pop psychology'.[11] After much controversy that followed her from California to Hawaii, Kalindi moved the main ashram around 2005 to eight houses in Colorado. MoL absorbed part of another movement called *Emissaries of Divine Light* (EDL). The EDL, centred in Colorado, was founded in 1932 by The Lady Gayle's father, Lloyd Meeker, a.k.a. Uranda.[12] Kalindi died in 2010, leaving MoL leadership to The Lady Gayle and a small committee. Ex-MoL members have been actively warning people about the potential harm experienced at intensives and as core members.[13] As in ADAM, core devotees in MoL were given new names. And, as in ADAM, thoughts about defection were avoided because of the danger of falling back into 'the illusion' of ordinary life. As one of the many affirmations suggested by MoL states: *I will do whatever it takes to break through the illusion, to move toward the Truth.*

Kalindi's self-published book *Ultimate Freedom: Union with God* (Gourasana 1998) is filled with pages of photographs of her, many sexually provocative, and some in the nude. MoL is registered as a non-profit but has managed through front groups to declare few assets leaving leaders to live relatively lavish lifestyles. Calls for donations were constant and with high pressure according to former members and investigative reports. MoL targeted the wealthy. One elderly woman complained to Legal Aid of Marin of losing $260,000 to bad investments through one MoL agent.[14] The group prohibited homosexuality. New members were to submit totally to sub-leaders called Masters, if they wanted to succeed in the quest for total freedom. This affirmation by MoL suggests the path is through 'direct experience' of gnosis, not faith: *Nothing can be believed about this entire phenomenon. It is only something you can know through direct experience.*[15]

Kevin, a young medical doctor ran an outpatient clinic that he owned. He decided to directly 'experience' MoL training around 1999. In subsequent years, he would take MoL intensives regularly until Kalindi asked him to sell his clinic and join her as her personal physician in Colorado. Kevin was ready – he told a girlfriend that he would do anything Kalindi asked of him. Kevin's father, Ben, also a physician and a professor of medicine, called me around 2005. He and his daughter, Kevin's sister Rita, were very concerned over this last turn of events. Ben was most concerned that for six years he was unable to mention anything to Kevin about MoL after an early dispute. As it stood, Kevin was still visiting with Ben at major family events, but relations were very strained. If Kevin moved to Colorado, his life would likely be micromanaged by Kalindi. Ben was not interested in getting Kevin out – he only wanted my help to re-establish normal communication with his son. Kevin's sister, on the other hand, wanted her brother out. Kevin would be coming home in a few weeks for his father's birthday gathering. Despite the tension, I gathered that Kevin retained respect for his father. We agreed that I would be introduced only as someone that would help father and son communicate normally again.

Rita brought me to the father's house for breakfast. Kevin was staying there and had arrived the night before. Note that over ninety per cent of my interventions had begun this way – by surprise to the cult member – so I had a good idea how to proceed. I coached the family the day before to act as if it were a normal event. Rita went upstairs to tell Kevin that Ben invited a guest.

Kevin was respectful but guarded with me at first. He seemed to loosen up after I recited some of my background and my reason for being there. I offered him my card, but he ignored it. We surmised that Kevin was never really comfortable with the MoL barrier between him and his father – we were correct. I broached the MoL story within the first hour. What grabbed Kevin's interest was my familiarity with MoL leaders from its earliest years.

[A colleague and I were hired to speak with an original MoL member in 1987 when the group called itself *Full Realization Eternal Enlightenment* or FREE. It became *Church of the Exodus* in 1990. That original member became clinically depressed and was sent home by the group to his mother's house in Arizona. His mother was concerned because he refused medical intervention and merely sat brooding in his room for a month. My colleague and I met with him, but he refused to communicate with us, so we gave up after two days of talking with his frustrated mother. One month later, the young man returned to San Diego and FREE where he tried to kill himself. While in the hospital, FREE members and his mother rallied around him. He emerged as a staunch group supporter, still immersed in the core group as late as 2007].

The inclusive approach to educate Ben, Kevin and Rita together moved the target away from Kevin. Although he was aware by then that I was no friend to MoL, Kevin was curious about my background with spiritual groups, so I recited my Agni Yoga and CUT experiences without condemning or judging any group at that stage. CUT had many parallels with the MoL experience and teachings. I also expanded on the Vedic foundations of MoL's odd, even wrong-headed interpretation of freedom or moksha.

Though I had informed Kevin that he could demand that I leave anytime, we sat conversing at that table through lunch and into late afternoon, taking only bathroom breaks. We broke for an evening party for Ben with a few family friends. I was invited. Rita took me back to my hotel after Kevin agreed to meet with me, Rita and Ben the following morning.

In this case, I had the advantage of exiting through intervention another doctor from MoL just the month before. The doctor knew Kevin. On the second day, Kevin permitted me to show and discuss a video about mass trainings and how they work. That video led to another that included the story of someone that had defected from Lifespring. Kevin's thinking wheels were turning as he saw directly a parallel to his own story. He noted how 'experience' could be easily manipulated. I asked him if he would speak with the ex-MoL doctor I counselled earlier. Kevin called him and they spoke for nearly four hours.

On the third morning, we debriefed for a few hours. Kevin's girlfriend, a former but fringe MoL member who was privy to the meeting, joined us. Kevin had a lot to think about, but he had to get back to his clinic – a six-hour drive. After giving his father a firm handshake and a hug, he drove away from Ben's home with his girlfriend. Two hours into their trip down the coast, Kevin called his father to tell him he was no longer selling his clinic and that he would end his relationship with Kalindi and MoL.

Now, Ben was somewhat shocked. Rita was happy. Ben told me that he had been hoping to talk sense to his son for over five years about MoL. He believed that Kevin would never leave the group. He just watched me help his son change his life around in less than three days. 'You are a magician', he said. I reminded him that I could have done nothing without his love and respect for his son.

Sometimes the fly leaves the fly bottle, when we show the way out.

Aesthetics

The art in this intervention business is in how we employ Wittgenstein's ordinary language to help someone determine what is ugly or elegant. Ordinarily, most people will not choose what they know to be harmful without belief in an overriding gain. If that gain proves to be illusory by evidence presented, the spell (influence) of the group over the believer's perception will evaporate. The transcendent wholeness promised by the group begins to look more like a hole – a bottled-up life. The suggested aroma of holiness lifts and the place begins to stink inside the now stuffy bottle. To describe the cult experience, we use aesthetic references from stories: down a rabbit hole, trapped on a yellow brick road, do not pay attention to the man behind the curtain, the emperor has no clothes and so on. Watching Alice trapped in a dream may be good entertainment, but no one save the mad Queen or Tweedle Dum wants Alice to be in Wonderland forever – that would be encouraging a mental or social disorder. That would be ugly and inelegant because life has difficulty flourishing under that condition – in a small bottle with a disconcerting way out.

Clients, including Alan and Kevin, often asked me what I think is a true religion or therapy, but I sense them angling for more, for what is the true religion, philosophy, etc. I cannot answer that because I do not think that human beings have the capacity to answer that. I think we do have the capacity to approach those answers through beauty and elegance. Elegance cannot be merely superficial. An elegant solution in mathematics tends to be the most useful for the most people and projects. Aesthetics is not necessarily about appearances which can easily fool perception – do not judge a book by its cover. However, anyone who specialises in new religions, new gurus and new approaches to old teachings should develop a taste for what might be working well and what is not in short order by examining evidence. By reversing the order of my model, by examining exit perils first, then circular tension and authoritarian leadership, I can better assess whether the initiation through ecstasy or the attractive goal of transcendence is worth the experience of self-sacrifice and devotion. I can only hope that my assessment will be useful to help my client choose well.

Notes

1 Professionals and para-professionals who discuss group affiliations with group members with the intent of educating them about possibly better choices have had

various labels including deprogrammers, exit counsellors, cult busters, mediators and so on. I have preferred cult intervention specialist or consultant. I also like the idea of *exit coach* as it is in keeping with the metaphor in this article 'to show the fly the way out of the fly bottle'.

2 www.icsahome.com/articles/razor-s-edge-indeed-a-deprogrammer-s-view-of-harmful-cult-activity. My model borrows from three sources: Zablocki and Robbins (2001) see especially Part 2 and Chapter 5 for Zablocki's clarification of 'exit costs'; Deikman (2003); and Lalich, (2007).

3 Wittgenstein (1958) (Article 309).

4 Wittgenstein advises that philosophy functions best when it is a kind of therapy that solves real problems in actual circumstances: 'There is not a philosophical method, though there are indeed methods, like different therapies' Wittgenstein (1958) (see Articles 107 and 133).

5 There are no Internet references to this group. I refer to personal files with my notes, original group documents and copies of documents issued by ADAM in the late 1980s. I found 2 references to artists that had exhibited at Thunderbear Gallery – one was E. J. Gold: www.gorebag.com/who/onlinebio/ejbio01.html.

6 https://en.wikipedia.org/wiki/George_Gurdjieff. For a thorough, outsider's critique of Gurdjieff and Fourth Way teachings, read (Webb 1987).

7 www.gurdjieff-con.net/2011/07/18/expose-of-ej-gold/.

8 Ex-MoL members relayed to me that small groups (5–6 people) devoted to Rajneesh/Osho would take MoL workshops.

9 'The Path Handbook' (*Miracle of Love* publication, 2005: 68).

10 'Miracle of Love' by Jill Kramer (*Pacific Sun*: 17–23 March 2006).

11 Email from concerned friend of MoL member, 9 August 2004.

12 http://emissaries.org/about-us/beginnings/.

13 www.miracleoflove.org/Home.

14 'Miracle of Love' by Jill Kramer (Pacific Sun: 17–23 March 2006: 13).

15 'The Path Handbook' (*Miracle of Love* publication, 2005: 66).

References

Deikman, A. 2003. *Them and Us: Cult Thinking and the Terrorist Threat.* Berkeley: Bay Tree Publishing.

Gourasana, K.L. 1998. *Ultimate Freedom: Union with GOD.* Miracle of Love Publications.

Lalich, J. 2007. *Bounded Choice: True Believers and Charismatic Cults.* Berkeley, Los Angeles, London: University of California Press.

Webb, J. 1987. *The Harmonious Circle: The Lives and Work of G.I. Gurdjieff, P.D. Ouspensky, and Their Followers.* Shambhala Publications.

Wittgenstein, L. 1958. *Philosophical Investigations* translated by G. E. M. Anscombe (1986 edition). Basil Blackwell, Ltd.

Zablocki, B. and T. Robbins (eds) 2001. *Misunderstanding Cults: Searching for Objectivity in a Controversial Field.* Toronto, ON: University of Toronto Press.

Part III

Member and former member experiences

8 Pagan experiences of counselling and psychotherapy

Vivianne Crowley

Mental health problems are one of the main causes of disease worldwide (Global Burden of Disease Study 2013). In England, for example, in any given year the percentage of people aged 16–64 meeting the criteria for at least one common mental disorder, such as anxiety or depression, is 17.6 per cent (McManus et al. 2009). The need for access to counselling and psychotherapy services is high, but the therapeutic relationships involved can present particular dilemmas for members of minority religions, such as Paganism, which are not well known or understood by others in society. Pagans seeking counselling and therapy may be concerned that a psychotherapist or counsellor will perceive their spiritual practices and any beliefs in magic or non-ordinary phenomena and states of consciousness as symptomatic of psychological disorder (Crowley and Winder 2015).

On the other side of the therapeutic relationship, Pagans who are counsellors or therapists must determine how 'out' they are in their professional lives, given that the majority of their colleagues and clients will not share and may not understand their beliefs. This chapter examines how Pagans negotiate issues of self-disclosure, authenticity and identity in therapeutic relationships and contexts, and how this impacts upon the therapeutic process. It draws on my ongoing research on Pagans and mental health ('Pagan Counselling and Psychotherapy Questionnaire' referred to hereafter as 'PCPQ 2015'), together with responses to a questionnaire on issues surrounding Pagan identity ('Pagan Census Responses Questionnaire' referred to hereafter as 'PCRQ 2013'), the first stage of which was reported on in Crowley (2014).[1] I argue that while Paganism is becoming more recognised in Britain as part of the spectrum of belief and practice of a multicultural society, lack of knowledge of and negative attitudes towards Paganism can create difficulties for Pagans in engaging in therapeutic relationships.

Attitudes to Paganism in Britain

Contemporary Paganism includes pre-Christian indigenous traditions and new or revived forms of Paganism (York 2003: 59–64). Some Pagans consider themselves simply 'Pagan'; others practise one or more different types of Paganism, such as Wicca (modern Pagan Witchcraft), Druidry, Heathenism, Goddess spirituality, Shamanism and/or indigenous traditions from their family culture, for example, Slavic Paganism among people of Polish descent (Crowley 2017). Though less than one per cent of the population, the most recent UK census data show over 85,000 Pagans, the seventh largest religious group in Britain (Crowley 2014). Census numbers reflect trends but underestimate the numbers of adherents, because many Pagans do not declare themselves on official documents. Generally accepted estimates are of around 200,000 Pagans in Britain (Crowley 2014).

Paganism differs from many other minority religions in that it is not the creation of a charismatic leader. Paganism is a 'bottom-up' grass-roots movement with nuclei of leadership and influence, which Michael York has characterised as a 'Segmented Polycentric Integrated Network' or SPIN (York 1995). Many Pagans are reluctant to join formal organisations. Only a minority are members of major Pagan representative groups. More are members of small informal religious groups, such as Druid groves, Wiccan covens or Heathen hearths, but many are content to be part of a wider community who attend public Pagan religious celebrations and other events, but whose spiritual practice is otherwise solitary.

Until recent years, the main way in which non-Pagans learned about contemporary Paganism was through the media. Media coverage on Paganism is often derogatory and belittling. The now defunct *News of the World* specialised in exposés of Pagans under headlines such as 'Satan Gran's Coven is a Cauldron of Sin' (Press Complaints Commission 1996) and *The Daily Mail* delights in relentlessly negative articles such as 'Pagans are on the march – but are they harmless eccentrics or a dangerous cult?' (Brennan 2010). Pagans are well aware of negative media interpretations of Pagan activities.

> The headline 'Ritual Cult to Get Rite to Marry' doesn't have the same ring as 'Persons who respect nature and generally believe in the spirits of place and the moon and honour them in a way similar to modern day druids but who do not wish to be labelled as such, to conduct marriage-like ceremonies which are legally binding'.
>
> (Anne, PCRQ 2013)

Pagans experience and anticipate experiencing stigma, prejudice and discrimination in the workplace and elsewhere and this influences how open they are about their Pagan identity (Crowley 2014; Tejeda 2015). The Equality and Human Rights Commission's report *Religion or Belief* notes that Pagans experience 'open hostility', and comments on the '(largely undocumented) existence of discrimination against socially marginal religious groups where ethnicity is not a factor' (Donald, Bennett and Leach 2012). Some National Health Service staff, for example, report experiencing prejudice if they are open about their Pagan identity:

> I described myself at work to a Muslim doctor who was my medical director as a pagan/goddess worshipper and he was shocked and nervously laughed and quoted an old saying about dirty pagans and asked did I know it?
>
> (Clare, PCRQ 2013)

The lack of formal group membership can be disadvantageous when coping with stigma and discrimination, in that Pagans do not necessarily have the support mechanisms of more conventionally structured religions. A sense of isolation can compound the caution many Pagans feel about revealing their beliefs to others:

> It is still a subject that draws negative responses from people when discussed even from people you would not expect it from, so it can be something easier to avoid talking about.
>
> (Brigit, PCRQ 2013)

There are second- and third-generation Pagans, but Paganism is predominantly a religion of choice rather than of birth. Although some may choose to wear religious symbols, those who considered themselves to be Pagan do not need to adopt a style of dress or other daily practices that make them distinctive in everyday life. The extent to which people reveal their religious choice is largely therefore a personal decision. Pagans often use similar language to the gay community, describing themselves as 'in' or 'out', or as some Pagans term it, 'in or out of the broom closet'. Given the potential for negative reactions, some Pagans conceal their Paganism from all but their closest circle of relatives and/or friends.

Like members of other stigmatised and non-visible minority groups, Pagans may choose to 'pass' as 'ordinary' or non-Pagan, but most Pagans have a continuum of identity-management strategies that regulate the level of disclosure they are willing to offer. Gradations of openness range from those who are open only with other Pagans, those who are open with family and/or close friends, those who are open with close work colleagues and those who are open or 'out' in all aspects of their lives. For many Pagans, there is a sharp division between private and public life and they may assume a pseudonym for online and other public Pagan activity.

Psychology, psychiatry and Paganism

Training courses and professional bodies emphasise that counsellors and psychotherapists should have an attitude of openness to clients' beliefs and religious practices. However, psychiatry and psychology as disciplines have a long history of estrangement with religion, paralleled by the personal disenchantment with religion of many psychologists who continue to be less religious than the population as a whole (Pargament and Saunders 2007). Pagans are not alone therefore in experiencing difficulties in having their spirituality understood by therapists, counsellors and mental health services. The Mental Health Foundation comments that:

> A survey published in 2004 indicated that 45% of mental health professionals felt that religion could lead to mental ill health, whilst 39% thought that religion could protect people from mental ill health.

> Clinicians often either ignore an individual's spiritual life completely or treat their spiritual experiences as the cause or manifestation of a service user's mental health problems.
>
> (Mental Health Foundation 2008: 1)

Ambivalent attitudes towards clients' religion and spirituality are compounded in the case of minority religions by a bias towards construing non-mainstream spiritual practice as symptomatic of psychological disorder (Buxant et al. 2007). Psychological explanations for joining new religions have tended to focus on negative psychosocial factors, such as poor relationships with parents and low self-esteem, which might dispose an individual to identify with a welcoming group (Granqvist and Kirkpatrick 2004).

Multiculturalism and European Human Rights legislation have been major drivers for more sympathetic approaches to the beliefs and practices of minority groups. In response to the UK's Human Rights Act (1998) and The Equality Act (2010), health bodies and professions have issued guidance on behaviour towards staff and patients from different ethnic and religious groups. Guidance from the Royal College of Psychiatrists comments, for example, that, 'A psychiatrist must provide care that does not discriminate and is sensitive to issues of gender, ethnicity, colour, culture, lifestyle, beliefs, sexual orientation, age and disability' (Royal College of Psychiatrists 2013). Subsequent to the UK Human Rights Act, the Royal College of Psychiatrists established a Spirituality and Psychiatry Special Interest Group to:

> provide a forum for psychiatrists to explore the influence of the major religions that shape the cultural values and aspirations of psychiatrist and patient alike. The spiritual aspirations of persons not identifying with any one particular faith are held to be of no less importance, as well as the viewpoint of those who hold that spirituality is independent of religion.
>
> (Royal College of Psychiatrists 1999)

By accident or design, however, the statement refers only to 'major religions' and the non-religious, leaving room for ambiguity in the approach to psychological distress and psychiatric illness among adherents of minority religions. Indeed, psychiatric attitudes may be becoming less favourable towards minority worldviews. The British Psychological Society has argued that recent developments in the influential psychiatric diagnosis manual *DSM-5* (American Psychiatric Association 2013) increase the risk that unusual behaviour can be pathologised:

> The putative diagnoses presented in DSM-V are clearly based largely on social norms, with 'symptoms' that all rely on subjective judgements … The criteria are not value-free, but rather reflect current normative social expectations. … the concept of 'attenuated psychosis system' appears very worrying; it could be seen as an opportunity to stigmatize eccentric people, and to lower the threshold for achieving a diagnosis of psychosis.

> Diagnostic systems such as these therefore fall short of the criteria for legitimate medical diagnoses.
>
> (British Psychological Society 2011)

While most National Health Service guidance is admirable in its even-handedness, some is surprisingly prejudiced. The South Devon Healthcare Trust has positive statements about equality and diversity on its website:

> Our aim is to promote good relations meeting the needs of our patients, service users, staff and visitors ... Unfortunately we recognise that particular groups in society may experience prejudice and disadvantage and it is all our responsibilities to work to prevent this.
>
> (South Devon Healthcare NHS Foundation Trust 2015)

In its guidance on religious, spiritual, pastoral and cultural care, however, it comments that, with regard to people who identify as Pagan:

> There may be some discomfort among some Christian service users and staff about the nature of these beliefs and terms used such as 'Goddess'.
>
> (South Devon Healthcare Trust and Teignmouth Primary Care Trust 2009)

The Trust creates the prejudicial expectation that unlike other religious beliefs, Christians may find Paganism particularly objectionable.

Paganism in the therapeutic encounter

Successful therapy requires deep levels of personal disclosure and authenticity, but a therapeutic encounter is a social interaction in which Pagans must decide the level of openness they feel comfortable and safe to engage in. The American Psychological Association's taskforce to identify what works in the therapy relationship evidences that the quality of the empathic relationship between client and therapist is one of the best predictors of treatment outcomes across a range of theoretical approaches, including psychodynamic, humanistic, cognitive, behavioural and systemic (Norcross and Wampold 2011). Pagan clients' relationships with their therapists will therefore play a significant role in treatment outcomes. Often clients report positive responses to discussions of their spiritual orientation, but clients can also experience negative or unhelpful reactions.

One problem is that while knowledge of the existence of Paganism has grown in recent decades, those who approach counsellors and psychotherapists often find that they know little about it.

> I told her, as I couldn't see the point in hiding my religion if I was going to be helped. But she had no idea about it at all and I felt it could have helped more if she had some knowledge.
>
> (Fiona, PCPQ 2015)

Lack of knowledge means that valuable and sometimes costly face-to-face time can be spent explaining Paganism to the therapist:

> Time spent trying to explain their beliefs to a non-Pagan counsellor increases the sense of nervousness that many people already have to overcome in order to seek therapy in the first place. As Pagans we have all experienced a certain amount of ridicule in the media, or from other people, about our beliefs and to reveal this information to others can sometimes be a risk. If a person is already feeling vulnerable, having to justify and convince a counsellor that their beliefs matter is not helpful.
>
> (Deidre, PCPQ 2015)

Clients can find that if they do disclose their spiritual orientation, the response is not necessarily positive:

> I found a counsellor who was local to where I lived and went to her for several sessions … I told her I was a Pagan. I thought perhaps it might unlock something but no, I was met with a blank stare … In the end we agreed that we weren't getting anywhere and called a halt. In retrospect telling her I was a Pagan was a mistake as I feel she didn't understand at all my way of life.
>
> (Elizabeth, PCPQ 2015)

Others reported receiving negative reactions to their Paganism:

> As a client, I spent two years being wary of having my involvement with Paganism interpreted as pathological. When I eventually began to share more of this aspect of myself he [the therapist] suggested that I was using magic to try and control the world with no effort on my part and without connecting with anyone (I'd talked about taking space to meditate/commune with 'the ancestors'). I was so taken aback and angry at this, and other assumptions, that I closed down.
>
> (Katharine, PCPQ 2015)

Many Pagan clients will have belief systems that embrace experiencing paranormal or unusual phenomena, such as clairvoyance, precognition, telepathy and seeing ghosts. Indeed, those who have the experiences may be attracted to spiritual groups that recognise and validate such experiences and contextualise them as 'normal', valuable and desirable (Farias, Underwood and Claridge 2013). The understanding of 'benign schizotypy' – normal dissociative, imaginative states – is growing (Crowley and Winder 2015), but when health professionals are unfamiliar with these experiences in a religious context, there is wide scope for misinterpretation. In theory, psychiatry and psychology recognise that religious and spiritual experiences are context-specific and that what is 'normal' or 'abnormal' will vary between cultures: 'what may be classified as a psychiatric disorder in one culture is revered as a mystical state in another' (Bhugra 1996). In practice, mental health professionals bring to their work their own experiences and preconceptions, which may predispose them to view some religious practices as more 'normal' than others:

> When my husband died … the psychiatrists and other staff did not understand me trying to talk in terms of my religion at all. I tried to talk about reincarnation, and his spirit moving to another state, but they just asked me if I was seeing spirits. The psychiatrist became irritated. I had my meds increased after that meeting!
>
> (Fiona, PCPQ 2015)

Lack of knowledge of minority religious practices can create the twin problems for counsellors and therapists of mistakenly pathologising spiritual practice that is commonplace for a particular religion, for example talking with spirits or having visions, and difficulty in distinguishing when such experiences go beyond the boundaries of religious practice and are symptoms of psychological distress. For those with less usual spiritual practices, it is important that health professionals can distinguish between 'normal' visions and delusions. The Mental Health Foundation's guide to mental health and spirituality highlights this point:

> People with psychosis may hold unusual beliefs (delusions), describe hearing voices or have other experiences that seem out of touch with reality, but people who are mentally well may also describe this kind of experience. Some people have spiritual experiences that are like psychotic symptoms, for instance believing in angels or identifying themselves as a white witch or hearing the voice of their god. When someone who has always held such beliefs becomes unwell, these experiences are not necessarily symptoms of their mental illness.
>
> (Mental Health Foundation 2007: 7)

In practice, however, mental health professionals may find the distinction difficult:

> When hallucinating, it was tricky explaining that they weren't a religious experience and I had to try to help them differentiate between the two. I felt I had to manage all the explanations and find the right words, as I was challenged on this, in an adversarial way, several times. On one occasion, the psychologist and two psychiatrists sat opposite me firing questions at me for quite a while, which when you are severely depressed is a very exhausting and deeply distressing thing to deal with.
>
> (Fiona, PCPQ 2015)

Pagan therapists can play a useful role in therapeutic settings in providing advice to colleagues on what is or is not a spiritual experience:

> I have been in a position to advise a psychiatrist that their client describing themselves as a witch was not delusional, that it was reality that they were a Wiccan Priestess, but they were a Wiccan Priestess who was also experiencing symptoms of psychosis.
>
> (Gareth, PCPQ 2015)

For clients to be open about their experiences and their spirituality, there must be trust between the client and mental health professional. The imbalance in power in therapeutic encounters influences how Pagans react, particularly when dealing with psychiatrists, who have ultimate power in a treatment team:

> When I saw a psychiatrist, I deliberately did not reveal that I was a Pagan. I felt the power imbalance between us – his power to judge me unfavourably or to section me if he decided to – and it felt like too big a risk to reveal a piece of information to which I did not know how he might react.
>
> (Deidre, PCPQ 2015)

Pagans can also be hesitant about sharing their religious beliefs with other service users. Group therapy can be particularly problematic for members of minority religions who must deal with the reactions to their spiritual practice of other group members as well as the therapist:

> I upset other members of the group, so stopped mentioning Paganism altogether. Having to explain it wasn't Satanism was tiring and boring!
>
> (Fiona, PCPQ 2015)

Resorting to concealing important aspects of identity may be an expedient strategy in the short-term, but in the longer-term concealment can be a source of psychological stress. Paganism can be construed as a concealable stigmatised identity (CSI), a socially devalued and negatively stereotyped identity that can be hidden from others (Quinn and Chaudoir 2009). The stresses of negotiating a stigmatised identity can have implications for psychological well-being (Plante et al. 2014). Anticipated stigma is a strong predictor of increased depression and anxiety among people with a variety of CSIs (Quinn and Chaudoir 2009). Research by Daniel Wegner and colleagues on the 'secrecy cycle' and the psychological effects of concealing a stigmatised identity shows that concealment increases the occurrence of intrusive thoughts and obsessive preoccupation with the secret, contributing to anxiety about self-disclosure and its potential consequences (Smart and Wegner 1999). Diane Quinn and Valerie Earnshaw point out that CSI is associated with decreased self-esteem:

> Because people with CSIs are aware of the societal negative stereotypes and beliefs about people with their identity, they may expect that others

> will devalue them even if they have never previously experienced discrimination. Moreover, if they have already experienced discrimination due to the identity, they may be particularly likely to anticipate future stigmatizing experiences.
>
> (Quinn and Earnshaw 2013)

The therapeutic situation is potentially one in which the psychological stress that can result from a CSI can be explored, providing the therapist or counsellor understands Paganism and is affirming about the client's self-identity. When the client's spirituality receives a negative response, this creates additional distress in what may already be a stressful encounter:

> So the effect of disclosure was met with disbelief, seen as part of illness, too much curiosity, too much questioning, assumptions about it being Satanism, assumptions about practices and blankness at different times. I think ignorance of my religion was difficult. I am not sure if I would disclose again. But that would be difficult as it's part of me. I felt very alone on this at times.
>
> (Fiona, PCPQ 2015)

Pagans as counsellors and psychotherapists

Most Pagans who are counsellors and psychotherapists have no doubts that it is crucial to the therapeutic encounter for clients to be able to talk about their Pagan experiences and identity. In relation to their own therapy or counselling, often as part of their training, they felt that this was an essential part of the process.

> I talked about it briefly quite early on as it's very much part of who I am and has had a profound impact on my development. I referred to it occasionally during the therapy whenever it came up. … I can't imagine not disclosing it and have no doubt that it was the right thing to do.
>
> (John, PCPQ 2015)

Where therapists had felt constrained to be less open about their practice, this was seen as impacting negatively on the authenticity of the client-therapist relationship

> When I first had therapy, I could not have imagined that there could possibly even be a counsellor who would understand Paganism, let alone be a Pagan themselves so I withheld it through fear of judgement as 'stupid' or 'deluded' or just through not wanting to have to explain what it all meant. As I have got older and trained as a counsellor myself, I have realised that there is no point engaging in the process if I am withholding too much information.
>
> (Deidre, PCPQ 2015)

In some cases, the choice of therapy was influenced by the therapy's stance towards spiritual experience, leading to either choosing a particular type of therapy and therapeutic organisation:

> Being very actively Pagan, it was natural to seek out a psychotherapy that is overt in taking spirituality seriously. I was then in my twenties with little experience of psychotherapy but knew that a Jungian approach was likely to be congruent to an extent with my own belief systems.
>
> (Gareth, PCPQ 2015)

or to avoiding particular organisations:

> It didn't occur to me to look for a specifically Pagan or Pagan-friendly therapist, though I made sure to find a secular organisation and avoided getting any counselling tinged with a mainstream religion 'flavour'.
>
> (Ian, PCPQ 2015)

For some therapists, finding a training organisation that is open to or has a compatible approach with a spiritual worldview was very important:

> I did two preliminary courses before my diploma – one at the ... centre and one at a local Further Education college and I was shocked at how dry and closed off the FE college course felt. The work was very shallow and we weren't encouraged to journey deeply at all. The college system is perhaps not able to add this element due to cost, regulations, and time! I did not feel able to be 'out' about being a Pagan at the FE college. I felt I would be judged as possibly unsuitable to be a counsellor if I were to reveal it. This may not have been the case, but it didn't feel safe to me to share this information.
>
> (Deidre, PCPQ 2015)

Therapists' attitudes varied with age and area. A younger therapist in an urban area was more relaxed about which training to choose and more confident about being open about his spiritual beliefs:

> Some of my teachers know that I'm a Pagan. However, we didn't discuss it in any detail, the course is secular, doesn't privilege any one religious belief over another. ... Plus some of my teachers deal with rites of passage, nature-based therapy and similar topics and while not active Pagans, could certainly be described as Pagan-friendly.
>
> (Ian, PCPQ 2015)

At work, Pagan counsellors and psychotherapists must determine their level of openness with their colleagues. This can be a dilemma for those employed by the National Health Service, but also for those in private practice who may be dependent on referrals from others:

> There is a certain amount of contradiction in my thoughts on this subject. I am both willing to be fairly open about my Paganism and fairly happy to deal with anyone who has an issue with it, but also willing to withhold the information and feel unsafe around certain types of people – usually 'authority figures' those I feel who hold a certain power over me – doctors, lawyers, those in positions which could stop me from getting work as a counsellor simply because of their ill-informed opinions that others may listen to.
>
> (Deidre, PCPQ 2015)

Estelle Seymour writes cogently about the dilemmas facing Pagan counsellors in dealing with colleagues' understanding of Paganism:

> As a Pagan who has spent the past eight years facilitating learning in counselling and counselling skills, as well as being a student counsellor in a college of further education, I have often been wary of sharing my beliefs with colleagues and students. Fantasies of being sacked for my beliefs and practices and publicising my case in the national papers as a Pagan martyr vied with my paranoia over losing credibility and paying the mortgage.
>
> (Seymour 1998)

There is some evidence that the religious background of providers of psychotherapy can have a significant effect on the likelihood of a prospective client choosing to see them (Gregory II et al. 2008). Most clients of Pagan counsellors and psychotherapists are not Pagans and in practising their profession, counsellors and psychotherapists must determine how 'out' to be as Pagans. Most counselling and therapy training does not encourage therapists to reveal personal information to clients, so for Pagans who are not 'out' in public life, the issues are fewer:

> I would be unlikely to reveal too much about myself in any area with a client as there are ethical issues around it and sessions can become more about me than about my client if I disclose too much information. This, for me, is about maintaining boundaries in the counselling relationship rather than a desire to hide my Pagan beliefs.
>
> (Deidre, PCPQ 2015)

For those who are active in running public Pagan groups or events, personal boundaries are not easy to maintain however in an internet age:

> Often they find out having Googled me on the Internet. I have found the best way to deal with this is to explain to them in great detail about the traditions I am involved with and by the time I have done so most do not ask again!
>
> (Gareth, PCPQ 2015)

As with other aspects of life, Pagans who are counsellors and therapists have different levels of disclosure depending on the social situation. They may be more circumspect when clients reveal that they practise religious traditions with a history of viewing Paganism negatively:

> I'm open about being a Pagan with anyone who asks although I tend not to talk about it if the subject doesn't come up in conversation. I have been asked by Christian clients on a couple of occasions if I am a spiritual person and I have simply said that I am without adding that I'm Pagan.
>
> (John, PCPQ 2015)

The location of the client sessions will also be a factor in how likely clients are to notice that their therapist or counsellor has some form of spiritual belief or practice. Where clients are seen in their therapist or counsellor's home, there are more triggers to ask questions:

> I only disclose where I feel the client will benefit. If they are asking about a certain statue or book they have seen on my shelves then that can be part of the work. If they ask me directly I will be honest as I have no need to hide. Often clients in this case are most curious about it and it can form a useful area for them to explore for themselves.
>
> (Linda, PCPQ 2015)

How open Pagan therapists are about their beliefs may also vary with different client groups:

> From a professional point of view I have to be a little careful in specific settings. For psychotic patients to know of my beliefs can be problematic. When dealing with some clients' spiritual issues it is helpful they do not know my orientation, while with other clients it is helpful they do know.
>
> (Gareth, PCPQ 2015)

Some Pagan psychotherapists and counsellors have other Pagans as clients, and in these instances there are fewer issues about the therapist's own beliefs, but treating Pagan clients can be problematic in other ways. As members of a small religious community, counsellors and psychotherapists must weigh the benefits for clients of a practitioner who understands their religious experiences against issues of boundaries, role conflict and confidentiality. The training of counsellors and psychotherapists emphasises the need to maintain boundaries, and most avoid entering into client relationships with people in Pagan groups in which they participate:

> Yes I have had Pagan clients and I treat them as I do any client. I do not typically provide therapy to those I work with magically and would usually guide them to find another therapist unless absolutely necessary.

> To enter into a therapeutic relationship with someone you relate to in another capacity will always raise boundary issues.
>
> (Gareth, PCPQ 2015)

Some Pagans do have therapy with members of their own Pagan groups, however, and find this is a positive experience:

> I had counselling and transpersonal therapy with …, who at the time was also High Priestess of our coven. It was pretty intense but very helpful in terms of getting me to examine in detail my past and how it set patterns and habits in my life.
>
> (Linda, PCPQ 2015)

Future developments

Interacting with psychotherapy and counselling services can present difficulties for Pagan clients that create barriers to an authentic therapeutic relationship and have implications for the successful treatment outcomes. To improve therapy and counselling for Pagans, two developments seem necessary. One is to create easier access to counsellors and psychotherapists with an understanding of Paganism. Pagans often ask other Pagans for names of 'Pagan-friendly' counsellors and psychotherapists. This should become easier with the spread of values that can be deemed 'Pagan-friendly' among the wider population (Moreton 2009), and the popularity of counselling and psychotherapy as professions among Pagans (Orion 1995; Crowley 2000). Since not all counsellors and psychotherapists advertise their religious beliefs, however, identifying a suitable one can be difficult, especially for more solitary Pagans.

To address this, some Pagan therapists advocate establishing a referral system for Pagans seeking counselling or psychotherapy (Seymour 2012). The Pagan Federation is currently collaborating with other Pagan bodies to create such a list. The numbers are unlikely however to become sufficient for Pagans to access the full breadth of counselling and psychotherapeutic approaches solely from within the Pagan community. Indeed, some therapists express concerns that Pagans' reservations about being treated by non-Pagans could create barriers to accessing the most appropriate treatment:

> Pagans tend to have a rather ghetto mentality that only a Pagan can treat a Pagan. The reality is that professional therapists treat patients of every creed, colour and orientation as their basic day job. Having a therapist you can relate to with the requisite skills to help you with the particular problems you face in your life is what is important. Pagans can easily end up excluding themselves from the mental health system and can run the risk of seeking out inadequately trained 'therapists' who do not have the skills to really help.
>
> (Gareth, PCPQ 2015)

A second beneficial development would be for counsellors and psychotherapists to be better informed about contemporary Paganism, so that clients' spiritual practices are better understood. Some educational materials and articles have been written for counsellors, psychotherapists and related professions (Reeder 2004; Yardley 2008; Seymour 2012; Moe, Cates and Sepulveda 2013), but primarily in the United States with its larger Pagan population and greater tendency to replicate mainstream religious infrastructure. Some Pagan therapists argue the importance of better coverage of Pagan and other spiritualities in counselling and psychotherapy training (Seymour 2005). This is a wider issue than that of Paganism. There are indications that most clients, whether of a majority, minority or no religion, would like their belief systems to be taken into account by professionals such as counsellors, psychologists and psychiatrists (Smith and Simmonds 2006), and there appears to be a more general need for educating therapy professionals about the spectrum of potential clients' religious and spiritual worldviews.

Note

1 Methodological Note: This chapter draws on responses to a questionnaire (PCRQ 2013) distributed though Pagan organisations and internet groups in 2013, following the release of 2011 census data on religious affiliation, the first analysis of which was reported in Crowley (2014). Over 1,700 Pagans participated, the largest survey response from British Pagan communities to date. These responses were supplemented by ten open-ended interview questionnaires (PCPQ 2015) completed by Pagan counsellors and psychotherapists, primarily from the Pagan Federation referral list. These were analysed using interpretative phenomenological analysis (J. A. Smith 1996). These participants commented from their perspectives as practitioners and recipients of counselling and/or psychotherapy. Also included are quotes from a case study of a mental health services user. All participants were allocated pseudonyms.

I am grateful to Mike Stygal, President of The Pagan Federation for his assistance in identifying Pagan counsellors and psychotherapists; to counselling and psychotherapy professionals, including Rufus Harrington, Adrian Harris, Estelle Seymour and Nerissa Shaw for their comments on the draft; and to Pagans who shared their experiences of Pagan identity and on delivering and using counselling and therapy services.

References

American Psychiatric Association 2013. *Diagnostic and Statistical Manual of Mental Disorders*. 5th ed. Arlington, VA: American Psychiatric Publishing.

Bhugra, D. (ed.). 1996. *Psychiatry and Religion: Context, Consensus, and Controversies*. London: Routledge.

Brennan, Z. 2010. Pagans are on the march – but are they harmless eccentrics or a dangerous cult? *The Daily Mail*. 10 November. Available at www.dailymail.co.uk/femail/article-1328968/Pagans-march--harmless-eccentrics-dangerous-cult.html (Accessed 1 June 2013).

British Psychological Society 2011. The BPS response to the American Psychiatric Association: DSM-5 development. *British Psychological Society (2011). The BPS response to the American Psychiatric Association*. June. Available at http://apps.bps.org.uk/publicationfiles/ (Accessed 26 May 2015).

Buxant, C., V. Saroglou, S. Casalfiore and L.-L. Christians 2007. Cognitive and emotional characteristics of New Religious Movement members: New questions and data on the mental health issue. *Mental Health, Religion & Culture*, 10(3): 219–38.

Crowley, V. 2000. Healing in Wicca, in: W. Griffin (ed.) *Daughters of the Goddess: Studies of Identity, Healing and Empowerment*. Walnut Creek, CA: AltaMira Press, pp. 151–65.

Crowley, V. 2014. Standing up to be counted: understanding Pagan responses to the 2011 British censuses. *Religion*, 44(3): 483–501.

Crowley, V. 2017. The changing face of contemporary Paganism in Britain, in: E. V. Gallagher (ed.) *Visioning New and Minority Religions: Projecting the Future*. London and New York: Routledge, pp. 87–99.

Crowley, V. and B. Winder 2015. Interpreting the unusual: how Pagans and Pentecostal Christians interpret and integrate paranormal experiences. *International Association for the History of Religions*, Erfurt, Germany, 23–29 August.

Donald, A., K. Bennett and P. Leach 2012. Religion or belief: equality and human rights in England and Wales, *Research report 84*. Manchester: Equality and Human Rights Commission.

Farias, M., R. Underwood and G. Claridge 2013. Unusual but sound minds: mental health indicators in spiritual individuals. *British Journal of Psychology*, 104(3): 364–81.

Global Burden of Disease Study 2013. Global, regional, and national incidence, prevalence, and years lived with disability for 301 acute and chronic diseases and injuries in 188 countries, 1990–2013: A systematic analysis for the Global Burden of Disease Study. *The Lancet*, 386: 743–800.

Granqvist, P. and L.A. Kirkpatrick 2004. Religious conversion and perceived childhood attachment: a meta-analysis. *The International Journal for the Psychology of Religion*, 14(4): 223–50.

Gregory II, C., A.M. Pomerantz, J.C. Pettibone and D.J. Segrist 2008. The effect of psychologists' disclosure of personal religious background on prospective clients. *Mental Health, Religion & Culture*, 11(4): 369–73.

McManus, S., H. Meltzer, T. Brugh, P. Bebbington and R. Jenkins 2009. in: Sally McManus, Howard Meltzer, Traolach Brugh, Paul Bebbington and Rachel Jenkins (eds) *Adult Psychiatric Morbidity in England, 2007: Results of a Household Survey*. Leeds: The NHS Information Cent. Available at www.esds.ac.uk/doc/6379/mrdoc/pdf/6379research_report.pdf (Accessed 3 October 2016).

Mental Health Foundation 2007. *Making Space for Spirituality*. London: Mental Health Foundation.

Mental Health Foundation 2008. *Executive Briefing: Spirituality and Mental Health*. London: Mental Health Foundation.

Moe, J.L., K. Cates and V. Sepulveda 2013. Wicca and neo-paganism: a primer for counselors. *Journal of Professional Counseling: Practice, Theory, and Research*, 40(1): 45–55.

Moreton, C. 2009. Everyone's a pagan now. *The Guardian*. 22 June. Available at www.theguardian.com/world/2009/jun/22/paganism-stonehenge-environmentalism-witchcraft (Accessed 1 June 2013).

Norcross, J.C. and B.E. Wampold 2011. Evidence-based therapy relationships: research conclusions and clinical practices. *Psychotherapy*, 48(1): 98–102.

Orion, L. 1995. *Never again the Burning Times: Paganism Revived.* Prospect Heights, IL: Waveland Press.

Pargament, K.I. and S.M. Saunders 2007. Introduction to the special issue on spirituality and psychotherapy. *Journal of Clinical Psychology*, 63(10): 903–907. doi:10.1002/jclp.20405.

Plante, C.N., S. Roberts, S. Reysen and K. Gerbasi Curr 2014. Interaction of socio-structural characteristics predicts identity concealment and self-esteem in stigmatized minority group members. *Current Psychology*, 33(3): 3–19.

Press Complaints Commission 1996. Report 37: Ms Marget Inglis. *Press Complaints Commission.* Available at www.pcc.org.uk/cases/adjudicated.html?article=MTkxNA== (Accessed 15 February 2015).

Quinn, D.M. and S.R. Chaudoir 2009. Living with a concealable stigmatized identity: The impact of anticipated stigma, centrality, salience, and cultural stigma on psychological distress and health. *Journal of Personality and Social Psychology*, 97: 634–51.

Quinn, D.M. and V.A. Earnshaw 2013. Concealable stigmatized identities and psychological well-being. *Social and Personality Psychology Compass*, 7(1): 40–51.

Reeder, J.M. 2004. Psycho-spiritual profile: Wicca. *Washington-Baltimore Pagan Clergy.* Available at www.washington-baltimore-paganclergy.org/wp/wp.../wiccaprofile.pdf (Accessed 18 May 2015).

Royal College of Psychiatrists 1999. Spirituality and psychiatry special interest group. *Royal College of Psychiatrists.* Available at www.rcpsych.ac.uk/workinpsychiatry/specialinterestgroups/spirituality.aspx (Accessed 26 May 2015).

Royal College of Psychiatrists 2013. Recommendations for psychiatrists on spirituality and religion: position statement PS03/2013. *Royal College of Psychiatrists.* November. Available at www.rcpsych.ac.uk/workinpsychiatry/specialinterestgroups/spirituality/publicationsarchive.aspx (Accessed 26 May 2015).

Seymour, E. 1998. Pagans and counselling. *philhine.org.uk.* August. Available at www.philhine.org.uk/writings/gp_pagcouns.html (Accessed 18 May 2015).

Seymour, E. 2005. Pagan approaches to healing, in: R. Moddley and W. West (eds) *Integrating Traditional Healing Practices into Counseling and Psychotherapy.* Thousand Oaks, CA: Sage Publications, pp. 233–45.

Seymour, E. 2012. A Pagan perspective. *Thresholds*, 4–8.

Smart, L. and D.M. Wegner 1999. Covering up what can't be seen: concealable stigma and mental control. *Journal of Personality and Social Psychology*, 77(3): 474–86.

Smith, A.F. and J.G. Simmonds. 2006. Help-seeking and paranormal beliefs in adherents of mainstream religion, alternative religion, and no religion. *Counselling Psychology Quarterly*, 19(4): 331–41.

Smith, J.A. 1996. Beyond the divide between cognition and discourse: using interpretative phenomenological analysis in health psychology. *Psychology and Health*, 11: 261–71.

South Devon Healthcare NHS Foundation Trust 2015. Equality & diversity. *South Devon Healthcare NHS Foundation Trust.* 14 May. Available at www.sdhct.nhs.uk/aboutus/equalityanddiversity/ (Accessed 26 May 2015).

South Devon Healthcare Trust and Teignmouth Primary Care Trust 2009. Religious, spiritual, pastoral & cultural care: A guide for staff in providing good religious, spiritual, pastoral & cultural care. *South Devon Healthcare NHS Foundation Trust.* 15 October. Available at www.sdhct.nhs.uk/pdf_docs/cultureandreligionhandbook.pdf (Accessed 26 May 2015).

Tejeda, M.J. 2015. Skeletons in the broom closet: exploring the discrimination of Pagans in the workplace. *Journal of Management, Spirituality & Religion*, 12(2): 88–110. doi:DOI: 10.1080/14766086.2014.933710.

Yardley, M. 2008. Social work practice with Pagans, Witches, and Wiccans: guidelines for practice with children and youths. *Social Work*, 53(4): 329–36.

York, M. 1995. *The Emerging Network: A Sociology of the New Age and Neo-Pagan Movements*. Lanham, MD: Rowman & Littlefield.

York, M. 2003. *Pagan Theology: Paganism as a World Religion*. New York and London: New York University Press.

9 Scientology auditing

Pastoral counselling or a religious path to total spiritual freedom

Eric Roux

Scientology auditing is one of the core practices of the Scientology religion. The goal of auditing is to restore one's innate abilities, oneself being understood as a spiritual being, the soul itself. This is accomplished by helping individuals rid themselves of any spiritual disabilities and by increasing their spiritual abilities. This religious practice is designed to help the person recover awareness of one's spiritual immortality, one's basic goodness and one's personal divine nature.

Auditing (from Latin *audire*, which means to listen or to hear) is done by an auditor, who is an ordained minister or a minister in training of the Church of Scientology. The auditor applies the 'processes' (spiritual exercises) of auditing to an individual to help him or her accomplish the goal of auditing, spiritual enlightenment and freedom. Auditing can be applied to an individual, to a group of individuals together (group auditing) and, in certain cases, is applied to oneself (solo auditing).

While auditing may be seen as a form of counselling, its purpose, effects and its practice are far from the field of counselling as normally understood in the common sense and even different from 'pastoral counselling' as sometimes defined. This possible misconception of what Scientology auditing is may stem from the earlier works of L. Ron Hubbard, the founder of Scientology, in which he wrote about Dianetics auditing in his bestseller, *Dianetics: The Modern Science of Mental Health* (1950), a few years before the discoveries which led to the founding of the Scientology religion.

In this chapter, I will outline how Scientology auditing differs from counselling in its usual sense, and also from pastoral counselling as described by some of the more common definitions, even though some of the incidental effects of auditing encompass the purpose of counselling and pastoral counselling. This is without derogating Scientology auditing from its religious status and concern.

Counselling definitions and Dianetics before the birth of Scientology

Counselling is usually defined in English dictionaries as the provision of professional assistance and guidance in resolving personal or psychological problems. The word is commonly used in the field of therapy, and refers to professionals trained in that particular field. The Merriam Webster dictionary defines counselling as 'professional guidance of the individual by utilizing psychological methods especially in collecting case history data, using various techniques of the personal interview, and testing interests and aptitudes'.

Pastoral counselling refers to the situation in which a clergy member engages in counselling. Pastoral counselling is usually defined as the use of psychotherapeutic techniques by trained members of the clergy to assist parishioners who seek help for personal or emotional problems.

Pamela Cooper-White describes pastoral counselling in these terms:

> Pastoral counselling, or psychotherapy, is defined as a distinctive form of counselling in which the full resources, theoretical knowledge, and clinical methods of secular psychology and psychotherapy are brought together with pastoral theological method and practice to provide a holistic approach to psychotherapy that honors and integrates the spiritual dimension of each patient's life and experience.
>
> (Cooper-White 2004: 131)

When L. Ron Hubbard wrote *Dianetics* in 1950, Scientology was not mentioned in the book.[1] He described Dianetics as 'a family of sciences embracing the various humanities and translating them into precise definitions', and amongst this family of sciences, gave an extensive description of Dianetics auditing, which he called 'Dianetics therapy' (Hubbard 1950). The purpose of the 'therapy' is described as the removal of the 'reactive mind',[2] in order to achieve the goal of 'Clear'. A 'Clear' is defined as an individual freed of his reactive mind, who 'demonstrates the basic nature of Mankind and that basic nature has been found uniformly and invariably to be good', with 'intelligence considerably greater than the current normal', with full memory 'throughout the lifetime, with the additional bonus that he has photographic recall in colour, motion, sound, etc., as well as optimum computational ability' (Hubbard 1950).

Needless to say, even if L. Ron Hubbard used the word 'therapy' to describe Dianetics auditing, he was not basing the use of Dianetics on 'clinical methods of secular psychology and psychotherapy', as Dianetics was a whole in itself, not to be combined with other techniques, and self-sufficient in creating what it promised.

However, this was in 1950, and the vocabulary of 'Dianetics', as well as the subtitle of the book 'Modern Science of Mental Health' played a role in placing Dianetics in the field of therapy, whatever the intention of the author may have been.

Nevertheless, at the end of the book, Hubbard outlined what would and should be the future of Dianetics, as well as the future of 'the therapy', including 'a further research into life force' as well as 'an effort to discover a higher echelon of universal origin and destination' (Hubbard 1950). Within the space of twelve months after the release of *Dianetics: Modern Science of Mental Health*, the first research had been driven to a conclusion, as Hubbard identified an animating force within every living thing, that he called 'Theta', from the Greek letter meaning 'thought', and distinguished it as life force existing separate from the physical universe.

That was the beginning of a new area of discoveries by Hubbard which he described in a 1958 interview with the American Professor of Religious History, Dr Stillson Judah, in these words:

> In the fall of 1951, I found out what was looking at the mental pictures… and described it. And found out that you could do things with it from a practical standpoint that nobody had ever done before, and found myself suddenly in the field of religion, whether I wanted to be or not, there I was. Very simple – the human soul was the fellow.
>
> (Hubbard 1958)

Scientology auditing as a religious practice

It was in the early 1950s that Hubbard started to develop Scientology, first as 'the science of knowing how to know' (Hubbard 1952), which rapidly developed into the religious field, without departing from its rational nature, as described by Hubbard: 'The Scientology religion is precise and exact, designed for an age of exact sciences' (Hubbard 1956b: 6).

The early 1950s were times of major breakthroughs in the spiritual field of Scientology. Hubbard developed several theories on the subject of the spirit. The spirit, called the 'theta body' or the 'thetan', was described as the person oneself, the 'I', separated from the body, the mind and even the physical universe itself. The thetan was described as having 'no mass, no wavelength, no energy, no measurable qualities and no time or location in space except by consideration or postulate' (Hubbard 1975). The thetan is immortal, and when the person dies, the thetan usually goes into a new body, for a new lifetime. Moreover, the thetan can exist separately from the body, with a full awareness of being out of it, a phenomenon which Scientologists call 'exteriorisation' (Hubbard 1952).

These new developments led Hubbard, and consequently Scientology, progressively into the field of religion. New auditing techniques were developed, addressing the thetan itself, designed to achieve higher spiritual awareness levels than the level of Clear as defined in Dianetics, and as described above. The purpose of auditing started to reach far beyond the goals of 1950s Dianetics, concentrating on the attainment of spiritual freedom. It is also worth noting here that at its very beginning Dianetics took a scientific approach to the mind and related observable phenomena, and so defined itself within these parameters and purposely did not enter into what was, at that point, the more speculative realm of religion. It was when Hubbard developed his research on the foundation of Dianetics, though beyond its original scope, that he found evidence of the spiritual nature of man.

In 1952, Hubbard expressed that 'The theta being is the principal target of the auditor' (Hubbard 1952), and the techniques of auditing began to focus on the goal of exteriorising the thetan, as a way to render the individual full consciousness of his or her spiritual nature. Further, many auditing techniques were designed towards gaining spiritual freedom by way of increasing the communication of the thetan with the physical universe, in order to develop freedom from that physical universe. These included spiritual exercises designed to help the individual change his 'considerations' (broadly speaking considerations are thoughts) with regards to the physical universe – considerations being described as a product of the thetan, superior to the physical universe and fundamentally as being causative over it.

> The freedom of an individual depends upon that individual's freedom to alter his considerations of space, energy, time and forms of life, and his roles in it. If he cannot change his mind about these, he is then fixed and enslaved amidst barriers such as those of the physical universe and barriers of his own creation… The goal of processing is to bring an individual into such thorough communication with the physical universe that he can regain the power and ability of his own considerations.
>
> (Hubbard 1954a: 25, 26)

Auditing was, and is, central to the religious practice of Scientology, and has been described as a sacrament, 'a process by which one becomes aware of the hidden spiritual barriers that keep one from becoming aware of one's essential spiritual nature as a thetan and from properly exercising that nature' (Bryant 1994).

In 1953, auditors were called 'Doctors of Divinity', and Hubbard made the announcement that they could set man 'free from pain, from grief, from suffering, from the endless despair of this vale of tears' (Hubbard 1954b: 273). Recognising that auditing had gone far further than dealing with materialistic goals, Hubbard made clear that Scientology was religious in nature, that 'it has taught us that a man is his own immortal soul', and that 'one cannot now play traitor to the men of god who sought, these ages past, to bring man from the darkness' (Hubbard 1954c: 279). The first Church of Scientology was incorporated in 1954. As soon as 1955, auditors were entitled to be called 'Reverend' and were the Church's ordained ministers.

Auditing, as a core practice of Scientology, had become a way to 'total spiritual freedom', as some Buddhist spiritual exercises are meant to lead to liberation, aimed at freeing the individual from the inherent sufferings of life. Nevertheless, Scientology auditing was developed in a rationalised manner, codified in order to offer 'Man a systematic and controlled endeavour to promote self-enlightenment and spiritual knowledge' (Wilson 1995: 29).

Many authors have recognised and acknowledged the genuine religious nature of the purpose of auditing. Frank Flinn has described 'Scientology's religious quest' as 'a sacred mission, addressed and available to one and all', and auditing as 'a religious instructional type of process by which spiritual guides (trained Scientology ministers) lead adherents through the states of spiritual enlightenment' (Flinn 1994: 9). In an earlier work he had called Scientology a 'technologized Buddhism' (Flinn 1983). Auditing has also been described as a 'sacred practice' and a 'detailed method of salvation' (Harley and Kieffer 2009). Wilson wrote of a 'rational means for salvation', comparing Scientology with Methodists in regards to a controlled, disciplined and methodical way of salvation, as well as with the the upaya ('right method') of the seventh stage of the 'bodhisattva way to salvation in Mahayana Buddhism' (Wilson 1995: 28).

Indeed, Scientology auditing is 'a set of spiritual exercises' (Hubbard 1955a: 23), extremely detailed, organised through a path designed to get an individual from a state of 'relative spiritual ignorance' to a state of 'spiritual knowledge' and 'total freedom as a spiritual being'. This path is followed step-by-step, going up what Scientologists call 'the bridge to total freedom'. Auditing uses processes – spiritual exercises – exact sets of questions asked or directions given by an auditor to help a person locate areas of spiritual travail, in order for individuals to find out things about themselves and improve their condition.

Even if Scientology auditing is also designed to help people increase their spiritual abilities and improve their daily life conditions, Scientology's ultimate goals 'transcend empirical proof, and the beliefs of its followers are transcendental, metaphysical, and spiritual' (Wilson 1995: 31).

I have outlined how there was a turning point in the passage from Dianetics to Scientology around 1952, which moved it further into the religious realm. While Dianetics has remained alive as a practice even nowadays, and became a sub-study of Scientology (Hubbard 1956b: 5), the critical juncture from Dianetics to Scientology has been described by Hubbard in these words:

> Dianetics was the forerunner of Scientology. By use of Dianetics, as early as 1950, it became apparent that we were dealing, not with cells and cellular memory, but with a beingness that defied time. Anyone using Dianetics properly would make the same discovery. For Dianetics reached deeper than Man had ever gone before in plumbing the mystery of life.
>
> The phenomena of past lives was followed by exteriorisation. Many of the things Man has always wondered about were suddenly very plain even to the most sceptical observer.
>
> The conclusion was inescapable: We were dealing with the human spirit.
>
> ...
>
> Scientology marked the point of change from a materialistic viewpoint to a spiritual one.
>
> ...
>
> Dianetics is defined as DIA (Greek) through, NOUS (Greek) soul.

> Dianetics is further redefined as WHAT THE SOUL IS DOING TO THE BODY.
>
> ...
>
> Dianetics, though it might not have guessed it in its early publication, was dealing with the human spirit and it is interesting that its name, as derived, meant that.
>
> (Hubbard 1981: 7, 8)

Scientology auditing as or versus pastoral counselling

Several authors have described auditing as pastoral counselling, and the Church of Scientology itself sometimes uses this term for auditing (CSI 2014). Bryan Wilson, for example, wrote:

> The means which Scientology employs constitutes a form of pastoral counselling, most specifically organized into the techniques of auditing (from Latin audire, to listen). The specific techniques and apparatus of auditing are organized as a technology which constitutes the core part of Scientological religious practice. (...) This method, like that of affirmation in Christian Science, is claimed to eliminate both the sense of sin and the effects of past suffering and wrongdoing.
>
> (Wilson 1995: 28)

Even some courts throughout the world have recognised, under the terms 'pastoral counselling', the religious character of Scientology auditing (for example Stuttgart District Court 1992), whether assessed for reasons of religious recognition or for tax exemption purposes.

However, it seems important to me that when using the term 'pastoral counselling' to describe Scientology auditing, we must make sure that what we have in mind is a correct definition of 'pastoral counselling'. Indeed, a commonly accepted (even if not exclusive of other meanings) sense of 'pastoral counselling', states 'clinical methods of secular psychology and psychotherapy are brought together with pastoral theological method and practice to provide a holistic approach to psychotherapy' (Cooper-White 2004). If we follow that definition from Pamela Cooper-White, then we cannot conclude that either Dianetics or Scientology auditing fits within that definition. Auditors do not use clinical methods of psychology and psychotherapy. Auditing is not to be mixed with any other practice, and is never done together with any secular psychological or psychotherapeutic method. Scientology auditing is based on Scientology scriptures, which are self-sufficient in order to achieve the purpose of auditing.

However, a more traditional and older definition of 'pastoral counselling', based on what religious communities have traditionally sought to provide in terms of religion-based solutions for those in trouble, would apply to auditing. This definition of pastoral counselling would refer to a normal function of pastoral duties, a function of pastoral care.

In fact, the ultimate goal of auditing, which can be described as the attainment of total spiritual freedom, inextricably results in what can be considered as the product of pastoral counselling, whatever definition is chosen. Indeed, it is said by Hubbard as well as by many Scientologists or Scientology observers, that auditing can and does actually bring real betterments for people in their emotional life, their problems and even their well-being. As Hubbard claimed: 'Scientology processing, amongst other things, can improve the intelligence quotient of an individual, his ability or desire to communicate, his social attitudes, his capability and domestic harmony, his artistic creativity, his reaction time and his well being' (Hubbard 1956b: 114).

However, the common results that can be observed both in counselling and in Scientology auditing, must not lead us to the wrong statement that they are the purpose of Scientology auditing. In Scientology, these results are incidental, and non-spiritual betterments are not to be considered as being part of the aim of auditing, while they can be the consequence of it. Scientology auditing is designed to increase the abilities, the knowingness and the freedom of the spiritual being, and this betterment of the essence of man will of course have pragmatic results in the daily life of the individual.

Scientology auditing, a world away from professional counselling

We have seen that Dianetics, when it started, was described with terms that placed it *de facto* in the field of psychotherapy. Indeed, as Wilson stated:

> When, in May 1950, L. Ron Hubbard first set out the prospectus of Dianetics, from which Scientology later developed, there was no suggestion that he was putting forward a pattern of religious belief and practice. Dianetics, an abreaction therapy, was not set forth in the language of faith. There is no reason to suppose that, at that time, Hubbard envisaged that Dianetics would become a system of religious belief and practice, or that his following would come to describe and organize itself as a Church.
>
> (Wilson 1995: 22)

Nevertheless, as outlined above, this description of Dianetics rapidly changed as Scientology developed in the 1950s. Moreover, at this time, Hubbard made it very clear that Scientology was 'not a psychotherapy. It is a body of knowledge which, when properly used, gives freedom and truth to the individual' (Hubbard 1954a: 351). During a lecture given in Washington in 1955, Hubbard said that the developments that had been happening in Scientology, 'have removed Scientology entirely from any classification as a psychotherapy'. In the same lecture, he even presented his classification of Dianetics as 'a science' as his 'biggest mistake':

> And the biggest mistake that I have made—and I've made mistakes, believe me, but the biggest mistake I had made was the day when I said, 'all right, boys, we will call this a science. All right. We will agree that the Western Hemisphere is not ready to accept anything spiritual or religious. All right. We will call it a science. And this science we will call Dianetics, which means "through mind"'.
>
> And that was myself approving with the society, and I never should have approved. Why? Because we went on a wide and large via. We associated ourselves with psychotherapy, and that was not good.
>
> (Hubbard 1955d)

Besides the concern that auditing could be misplaced in the field of psychology or psychotherapy, there was a practical concern which had to do with the reason Scientologists should get auditing: it was important that Scientologists not be misled by their own misinterpretations of what auditing is. Indeed, for Hubbard,

> to use Scientology 'to get well', to 'become less nervous', is like using an alpine stock[3] to dig a ditch for a water pipe in the back yard. To use Scientology as a guidebook to the discovery of the infinity of infinities is a proper use.
>
> (Hubbard 1955c: 155)

Hubbard, on the other hand, had never been afraid of psychology and felt very free to comment on it, as he commented on many societal topics. He sometimes pointed out that the etymology of the word psychology was referring to psyche, the soul and that modern psychology, by negating the existence of the soul had lost its own meaning. He was very much more comfortable with the fact that ancient psychology was associated with religion.

> Neither Dianetics nor Scientology should be confused with 'modern psychology'. More acceptable and normal psychology, such as that begun by Saint Thomas Aquinas and extended by many later authors, was (in 1879) interrupted severely by one Professor Wundt... Scientology is actually a new but very basic psychology, in the most exact meaning of the word - a study of the spirit.
>
> (Hubbard 1956b: 5, 6)

He even advised that some discoveries and Scientology auditing processes be 'coached to analysts in the hope that the field of psychoanalysis could be made into a successful psychotherapy, for Scientology is not a psychotherapy and does not intend to take the place of any existing psychotherapy' (Hubbard 1955b: 140). This, while distancing Scientology from the secular field, could be seen as an assumption that the discoveries he made in the frame of his research in the religious field of the human spirit, could benefit and have influence in the secular field of psychotherapy.

He went as far as writing a full critique of psychoanalysis in 1956, in which, after having acknowledged the fact that he was indebted to psychoanalysis and its originator Sigmund Freud, he endeavoured to point out the limitations and errors inherent in the subject as developed by Freud and as practised thereafter (Hubbard 1956a: 443–449, 455–463).

Needless to say, in Hubbard's discourse, the fact that as a religious figure, he was communicating on subjects that were not to be considered as religious, is not to be taken as even temporary abandonment of the religious sphere. The incorporation of modern scientific terms and topics of 'Scientological discourse', 'does not derogate from its religious status and concerns' (Wilson 1995: 31).

Scientologists and the use of auditing

Having been myself a member of the clergy of Scientology for more than 20 years, and having met personally more than a thousand Scientologists, be they new ones or old-timers, I can say that I have a personal and in-depth knowledge of the reasons for which Scientologists practise auditing. Having said that, it appears that these reasons, at least at the beginning of the practice of Scientology by a newcomer, may be of various natures, depending on the background and the personal interests of the individual.

Even if huge efforts are made by Scientology Churches to let the newcomers know that they are at the point of starting a religious study which intends to drive them towards upper levels of spirituality, it might happen that some of the new Scientologists are more interested in auditing as a way to solve personal problems or daily life difficulties than to attain total spiritual freedom. The Church will not close the door to them and on the contrary, will consider that the wisdom of Scientology should be available to all, and that its study and practice should not be conditioned by the fact that the applicant must be fully aware of his own desire to be spiritually free, his own desire to rediscover his divine nature. However, as Bryan Wilson wrote:

> Thus although much of the initial practice of Scientology is concerned more narrowly with more personal spiritual benefits for those (preclears) who seek Scientological assistance, ultimately the Scientologist must realize that his present life is but a fragment of his continuing existence as a thetan, and that the life of the individual is linked to each of these ascending levels described in the eight dynamics, and so ultimately to the existence and survival of the Supreme Being or infinity.
>
> (Wilson 1995: 25)

L. Ron Hubbard identified eight human impulses which he termed dynamics of existence. They are subdivisions of the fundamental impulse towards survival that is the basic principle of existence itself.[4]

There is a strong determination that Scientology should be used to help one's fellows, whatever they want to resolve, and that people should encounter Scientology at their current level of interest, in a way that does not close the door to people who are not particularly spiritually oriented. It is also postulated that by experiencing the power and the wisdom that stems from auditing practice, every man or woman will sooner or later discover for him or herself that s/he is a spiritual being, that spiritual heights are attainable and desirable. However, as stated above, in Churches of Scientology, the emphasis is placed on the religious nature of Scientology even before someone starts any auditing or study, so that the person knows that everything he or she will gain from Scientology is the result of a full body of knowledge that is a real understanding of the true spiritual nature of Man.

On the other hand, I know a great number of Scientologists, amongst whom I count myself, who started their study of that religious philosophy and the practice of auditing as a true research of the Absolute, with a strong personal desire to discover metaphysical answers to life, a desire which preexisted their encounter with Scientology, a desire that was later increased and fulfilled by the practice of auditing.

For Scientologists, Scientology applies to life itself, in all its dimensions. Scientology is defined as an applied religious philosophy. It should be used for the betterment of the eight dynamics, without excluding any of them. So there is no contradiction in using it to improve any aspect of one's daily life whilst at the same time to practise it with the purpose of reaching higher states of consciousness and to attain spiritual freedom.

Conclusion

So can we assume in Western countries that Scientology auditing is a form of pastoral counselling in order to understand it through the prism of other denominational pastoral cares? Indeed, if we refer to the normal function of pastoral duties in our societies, which is to provide help in terms of religion-based solutions to the one who needs it, I think auditing can be seen as a form of pastoral counselling.

It is also interesting to see that Hubbard described auditing processes as 'spiritual exercises', and that the West has its own tradition of 'spiritual exercises'. Amongst the foremost of these are the Spiritual Exercises developed by St Ignatius of Loyola, which are a set of meditations, contemplative practices and prayers to help people deepen their relationship with God, 'to conquer oneself and regulate one's life without determining oneself through any tendency that is disordered' (St Ignatius 1522–1524). These became the central component of the Jesuit training programme for novices, when the Society of Jesus was founded.

The 'Bridge to Total Freedom', which is a path to liberation as a spiritual being, a path to knowingness and enlightenment, consists of thousands of detailed processes. These processes are designed to increase progressively the awareness of the individual, one's recognition of one's spiritual and divine nature and to free one from the entanglement of the essence of man with the physical universe. These processes do have concrete effects on the daily life of the one who practises. The ability to confront life's problems increases, as does the handling of life's vicissitudes. This can also be perceived as having an effect on the physical health of the person, and whilst Scientology does not claim to heal any physical disorder, it will not be the first religion to demonstrate that spiritual enlightenment can have an effect on physical health. If you run through 'success letters'[5] written by Scientologists who received auditing, you will see that most of them illustrate the spiritual changes and betterments they have undergone with pragmatic changes that they experienced in their daily lives. This should not overshadow the essentially spiritual and religious character of the source of these changes and of the auditing practice itself. The objective changes in daily life are the results of the subjective changes that originate from religious exercises addressing the thetan itself.

Scientology is an applied religious philosophy which encompasses all the facets of life. Scientology auditing – addressing the spiritual being itself, increasing its freedom to alter its considerations of space, energy, time and forms of life, and its roles in them, enhancing its communication with the physical universe – also embraces all facets of life, but is aimed at total spiritual freedom, and full knowledge and awareness of the thetan as regards to its spiritual and divine nature. In that regard, Scientology auditing is more than a form of counselling, it is undoubtedly a method of salvation.

Notes

1 In 1954, in the magazine 'Scientology', published by the Hubbard Association of Scientologists, it was written that L. Ron Hubbard had named the product of his research 'Scientology' in 1938, but that he changed its name to Dianetics in 1947 'in order to make a social test of publication and popularity' before coming back to the original name in 1952.

2 Scientologists consider that the mind has two very distinct parts. The part that you consciously use and are aware of is called the analytical mind. This is the mind which thinks, observes data, remembers it and resolves problems. It contains standard memory banks with mental image pictures and uses the data in these banks to make rational decisions. However, two things appear to be, but are not, recorded in the standard banks: painful emotion and physical pain. In moments of intense pain, the action of the analytical mind is suspended and the second part of the mind, the reactive mind, takes over. When a person is fully conscious, his analytical mind is fully in command. When the individual is 'unconscious' in full or in part, the reactive mind cuts in, in full or in part. 'Unconsciousness' could be caused by the shock of an accident, anaesthetic used for an operation, the pain of an injury or the deliriums of illness. Scientology considers that when a person is 'unconscious', to a lesser or greater degree, the reactive mind exactly records all the perceptions of that incident, including what happens or the words pronounced around the person. It also records all pain and

stores this mental image picture in its own banks where it is unavailable to the individual's conscious memory and outside of his direct control. For Scientologists, reactive mind is the source of aberration, undesired emotions, psychosomatic illnesses and more.

3 A variation of the term 'Alpenstock', a long iron-tipped staff used in mountain climbing. The term alpine means of or pertaining to the Alps, and the term stock comes from a German word meaning stick or staff.

4 In ascending order the dynamics of existence are: the first dynamic which is the urge of survival as an individual, the second dynamic which is the urge of survival through one's family, the third dynamic which is the urge of group survival, the fourth dynamic which is the urge of survival for all humankind, the fifth dynamic which is the urge of survival for all life forms, the sixth dynamic which is the urge of survival of the physical universe, the seventh dynamic which is the urge of survival for all spiritual beings and lastly the eighth dynamic which is urge of existence as infinity. God is infinity but Scientologists do not describe God in anthropomorphic terms. All Scientology practices are aimed ultimately at complete affinity with the eighth dynamic or infinity.

5 It is a common practice amongst Scientologists to write 'success letters' in which they depict the spiritual gains they make through auditing or scriptures study. While they are encouraged to do so at the end of each attained level of auditing, they usually originate their own success letters all along their spiritual journey. With the authorization of their author, these letters may be shared with others, and you can find some of them in various Scientology magazines and publications.

References

Bryant, D. 1994. *Scientology, A New Religion*. Available at: www.scientologyreligion.org/religious-expertises/scientology-a-new-religion/ (Accessed 6 June 2017).

Cooper-White, P. 2004. *Shared Wisdom*. Minneapolis: Fortress Press.

CSI (Church of Scientology International) 2014. Available at: www.scientology.org/faq/inside-a-church-of-scientology/what-goes-scientology-church.html (Accessed 6 June 2017).

Flinn, F.K. 1983. Scientology as technical buddhism, in: J. Fichter (ed.) *Alternatives to American Mainline Churches*. New York: Rose of Sharon Press, Inc.

Flinn, F. K. 1994. *Scientology: The Marks of Religion*. Available at: www.scientologyreligion.org/religious-expertises/scientology-marks-of-religion/ (Accessed 6 June 2017).

Harley, G. M. and J. Kieffer. 2009. The development and reality of auditing in Scientology, in: James R. Lewis (ed.) *Scientology*. Oxford: Oxford University Press.

Hubbard, L. Ron. 1950. *Dianetics, The Modern Science of Mental Health*. California: Bridge Publication 2007.

Hubbard, L. Ron. 1952. *A History of Man*. California: Bridge Publication 2007.

Hubbard, L. Ron. 1954a. *The Creation of Human Ability*. California: Bridge Publication 2007.

Hubbard, L. Ron. 1954b. An Invitation to Freedom. Man can save his Soul. *Technical Bulletins volume II*. California: Bridge Publication 1991.

Hubbard, L. Ron. 1954c. Man's search for his Soul. *Technical Bulletins volume II*. California: Bridge Publication 1991.

Hubbard, L. Ron. 1955a. Professional Auditor Bulletin 44. *Technical Bulletins volume III*. California: Bridge Publication 1991.

Hubbard, L. Ron. 1955b. Straightwire. *Technical Bulletins volume III*. California: Bridge Publication 1991.

Hubbard, L. Ron. 1955c. The adventure of Scientology. *Technical Bulletins volume III*. California: Bridge Publication 1991.

Hubbard, L. Ron. 1955d. *The Hope of Man*. The Anatomy of the Spirit of Man Congress, Compact Disc, Golden Era Production 2004.

Hubbard, L. Ron. 1956a. A Critique of Psychoanalysis. *Technical Bulletins volume III*. California: Bridge Publication 1991.

Hubbard, L. Ron. 1956b. *Fundamentals of Thought*. California: Bridge Publication 2007.

Hubbard, L. Ron. 1958. *Interview of L. Ron Hubbard by Dr Stillson Judah*. Excerpt available at: www.ronthephilosopher.org/phlspher/page40.htm (Accessed 6 June 2017).

Hubbard, L. Ron. 1975. *Dianetics and Scientology Technical Dictionary*. California: Bridge Publications.

Hubbard, L. Ron. 1981. Dianetics and Scientology definitions. *Scientology 0/8, the Book of Basics*. California: Bridge Publication 2007.

St Ignatius of Loyola (1522–1524). The Spiritual Exercises of St Ignatius of Loyola.

Stuttgart District Court, 1992. *Peter Graf v. Dianetic Stuttgart e.V.*, 9 December 1992. Excerpt available at: www.bonafidescientology.org/Append/09/page04.htm (Accessed 6 June 2017).

Wilson, Bryan R. 1995. *Scientology: An Analysis and Comparison of its Religious Systems and Doctrines*. Available at: www.scientologyreligion.org/religious-expertises/scientology-analysis-and-comparison/ (Accessed 6 June 2017).

10 How counselling can help faith and families

Simon Cooper

Until recently, I was a full-time lay pastor for a church congregation that's part of Reverend Moon's Unification Movement. In this chapter I present a case study, taking you through a journey that I went on as I found faith in my life and then also found how useful counselling or psychotherapy can be in addition to that. It is also an account of how my family and I could overcome some of the dysfunctional conflict that we were experiencing. Conflict can often be healthy, but if it is not dealt with properly, it can become counter-productive. This story is about working out family conflict and the blessings that can spring from such efforts.

I started out life essentially very happy and, as far as I can remember, life as a child was wonderful until I became a teenager. I got expelled at 15 after I'd worked very hard to get into Kings College School (KCS) Wimbledon, a top private school. That was very disappointing, although my parents were very understanding. But it just got messier from there. I remember on my 16th birthday getting arrested in a car park with some hash and my mum having to pick me up from a police station in Chelsea. That is just a couple of experiences that I had in my life as a teenager that reflected my slightly unsuccessful attempts to figure out what I could do to make my life interesting. Then I went off to Newcastle, to university. I got suspended at the end of my first year, and was still finding it difficult to figure out a personal sense of my purpose and direction in life. I continued at Newcastle University and at the end of my second year, my parents bought me a ticket to go travelling for the summer in Central America, probably hoping it would help me grow up a bit.

I never got to Guatemala. I had a one-week stop-over in New York, and I ended up staying.

I met the Unification Movement, and I found, more importantly than the organisation, a personal faith in God for my life. I had a rebirth experience, what I would say was a personal encounter with the living God, and that changed my life completely. It also changed our family dynamic. I came from a very 'good', *Guardian*-reading family that was cultured but certainly not religious, and that had never really had a tradition of sharing faith in God together. My parents had had faith experiences when they were young, but they turned out to be quite sour experiences in the end from what I could gather, and so they had left that behind, so bringing religion back from my journey abroad was a bit of a shock.

I had found something that was for me priceless and incredibly precious, and yet at the same time was abhorrent, at least initially, to my parents and my brother. And it was a messy start; they tried and managed to get me deported from America back to England where I had met the movement. With hindsight, I am glad in some ways that they did that. It meant I wasn't able to just drop my university degree as a consequence of becoming very excited about my new faith, and instead found myself back in my English Literature course, in the same student house with the same friends from the previous term.

At some point lawyers got involved, and social workers and anti-cultists (I am not really sure what an anti-cultist is, but someone who basically tries to help people leave a religion or a new religious movement). My parents weren't sure what to do so they even considered having me sectioned. All of those different elements did not really help – they essentially increased the level of distrust that we were experiencing as a family. Of course it was also hard for my church in the UK to manage because it is hard to know what to do: you want to support someone who's found faith but at the same time you want to respect their family. The student wing of the church that I had met in the USA had also been very 'gung ho', living in its own closed world, and with hindsight, I know I behaved badly towards my parents.

In the end, I went back up to Newcastle University just a few weeks late for the autumn term and things seemed to quieten down a bit.

Going back to Newcastle was formative for my faith. I went from being in what had been a bit of an idyllic cocoon in New York with all the new friends who were my age who had also recently met the church, back to where I had been just a few months earlier studying with my friends at university, and I had some big lifestyle changes. I had given up alcohol, lots of other drugs and sex outside marriage. But it was in many ways one of the most precious years of my 'faith life' as I got to experience what it means to find and deepen faith on my own. There was just one family from my church in Newcastle and they used to invite me for Sunday lunch. But, I have always been glad, looking back, that I went through that year to some extent isolated from members of my church. After the very spiritually rich and supportive experience that I had been given in the USA, it was a healthy experience to find myself working things out on my own.

Looking back, I can see how I was still very new to religious life, and that final year of university helped me to learn about taking responsibility for my faith rather than simply relying on the support of others.

Somehow everybody at Newcastle University seemed to have heard that I had been 'kidnapped by a religious group' and everyone had lots of questions. People I didn't even know would come up to me and ask about it. Most people thought that by the end of the year I would be 'back to normal'. They were surprised to see my beliefs ran a bit deeper. I did try once smoking hash again in that final year after I had become a member of my church, but it felt vastly different since I had been 'clean' for so long, and I stayed well clear of the drug, finding it quite disturbing.

For the friends that I house-shared with, it was challenging at times – for them and myself. But I am glad to say some of us are still close friends and we still get to hang out with each other, now with our kids as well. One of my boys now plays in the same football team as one of my university friend's sons, and I'm very grateful that our friendship has lasted into our 40s. We have had several reunions back in Newcastle, and I have occasionally broken my rule of no alcohol and had the odd half pint of lager.

For several years things continued to be difficult with my family. In their eyes, all the decisions I was making were more than a waste of time, and I was misguided and lost. To me they simply couldn't see what I saw and therefore all of their perspective was faulty. I decided to volunteer for my church full-time after graduating university and despite having lots of good experiences doing this, they weren't ones that I could share positively with my family, and neither were they experiences which they felt able to relate to. My dad did his best to try and understand but it was hard.

There was a process of healing that started at some point along our journey as a family, and I think what helped us along that path was my marriage. As with the original conversion, the way I met my wife – through a suggestion by Rev Moon – was initially very tough for my family to deal with. I did an interview in *The Times*, and then my dad had a response published a few days later in the letter's page, which was very critical of my decision. That was not easy to take.

My wife, who is Japanese, spoke Italian which was a language both my parents spoke as they had met in Rome, so that was good. Nevertheless, my family and I still struggled enormously with various things, and there was often a lot of tension as a result. Chieko, my wife, has over the years not only earned their respect, but also their affection.

Also, when Chieko and I started a family of our own, my parents became grandparents, and despite difficulties remaining, we had started to find things in common. My parents had obviously lots of experience of being parents, particularly my mum, so we now shared a love for my children. We started to do family holidays, and then a few months before my youngest (our daughter) was born, my brother had a girl, and so I also started to share common experiences with my brother (including dealing with family life and raising children).

What I realised eventually was that behind all this dysfunctional conflict that my parents, my brother and I experienced, was a deep, powerful and wonderful love that we had for each other. We are a very close-knit, very 'in-your-face' kind of family. One of the advantages that my wife brought to this Cooper family scenario was the fact that she was from a family where everyone tended to respect each other in a rather unusual way. They did not interfere in each other's business, or interrupt each other, but instead gave each other a lot of space. To my family it almost looks like too much space. However, she brought that kind of influence into our family that was very helpful.

But one of the things that really helped to change the dynamic for our family was therapy.

At one point, my relationship with my parents had gotten so bad that I thought of returning to Metanoia, the counselling practice they had sent me to when I was expelled from school at 15. It was near Ealing Common, not far from where Chieko and I were living. Metanoia uses a psychotherapy practice called TA (Transactional Analysis). I am simply a layman in respect to this approach to therapy and just someone who's been counselled in the context of this practice, but essentially TA tries to describe in quite a practical way how people are structured psychologically. It uses perhaps its best-known model, the Parent, Adult, Child Model, to do this. The model helps explain how people function and express their personalities in their lives. These three ego states of parent, child and adult are modes that we dip into at different points in our daily life. For example, in the parent mode I will rely on thoughts, behaviours and feelings copied from my parents or parental figures in my life. When in the child ego state, I will dip into the emotional world of my childhood. When I am in the adult mode I will have behaviours, thoughts and feelings that respond simply to the here and now around me. TA also describes four basic states that we often find ourselves in when conducting relationships:

1 I'm OK and you're OK. This is essentially seen as the healthy model.
2 I'm OK and you're not OK. This is essentially that I see others as more damaged than myself and this is normally not very healthy.
3 I'm not OK and you are OK. This is essentially that others are automatically right and I am wrong and I can potentially be open to abuse as a result of this perspective.
4 I'm not OK and you're not OK. This is really the worst state because I'm not very good and the world is a mess as well and there's really not a lot of hope.

So, that's the theory and I had some very healthy and quite useful counselling there, when I went back all those years later after my original visits as a teenager. Some of the most profound moments were when the counsellor and I sat in silence, after a conversation had come to an end. In those moments, I would get the chance to observe my emotional world, to go down the rabbit hole and get the measure of my vulnerability, and through that, also find a deeper confidence in myself.

The first thing this counselling helped me to do was stop reacting all the time to my mother when she called up on the phone and said something that would trigger an argument, that would end up with an avalanche of attacks on each other – which I am sure many of us have experienced with our mothers at some point in our lives.

I started to learn to not always get caught up when she spoke to me as if I was a child and of course to understand that to her I would always be a child, and just to get over that often annoying reality. I managed to start to separate my emotional life from my mother's very powerful feelings for me, and in the process, became a more responsible adult who didn't need to react to the emotions of another person just because they felt something very powerfully. Instead I could choose to respond if I felt like it.

I used to get into complicated stand-offs with my mother. For example, I would be meeting her half way between my parents' house and ours, somewhere in Barnes by the pond, to drop off the kids so that she could have them for the day. She would say something that would challenge my identity or my sense of security, and I would lay down the law very heavily in response. It is very hard now to remember the things that would spark these painful battles, but they were ultimately really about deeper anxieties we both had about each other and ourselves. But as I worked my way towards the 'I'm OK and you're OK' state of mind, I was able to extract myself quicker from these nasty little scraps, and eventually I was able to start avoiding them before they even got going.

Part of what motivated me was a sense of how unhealthy it would become for the children as they got older to see me and my mum snapping at each other. Not that it never happens anymore, but it is generally rare now.

I also went along to my parents' psychotherapist, who was also helpful. My parents have also always been interested in psychotherapy and used it for their own relationship. I think that even when I was a young teenager we had some family counselling, which was very progressive and proactive of my parents.

Their psychotherapist, who they had found independently (and who I went to visit with them just a few years after I had been to Metanoia the second time around), said at one point something very interesting to my mother. I was there with both my parents at that particular session, and she said that actually all the conflict we were experiencing really had nothing to do with the church *per se*. It was more to do with deeper fundamental issues that we had already been dealing with when I was a teenager. This really hit the nail on the head. She said it was much more to do with where my mum stopped and I started and that line being just a little bit too grey. And then she said this killer line:

'Maybe Simon joining the UC was the only way that he could find to separate himself from his parents and become his own person.'

That is quite a statement for a religious person to take with regards to the origins of their faith, but I thought nevertheless it was still quite a good one; and it sent me home with a lot of reflection and prayer.

As a person of faith, one can reject suggestions like that as having nothing to do with what God was doing in one's life. But perhaps it is worth being a bit more liberal with the narrative we have built up around our journey in life. I think that because I was able to do that (to not just react against and reject what she had said about my subconscious motivations for joining the church), the consequence was that my perspective on how God is working in my life became a bit broader and more interesting. It was no longer an immature and limited battle to defend a theist belief from an atheistic, secular attack.

Of course, when these opposing themes come up in conversation with my family they are far from resolved, but I feel more able to avoid becoming antagonised.

Any religious person who is able to honestly consider different world views that don't fit easily with their own tends to become healthier and more robust in their own world view rooted in their faith.

Many people, whether religious or secular, weaken the foundations on which their beliefs are built by being too nervous and afraid of views that oppose their own. You know you are speaking to someone who has built their house on a rock, when they are comfortable to consider viewpoints that generally they object to, and even somewhere in the discourse, they amend or perhaps develop their outlook as a result.

Basically, the whole process of therapy was very positive for my parents and myself. One of the first benefits was that we started to respect each other much more, and as a result, we of course behave better towards one another, which is not always easy in our family because we tend to just let it all hang out. To behave in a much more civilised way with each other gave us scope to come to understand a little more of the other's perspective.

So learning this ability to not react was a process of growing up for me. One of the interesting things I found was how, as my relationship with my father was restored, there was a big shift in the way I did my work at my church.

The father–son relationship is one of the fundamental relationships that we experience in our lives as boys and men. We discussed this issue with my parents' psychotherapist (when my dad and I went alone). We looked at how his dad had never had much of a father, because my grandfather's father had died at sea when he was in the Navy; and then my dad's father, my grandfather, had been divorced from my grandmother when my dad had been quite young, and remarried and had a second family. And so we asked ourselves this question: from where do we learn to be fathers? That really enlightened us. It helped us to see we had a chance to buck the trend and so we looked at how my relationship with my father might affect my relationship with my boys, and so forth.

I found that this new lease of life in my relationship with my father meant that I became a lot more confident in my work. I was leading our UK church movement at the time when our relationship began to improve bit by bit.

I realised that previously I had been much more defensive about my faith because of the way my parents and my brother were so against my church. Those experiences over the years when my faith had been ridiculed, harshly questioned, aggressively put down as nonsense and almost regarded as an evil force had impacted on me unconsciously.

I used to get very nervous sometimes speaking with some of the other parents in the school playground. It seemed especially to be those who I somehow labelled mentally as having an air of authority to them. I remember not fee ling like I could just relax and talk to them as myself, but instead felt under pressure of being found out in some way and unconsciously worried about being disapproved of, as had happened in my family.

This easing and improving of relationships with my family (and especially my relationship with my father) allowed me to increase my level of critical thinking. I became much more constructively critical of the organisation for which I worked. I was able to point out when things were being done badly, or didn't make sense. For example, I argued that it was much better for the national director of the church to establish a finance committee for the national HQ that was independent and could make decisions free from the pressure of senior leadership. Up until that point, senior leadership had been almost expected to assert their will on how finances were used and, as a consequence, decisions were very much influenced by short-term needs and not long-term planning.

This meant that as the director, I was no longer under pressure from those above or below me in the management structure, and when requests for finances came, I would refer people to the finance committee who had become properly responsible for making the financial decisions. And I would explain, 'it's not just up to me to take the decision unilaterally'. The committee would listen to me, but then they would vote, and I would not have a vote.

In a similar vein, I also helped to give significance and meaning to the trustees of our church charity. Up until that time they had been a group of respected elders who essentially rubber-stamped what the leadership asked of them, admittedly because they had faith in the leadership. But it has now become a committee that provides genuine oversight of our movement's workings, holds leadership to account as best it can and is made up of people who have a variety of professional capacities as a result of their careers that allows them to contribute in a robust and serious manner to how our assets are managed. They now have teeth.

The changes I made to the running of the finances and the role of the trustees, although I wasn't fully aware at the time, were probably two of the most valuable things I did as the national director of our UK movement.

I felt free to think outside of the box about what, in my mind, were the priorities in my job, and focus on the issues that I believed needed to be addressed. Communication was an important issue, and I worked hard to improve accountability and discourse between the membership and people like me who were in a leadership role. I used to write to the membership on a regular basis and inform them of what I was doing and thinking. Many of them often wrote back and appreciated what was something of a new culture. I wonder if I would have had the confidence to develop my role in the way I did if I had not experienced some healing in my family relationships that had allowed me to discover a deeper confidence in who I was.

Another area of communication that I poured a lot of energy into was encouraging our movement to improve its relationship with the media, which had been poor in the past. I worked with others who felt similarly that we needed to learn to trust the media on some level if we realistically expected them to begin to trust us more. As the media spokesperson for our UK movement, I was eventually able to get involved with a production company in making a prime time documentary that was broadcast on Channel 4. The documentary followed the lives of some young people in our movement on their journey towards marriage. It was certainly a challenge to get the support of many in the church who were very suspicious of the cameras and the production team. But in the end, what went out on TV was a big step forward in terms of previous media efforts, and it managed to show the human face of our community. Our founders, Rev and Mrs Moon, got to see it too, and I heard that they enjoyed it enormously. It was generally quite well received around the world by others too.

Again, there were echoes here of building the bridges that I had been building with my parents. My father had always had a bit of a campaigning journalist's bent and so I started to see how some of the blog posts I was writing began to inherit some of this character. I would call out decisions that I believed were wrong, and write about them.

Often when giving the message on Sunday I would raise contentious issues from within the wider church community which I felt needed addressing and it would often touch a nerve that many in my congregation (but certainly not all) felt needed touching on. And so indirectly the therapy that I was having with my parents was impacting on the life of my community as well.

Where am I today?

Therapy in its different forms has helped my faith to mature. There is obviously still a tension between psychotherapy and spiritual institutions or some religions, and I can sense that when I talk to some people with particular, strong beliefs, they see the two as incompatible. I always remember walking out of the counselling sessions asking myself how the experience I had just encountered reflected on my religious life. Did it shed light? Did it bring my faith into doubt or question? Was this another way of interpreting my existence?

I often felt that what the counsellor had been doing in my counselling session was almost parallel to what I was trying to do in my work sometimes when, as a pastor, I would work with someone on trying to understand where he or she is going on their path of faith. When the psychological and spiritual approaches to self-awareness are able to come together, it's a very exciting exploration.

There is still conflict between my family of origin and myself. It would be boring if there were none at all. But it is much more constructive these days, and rarely unhealthy. It is also not all targeted towards 'me and my church'; there is much more space now for other areas of conflict, such as something my brother might have said or done, or something that my parents might disagree on and so there is a healthier balance. Generally, my family have also learnt to see that whatever they might feel about my religious beliefs, 'I am

OK'. In respect of the transactional analysis model we have moved towards a healthier model when assessing the quality of Simon's life. Now my mum will say, regarding her grandchildren: 'They need more than just Church and football in their life, Simon!' (I manage the team that my youngest son plays in, and three of my four boys play for our local club.) What she's really emphasising is the need for cultural input, the theatre and so forth, and generally I am grateful for the feedback. The volume levels on conflict have been turned down significantly, and it's on a much more manageable level.

My mum has emphasised the importance of playing musical instruments, and that is something we have been able to work on together in a very positive way. She has helped with the cost of the lessons, and the children practise without being coerced; in fact, they do it of their own accord, which is a world apart from what my brother and I experienced when we were young. Perhaps this is what evolution is about for humans: different generations (like my mother and I) working things out, so that the next generation can progress and avoid the problems of those that came before them. Instead they can reap the fruits of the struggles that we have resolved.

In the last couple of years, I have stepped down from the paid leadership roles that I held in my church as I felt that I needed a change in terms of my work environment. A number of factors led to this decision. One was that I had reached a point where I felt I was limited in what I could really contribute. Part of that was a sense that I needed more training, and there was little available at the time from within my church. I also decided to start work part-time for my father and help him with his business because he is in his late 70s and still sometimes works a six-and-a-half-day week.

This stepping down meant that I could also improve my financial stability at a time when the children were growing quickly but, just as importantly, it was an attractive proposition to see how my father and I could work together in a business environment after all the time we had put into fixing our relationship in other respects.

I imagine I would be grateful to go back and work more for my church again in the future. I would like to take advantage of learning from church leadership programmes outside the Unification Movement, in order to bring something more to the table, if the chance arose. But I can also see that our Unification Church movement has gone through a lot of emotional and organisational conflict, trying to grow up and become a movement that evolves and develops for the next generation that is now being raised within it.

And I guess the only question I have remaining is whether to go back to Metanoia to maybe aid me in working on my relationship with my children, as they are now becoming teenagers and starting to ask questions about what they believe in. Having teenagers is making me feel much more middle aged. I think I am entering with my wife a new phase, or part of our journey where our children (two of whom are now teenagers) are no longer only cute (one of them at 16 is taller than me...) but also wanting to define their own identities and lives. It has meant that I have started to ask myself some of the existential questions that they are dealing with as they go from just following their parents to considering all the different ideas that they are given at school, in the media, on YouTube, etc.

I recently bought a book that looks at the 'six numbers' that needed to be fine-tuned to an almost infinite degree in order for life to be possible in our universe and for it not to turn into an anaemic wasteland. This is a consequence of me being an English Literature graduate and not understanding much about maths or physics which are the two subjects my eldest is planning to concentrate on at A-level. But it is also my desire to approach my belief in God from another angle, so I can talk with my son in a language that he relates to.

I can see how as my parents were heartbroken I might be in danger of feeling the same if my children don't believe what I believe. Isn't it ironic? I say it is a danger, because it is not a foregone conclusion. As a parent, I would like to 'believe' in my children, as much as, or more than I believe in my theology. In that way, my expectations for them can be much broader and more enlightened, and perhaps so can my theology. I am looking for ways to avoid ending up in a reactionary relationship like the one my parents and I ended up in.

The other weekend it was a rainy Saturday when all seven of us (my wife and our five kids) were at home. I was dealing with some of the tensions that build up in me when everyone is on a different screen or console, and eventually we did all watch 'Planet Earth' on the actual TV together. But at one point in the afternoon I got a sense that although my faith is genuine, I can start to see a lot of the personal, emotive reasons for grabbing hold of faith so strongly all those years ago when I met 'the church'. I don't remember particularly sitting with my parents and discussing what life really meant to them. I can remember campaigning in Putney High St, aged eight, with a paper gas mask, for lead-free petrol, and other political ideas, and opinions being expressed. But we never really had a personal one-to-one confiding or opening of the heart about what they understood or possibly didn't understand about their lives.

And so, perhaps that was something I would have appreciated talking about with them. And so from a therapy perspective, I derive a lot of reassurance from my faith: that it tells me there is purpose and meaning to life, and that life is not only relative in a postmodern subjective fashion, but there are some absolutes. The knowledge I feel I have that God has a way of working – a steady hand as he guides this world, slowly, towards a better place, out of the seeming chaos of human contradiction, is like an anchor and compass for my sanity.

And as I thought these thoughts on the rainy Saturday afternoon, I found myself calling my dad up to see if he wanted to go out for a drink, so that I could fill in that gap about his inner life. I wanted to tell him that it would have been good for us to talk more when I was younger, and maybe we could do that talk now. Part of me felt that unless I do that with him, I might not do it with my own children very well.

Certainly, I know that it would help my dad get to grips with my nonsensical, false religion and belief, if he got a picture of how I was only wanting to make sense of my world when I went 'all religious'. Possibly he might also become aware that his atheism is not as fool-proof as he likes to make out, and his certainties are not so different from mine in terms of the emotional needs that they meet.

But together with the need for possibly another stint of therapy, there is a need to rediscover some of my personal religious practice that gets frayed at the edges and sketchy over time. Finding ways for God to be a part of my life in the office in the same way as I did when I worked as a pastor for my community; to pray for my youngest son's football team that I am managing as I did for the members of my congregation when I was ministering there. The reality is I am rarely at church on a Sunday morning these days because of our football matches. My mother's reaction interestingly is not relief, but a disappointment that my life seems to be 'all about church and football', and why is there no 'culture, theatre, etc?'.

Her anxiety is more to do with her superimposing on to my family the economic and emotional poverty that she experienced growing up in her family in Rome having been displaced from Germany after the Second World War and the Holocaust. One of the lessons my wife has been teaching me with our kids is a philosophy which says (whenever there is something to worry about): 'basically they are really good kids', 'trust them'.

Recently when our son turned 16, he didn't want to do our traditional birthday prayer we do with our children when they wake up in the morning on their birthday before school. I was a bit heartbroken. But I got into work, and something in my head reminded me that when I turned 16 and went away for the weekend, my mum ended up having to pick me up from the police station for possession of class C drugs. So I told myself, actually they are really good kids and doing much better than me when I was their age: better at school and in terms of emotional intelligence. Perhaps that's progress, and maybe I do a good job as a dad too. And even if they don't end up believing exactly what I believe, the way we express our trust and love for one another is possibly more important.

11 Counselling practices within The Family International (Children of God)

Abi Freeman

Introduction

The Family International (TFI) is a Christian-based new religious movement that began in 1968 as the Children of God (COG), drawing its first membership from the counter-culture youth of North America before spreading thinly worldwide (Melton 2004; Bainbridge 2002). The full-time membership was rarely more than 10,000 adults at any one time.

For the most part, full-time members lived in communal homes. However, the movement has been punctuated by internal change, and the communal living requirements were dissolved amongst other far-reaching alterations in the 'Reboot' restructuring of 2010 (Shepherd and Shepherd 2009; Freeman 2017). This chapter is mostly written within the context of the communal environment that existed between 1968 and 2010.

The Letters hold the key to understanding life in TFI. *The Letters* are the writings of the founder, David Berg, also known as Moses David or 'Dad'. After he died in 1994, the new directors of TFI, Karen Zerby (Berg's wife) and her new partner, Steve Kelly, took over writing *The Letters*. The couple are known in the movement as Maria (Mama) and Peter. Along with the Bible, *The Letters* were the foundation of the movement's theology, but they also went further, extending into every aspect of TFI's religious practice and daily life. Therefore, I will be drawing upon *The Letters* in order to analyse the movement's counselling practices, along with observations from my life as a member of TFI communities from 1973 until 2007.

This chapter will only discuss the practice of counselling of adults, by adults. The important topic of counselling and support of teenagers and children is beyond the scope of what follows, due to space limitations.[1]

Personal counselling within the movement

One of the blights of modern living is social isolation and loneliness, as observed by Killeen (1998: 762). This was not usually the case for the communal-living members of TFI. Living in a household with an average of six to twelve other adults, a member could usually find someone to talk with, someone who would listen to their troubles and offer a word of comfort.

Counselling in TFI and the COG went further than this informal peer support. Referred to as 'personal shepherding', it was delivered with the best of intentions, but could at times be intrusive and arguably harmful.

'Personal shepherding' in TFI extended to teaching, offering advice and guidance, supervising the members' spiritual and practical life, mentoring, offering correction and more. However, there were elements of shepherding more closely akin to counselling, as the 'shepherds' – those in positions of leadership at any level – were expected to be compassionate and ready to listen to those who opened their hearts.

> BUT HOW ARE YOU GOING TO [help and encourage members], how do you know what Scripture they need, what solution they need or what they need, if you don't listen to what their problems are when they need help? … Sometimes that's the best thing you can do for them, just give them somebody to talk to, to pour out their hearts to … for the greatest example of loving-shepherding, just read the Gospels and see how Jesus fathered His little flock and taught His little disciples!
>
> (Berg 1977b)[2]

Any TFI member could find him or herself in the position of counsellor, or of the one being counselled. No formal training was provided for the counsellors. Instead, shepherding was guided by *The Letters* and peer support.

The counsellor – or shepherd as he or she was referred to in TFI – was expected to offer prayer and spiritual support, such as the sharing of relevant scripture portions or prophetic messages.

Counselling sessions took place in a quiet, private room, although they could just as easily have been part of a 'walkie talkie' – walking and talking in the garden if the property was large, or out in a park or another open space. However, if it was likely to be a sensitive conversation, with tears shed, it was probably indoors.

Depending on the reason for the session, the shepherd would listen and draw out the thoughts and feelings of the member. He or she might ask probing questions, or just let the member talk. In response, the shepherd would share his thoughts, but also quote or refer to passages of the Bible or *The Letters* as a means of offering counsel. If the member's concern involved someone else, the shepherd might refrain from offering too much comment until he or she had a chance to find out more, bearing in mind the Biblical proverb, 'He who answers a matter before he hears it, It is folly and shame to him'. (Proverbs 18:13, New King James version).

As a faith-based Christian community, almost every activity within TFI began and closed with prayer. Counselling was no different. Usually the shepherd would open with prayer, and then might ask the one counselled to close in prayer at the end of their conversation. The two may also spend a little time quietly waiting for a 'prophecy' – words inspired by Jesus or another personality from the spirit world. A sentence or two, perhaps of paraphrased scriptures, might come to mind and then be spoken, either by the shepherd or the one being counselled.[3]

The aim of this shepherding was to bring about improvements in the member's life: to reach a resolution about a conflict or achieve some personal growth. With this in mind, at the close of the session the shepherd may have also given the member some follow-up assignments, such as reading certain *Letters*, memorising scriptures or receiving prophecies.

The supportive environment of the communal home was considered by members to be one of the benefits of TFI life; personal shepherding likewise was often appreciated.

It should be noted that this was virtually the only form of support available; there was rarely a possibility of obtaining emotional or psychological support from outside of TFI, as conventional psychiatry was generally spoken against:

> YOU WANT TO GET YOUR PSYCHOLOGICAL TROUBLES CURED? You think you can go to a psychiatrist who studied Nietzsche & Freud & some of those nuts? Let me tell you, they were nuttier than a fruitcake! They're nuttier than you!
>
> (Berg 1981c)

The Letters could, however, be contradictory. While one Letter portrays psychologists as 'atheistic' and 'teaching the doctrines of the Enemy' (Zerby 2003b), in another Letter Berg wrote: 'So you can gather a lot of good things from psychology, psychiatry, positive thinking, meditation, oriental religions, etc.' (Berg 1978).

In any event, TFI shepherding was considered superior to what existed outside, as Zerby puts it:

> ... whether in the Family or out of the Family, you need shepherding and help in your personal life in order to be happy and continue growing. You'd be surprised at how many people in the System [mainstream society] see a psychiatrist – their version of a 'shepherd' – to get advice and help for their problems ... But, as someone put it, in the Family you have free in-house shrinks, ha! Of course the big advantage is that our 'shrinks' are people who love you and care about you, who understand and often relate to your battles (having gone through similar ones), and try their best to help you ... Most of all, your shepherds can point you to the greatest 'shrink' of them all – Jesus – and His Heavenly answers in the Word and through prophecy!
>
> (Zerby 1998)

Intrusion into personal space

Even in conventional counselling practice, a client may not always find counselling is to their liking. They may not find the sessions helpful, or they may not feel comfortable with a certain counsellor. In such cases, they will often cease attending the counselling sessions, perhaps seeking a different counsellor or an alternative approach to their problems, such as a peer-based support group.

This autonomy of the client is an important part of the therapeutic relationship (British Association for Counselling and Psychotherapy [BACP] 2013: 2). This was not the position for TFI members. Shepherding and counsel were not only available, but at times they could also be imposed.

There was an element of intrusion into the inner thoughts of TFI members, or 'meddling with what you consider very personal matters' (Zerby 2004b). 'Open Heart Reports' (OHRs) are an example. Members were expected to write these daily or weekly reports to their shepherds, telling not only their activities, but also sharing their deepest thoughts and feelings. In his landmark ruling in the custody case of a child who was being brought up by his mother in TFI, Lord Justice Ward[4] criticised OHRs as 'capable of unfair exploitation to the disadvantage of those who felt compelled to give some disclosure lest they be punished for pride and self-righteousness' (Ward 1992). (The requirement for OHRs was discontinued with the adoption of *The Love Charter* in 1995).[5]

The shepherd might respond by returning the OHR with a few notations such as, 'IPFY' ('I'm praying for you'), 'GBY' ('God bless you') and so on, or invite the member to meet to talk and pray. If a member was unhappy or struggling, the OHR would likely be followed up with a talk with the shepherd, whether requested or not. He or she might listen and sympathise, but also offer suggestions or correction.

Whether initiated by an OHR or other circumstances, helping the member to 'get the victory' was the aim of the counselling. This might have been through encouragement, but could also be through a 'telling off'. The shepherd might suggest that the individual asks to be prayed for in public by the members of that community. If the shepherd felt that the problem was due to evil spirits, this prayer might have included the laying on of hands to 'cast out the demons'. This could be followed up by a disciplinary procedure, such as loss of privileges or demotion from a leadership position. For lesser matters, the member might be advised to memorise a certain passage of scripture, read certain *Letters* or miss the weekly movie showing.

Zerby explains the position on more serious correction in this extract:

> **SPECIFIC STEPS TO HELP'M GET THE VICTORY!**
> We've done all kinds of things to help people pull through their problems & make it: We've counselled them, put them on reading lists, had united prayer for them & exorcisms & prayers of deliverance, even given some people a fulltime buddy to help them over a particularly difficult time, a reading buddy that they can read out loud with. We've asked people to write their OHRs daily, prayed for them country-wide or worldwide, had different leaders writing them *Letters* counselling & praying with them, or other of their peers writing them encouraging notes & *Letters*.

> We've taken some people off their regular work, given them time by themselves, put them in a different job in the same Home, changed their location so they'd be under other leadership & with different people, given them ultimatums, etc. We've also disciplined people in various ways: Put them on Babes' Status, put them in Victor Programs, put them in Retraining Centers (RTCs). People were warned when brought into the RTCs that they desperately needed to make progress & gain some genuine victories in their lives, or they would be asked to move out of our DO [ed. Full-time] Homes!
>
> (Zerby 1991b)

The ultimate disciplinary procedure was expulsion from TFI. Although expulsion was codified in *The Love Charter* (1995) to be for specific offences and not as discretionary as it had been up until that point, even in 2015, 'activities that foster schism' – presumably such as spreading doubts – can still result in loss of membership (The Family International 2010).

Expulsion from TFI communities was a serious threat because of what the member stood to lose on a personal, practical and emotional level. A former member who read an unfinalised draft of this chapter told me:

> The threat of being expelled hung over us. It could mean losing something you'd spent years working to build. You'd raised support, got donations, got some mission work going. And much worse, getting kicked out would probably mean separation from your spouse and your children. You would leave alone and feeling like a failure. – And all because you expressed doubts about some doctrine or requirement.
>
> (Conversation with C. H. 2014)

Members were taught to be confident that having received Jesus as their Saviour, they could not ever lose their 'salvation'. Yet Berg also warned 'backsliders beware!' and that one may still 'suffer for their sins' both now and in the next life (Berg 1981a). Naturally, this was an added pressure.

Problems to be solved

'I don't have a sad God! I have a happy God, who wants me to be happy too, and you as well!' (Berg 1977a). Berg's statement leads to an important theme that underpinned counselling in TFI. To be unhappy or 'out of the victory' was seen as a problem to be solved. TFI members were expected to have a positive and cheerful attitude, regardless of their circumstances, and if they repeatedly could not maintain this, they became a 'problem case'.

There was a sense from early on in the movement's history that members should be of sufficient calibre to not need a lot of support, either psychologically or physically. For instance, in 1975 Berg wrote *Who To!—Pushers or Problems?,* exasperated with those who were so determined to expand COG membership that they were encouraging just about anybody to join, even those who did not have what were considered the requisite mental or physical abilities.

In general, Zerby seems to have had more patience. Even in her comments about T, a young man who was the subject of a series of strongly-worded *Letters* about his alleged problems of 'murmuring' (complaining) and doubts, she tries to strike a balance:

> So I want to make it clear that it's not wrong for a Shepherd to spend his time with one of his sheep in counselling them & reasoning with them & praying with them & reading with them & pouring a lot into them ... The problem occurs when this kind of intensive treatment doesn't happen only once, with the Shepherd spending hour after hour with the one sheep who's having problems.
>
> (Zerby 1991b)

The 'problems' being referred to might well be interpreted differently outside of TFI and merit further exploration.

If a member was not happy, it was generally considered to be their fault or due to an 'attack of the Devil'. As Zerby observed: 'No matter what the circumstances or conditions, right from the start you've got to recognize depression for what it is – an aggressive attack of the Enemy' (Zerby 2003c).

'Negative thinking' was a catch-all term that could encompass discouragement, unhappiness or doubt. In a 'message from Jesus' in Zerby's *Letter, Full Possession*, negative thinking sits alongside other problems to be condemned and fought against:

> (Message from Jesus:) The sins that bring you down all filter through the mind: pride, the root sin of all; jealousy; lust; selfishness; lethargy; bitterness; disunity; comparing; discontent and murmuring; negative thinking; worldliness; disobedience; doubt; putting other gods before Me; self-righteousness, etc.
>
> (Zerby 2001a)

If a member was doubting, this might be attributed to negative thinking or lack of reading 'The Word' – meaning both the Bible and *The Letters*; it might have been blamed on a demonic attack, or on the person's attitude or actions (Zerby 1996). 'At the root of every doubt, there is sin, the heinous, diabolical sin, of rebellion against God's will!' wrote Berg (1971), while three decades later, Zerby published a 'message from Jesus' saying: 'You might not understand or agree with every single thing in My Word or the ways of My Spirit, but it's not your place to criticise My ways or to assume you know better than Me' (Zerby 2000). The battle against doubts was a recurring theme, as evidently many, if not most, members struggled to accept the totality of Berg, Zerby and Kelly's teachings. The word 'doubt' and its derivatives occur in more than half of *The Letters*.

Even the lethargy and tiredness that often accompanies depression and other medical conditions was seen as a spiritual attack (National Health Service website 2014):[6]

> That is a major way that spiritual lethargy manifests itself in you. You're too lazy and lethargic to go on the attack and hit that punk where it really hurts! I know that this is quite a challenge and it's hard for you to fight the Devil when he throws this discouragement at you. But this is a goal that I've set before you, and a mountain that you must climb in order to continue to grow spiritually and turn into what I want you to be.
>
> (Zerby 2003c)

'You can get the victory'

It can be seen from these examples of 'problems' that a member who was suffering from depression or another mental health condition could additionally struggle with self-condemnation, as the individual was expected to 'get the victory' through prayer, reading and occasionally fasting. The 'victory' was to be manifestly cheerful, positive and full of faith. Anything less denoted an ongoing personal problem. Outcomes were seen as almost entirely based on the individual's own actions. Lack of achieving 'victory' was down to their failure in some way.

> THEY CAN [GET] THE VICTORY IF THEY CHOOSE to, because God's got it for them, and there's oodles of promises on it. So they have absolutely no excuse for not getting the victory. If they will do their part and forsake their sins and make the right choice to do God's will, He'll give it to them – If not, nobody can!
>
> (Berg 1975)

There was no consideration given to the idea that an individual's psychological or emotional state might not be that simple to either diagnose or treat. This random sampling of Letter titles gives a flavour of how this simplistic view-point was repeated: *Get the Victory or Get Out* (Berg 1981b), *Getting the Victory over DeepRooted Problems* (Berg 1985a), *You've Got the Victory—Don't Give Up* (Berg 1985b), *Don't Be Discouraged!—Keep the Faith and Trust the Lord!* (Berg 1987), *Praise and Sing Your Way to Victory* (Berg 1991c), *Victory Over Depression and Drug Addiction!* (Berg and Kelly 1989), *Overcoming the Past! More on How to Get the Victory over Bitterness!* (Zerby 1992), *Positively Positive* (Zerby 2005).

In Death to Depression (2003a), Zerby published a selection of prophetic messages offering solutions for depression. Attributing these words to Jesus heightened their impact for members and makes uncomfortable reading for a depressed person:

> (Message from Jesus:) Depression is a form of anger at Me. It is not agreeing with what I've chosen for you to experience and go through. This overwhelming sadness you feel when you're depressed is often rooted in anger and unyieldedness. It's like sand that sinks deeper the farther you walk into it, sucking you into its depths of death.
>
> (Zerby 2003a)

In this Letter, there is a constant theme that depression can be overcome if you do the right things. Zerby again:

> Though I haven't had firsthand personal experience with depression, quite a number of years ago Peter [Kelly] battled serious discouragement and debilitating depression, as have others that I've known and worked with over the years – including some folks in my Home now … I believe that these experiences have helped me to gain a better understanding of depression, how difficult it is to fight, as well as the Lord's unfailing ability to deliver … Thank the Lord that due to Peter's faith, prayers, yieldedness, fight, and desire for victory, coupled with the Lord's miracle-working power and our prayers, he was wonderfully delivered.
>
> (Zerby 2003a)

Other serious mental health problems, such as anorexia, were seen in much the same light. The 'victory' was yours, if you did the right things. In a series of *Letters* entitled Fight for Life, Zerby described the struggles of a member who apparently overcame anorexia:

> She's endured an extremely difficult and long-term battle, and when the Lord asked her to go on a new and wholehearted offensive, she yielded and responded beautifully, threw herself into it, and has been rewarded with a wonderful victory!
>
> (Zerby 2001b)

Zerby explains what this 'battle' entailed:

> … lessons on yieldedness; desperation; honesty; openness; gaining victories, and how victory IS possible; rising above; how serious problems can be overcome; exposing the Enemy's devices and lies; shepherding and helping those who are going through serious battles, and how far the Lord expects and asks us to go to help people; negativity and its dangers; being a clear channel even when you don't feel like it; and the straightforwardness and yet mercy of the Lord when He chastens us in love, just to name a few.
>
> (Zerby 2001b)

This is in marked contrast to conventional guidance on the treatment of anorexia.[7]

The lack of access to professional support or treatment may seem reprehensible and begs the question why members allowed it to continue. Perhaps one reason is that efforts at shepherding were for the most part well-intentioned. The goal was to help each other, to 'bear one another's burdens, and so fulfil the law of Christ' (Galatians 6:2 NKJV). Shepherding was seen as an act of love.

It should also be understood that members living within TFI communities during this time were so totally immersed in TFI culture, that they had little exposure to alternative viewpoints. Most adult members had joined the movement in their teens or early twenties with limited life experience. Many lived outside their country of origin, and much of this period (1968–2010) was before widespread internet access could have opened up wider sources of information. Hence, members could only interpret their experiences through the prism of TFI culture and writings.

Still, there were undoubtedly occasions when members disagreed with certain *Letters*. In such events, they would likely have kept their opinions to themselves, but quietly ignored what was written. Such *Letters* might have been read only once and then forgotten. Despite the importance attached to *The Letters*, there was a constant flow of new reading material, sometimes contradicting what went before, so an occasional – perhaps unconscious – decision by a member to 'read and try not to remember' was not as surprising as it might seem.

The leadership themselves also showed a gradual change of attitude regarding more serious mental health problems, culminating in Zerby eventually admitting that there are cases when the sufferers would benefit from medical attention.

In 2004, Zerby wrote a series of *Letters* called Choices and Consequences, part of which was centred on J., a young man who had been hospitalised with what sounds like a psychotic episode in connection with bipolar disorder, although this is not how Zerby explained it. This followed several exorcism prayers, which had initially seemed to help, but the local shepherds could not manage J.'s subsequent violent outburst. Once in mental hospital, J.'s condition did improve. 'Prophecies' in this Letter acknowledged that J. had been helped by medication and his stay in hospital, whilst emphasising that prayer was still the main reason behind his improvement.

Considering all that had been written earlier – including Berg's, '*The psychiatrists in psychology are the priesthood of the Devil!*' (Berg 1992) – this was a remarkable development and provoked questions amongst some members. Zerby clarified: 'The reality is that I do endorse going the medical route when that's the way the Lord is leading'. Nevertheless, the bottom line was still that the 'healing' depended on J.: '… it was important to seek medical help for J., because he was not yet ready to humble himself and do his part in order to be delivered' (Zerby 2004a).

The impact of Berg's writings and example

The apologies and at least limited change of attitudes towards mental health problems were a long time in coming. The root of why things got to this stage lay in Berg's views and how he personally dealt with individuals. The theoretical basis for counselling within TFI sat firmly in its own writings. The practical application was also drawn from *The Letters*. Although very few members ever met Berg, much less lived under his roof, the example he set in *The Letters* was intended to influence the shepherding that took place throughout the movement.

Although Berg claimed that he had taken a course in 'abnormal psychology' in college (Berg 1985d), he viewed serious emotional and mental problems as having a spiritual origin.

> These people who have phobias are demonic, because it's spiritual! There's no real cause for most of it, but they said it's the second highest cause of mental illness in the U.S. today next to schizophrenia, which is demon-possession!
>
> (Berg 1985c)

Whilst it was often repeated that 'love is the most important thing' (Zerby 1983), Berg himself did not always exhibit a great deal of patience with people's problems. This is illustrated by a series of *Letters* he wrote in response to a letter he received from a discouraged mother of four young children. She felt that having a family was hampering her missionary efforts. Although he begins his response sympathetically, by the end of the series he rebukes her:

> GOD IS ANGRY WITH YOUR MURMURING! [complaining] – And He's displeased with your blaming it all on others instead of yourself! Your poor husband has worked hard to try to keep you & his little family together, while you've done a lot that could've broken it up!
>
> (Berg 1979)

There was no respect for confidentiality whatsoever. The woman's letter to Berg was reprinted in full; she was named and shamed in his response that was published for all the membership to read.

There were numerous examples of Berg dealing with personal problems in this way. There were fourteen *Letters* alone about one couple (Berg 1974a–m); five about a woman in a leadership position who was a lesbian (Berg 1984a–e); and at least four about T., a young man unhappy with his life, who had expressed his feelings in an OHR (Berg 1991b,c and Zerby 1991a,b). In each case, their identities and personal issues were exposed to TFI at large to serve as an example.[8] The treatment of T. was of specific concern to Lord Justice Ward (1992) who was troubled about T.'s 'public humiliation' amongst other concerns.

However, the practice of public exposure did not stop. Zerby did much the same as late as 2004, regarding J., the young man hospitalised with bipolar disorder. *The Letters* about his situation included his name and location, so that he was identified to TFI at large. Although J. apparently gave his permission for this, it is questionable whether he was in a sufficiently competent mental state in which he could give his informed consent.

This lack of respect for privacy and confidentiality is a serious breach of ethics.[9] Zerby and Kelly did finally appear to realise this, as in 2009 they apologised for occasions when private matters were made public:

> In the process of addressing what was considered problem behavior, some teenagers or young adults were strongly reprimanded in Family publications. Adult members were also highlighted from time to time, and their troubles made public. Public reprimands of this nature were inappropriate. Peter and I apologize to any young person or adult who had their private lives made public in this way.
>
> (Zerby and Kelly 2009)

Conclusion

In my view, despite the majority of TFI members being well-meaning and sincere, much of the teaching and practice regarding counselling and mental health in TFI was irresponsible on the part of the leadership, and perhaps on occasion negligent to a serious degree. The bias of the counsellors, the lack of professional training, the disregard of confidentiality, the infringements on personal space, the simplistic notions of psychological disorders and the laying of blame on the individual are some of the problems I have identified regarding counselling practice.

On the other hand, daily life within communities was largely supportive and encouraging. The sense of inadequacy and low self-esteem that are sometimes observed amongst former members tell only part of the story. Others have a commendable 'can do' attitude that enables them to make a success of their post-TFI endeavours. Many former and current members have good memories of their lives within communities, and even lament the loss of the communal milieu since leaving the group voluntarily or as a result of the restructuring 'Reboot' in 2010.

It is rarely understood by those who have not lived through the experience just how much of a loss is felt by former members – whether or not they left TFI of their own volition, or were still members at the time of the 'Reboot' when the community structure was abolished. The loss of community, of living with friends, side-by-side and of a sense of daily purpose, are just a few of the adjustments that have to be made in a post-TFI life. The post-TFI individual needs to come to terms with these losses, make sense of past experiences and adjust to life outside of their former support structure. It is, in a sense, a bereavement, and grief counselling can be a helpful model for supporting such individuals, providing a safe and non-judgemental space to explore memories and work through typical grief responses such as anxiety, depression, regret and anger.

The grief counsellor works toward helping the bereaved accept the reality of their loss, process the pain of grief, adjust to their changed life circumstances, overcome obstacles to readjustment and find a way to remember the deceased whilst feeling comfortable reinvesting in life (Worden 2010). For the post-TFI individual, similar tasks exist. Recognising that their tenure in TFI included both positive and negative experiences can help them move forward.

Managing the practical aspects of a post-TFI life can be a daunting task; re-establishing identity is a further challenge. The process of 'relearning the world' and recovering a 'sense of daily purpose' as described in the context of grief (Attig 1996) are apt for an individual whose life has been framed by TFI's teachings and structure for decades.

Notes

1 Counselling of children and teenagers in TFI did take place, not without problems. The wider context of children in the movement is described by Bainbridge (2002:141).

2 The capitalisation, italics, bolding and underlining in all quotes from *The Letters* are in the original texts.

3 TFI understand prophecy as an inspired utterance that may originate from God, Jesus, angels, other personalities living in the spiritual world or departed believers. According to their statement of faith:

> We believe that God seeks to communicate with people. … God has promised to make His words known to His children through His Spirit (Proverbs 1:23). The ability to receive direct messages from God is referred to in the Bible as the gift of prophecy. Prophecy is a gift of the Holy Spirit, which is available to believers, and can play an active role in their daily lives.
>
> (Acts 2:17)
>
> We believe that … God also empowers the spirits of departed believers to minister to and deliver messages to His people. An example of this is found in the Biblical account of the spirits of the departed prophets, Moses and Elijah, appearing and conferring with Jesus (Luke 9:28-31). Paul referred to departed believers as "a great cloud of witnesses" watching over those on Earth (Hebrews 12:1).
>
> (TFI 2010)

4 A grandmother went to the British family court to ask for custody of her newborn grandson, whose mother was a TFI member. The mother's membership became the crux of the matter as the judge initiated a wide-ranging investigation into the movement involving hundreds of pages of documents and many hours of testimony. Lord Justice Ward's final 300-page judgement criticised TFI and its leadership in no uncertain terms, yet ultimately concluded that the child was safe with his mother and denied the grandmother her petition (Ward 1992 and see Melton 2004).

5 *The Love Charter*, usually referred to as *The Charter*, codified the movement's basic beliefs, rules and structure. First published in 1995, this was the first formal written constitution for the movement as a whole. The Charter has been updated

on numerous occasions since then, with the most extensive revision following the Reboot of 2010.

6 National Health Service, Medical Causes of Tiredness. www.nhs.uk/Livewell/tiredness-and-fatigue/Pages/medical-causes-of-tiredness.aspx (Accessed 2 December 14).

7 National Health Service, Anorexia Nervosa. www.nhs.uk/conditions/anorexia-nervosa/Pages/Introduction.aspx (Accessed 1 December 14).

8 Those who joined TFI adopted new names, and it was these 'Family' names that were used in the *Letters*.

9 British Association for Counselling and Psychotherapy. *Ethical Framework for Good Practice in Counselling and Psychotherapy*. 2013: 6.

References

Attig, T. 1996. *How We Grieve: Relearning the World*. Oxford: Oxford University Press.

Bainbridge, W.S. 2002. *The Endtime Family, Children of God*. Syracuse, NY: Syracuse University Press.

Berg, D.B. *The Letters*. Zurich: World Services.

Berg, D.B. 1971. *Third Epistle to Pastors!* Letter 49.

Berg, D.B. 1974a. *The Genesis Story Part 1*. Letter 1431.

Berg, D.B. 1974b. *The Genesis Story Part 2*. Letter 1432.

Berg, D.B. 1974c. *The Genesis Story Part 3*. Letter 1436.

Berg, D.B. 1974d. *The Genesis Story Part 4*. Letter 1438.

Berg, D.B. 1974e. *The Genesis Story Part 5*. Letter 1442.

Berg, D.B. 1974f. *The Genesis Story Part 6*. Letter 1443.

Berg, D.B. 1974g. *The Genesis Story Part 7*. Letter 1444.

Berg, D.B. 1974h. *The Genesis Story Part 8*. Letter 1448.

Berg, D.B. 1974i. *The Genesis Story Part 9*. Letter 1452.

Berg, D.B. 1974j. *The Genesis Story Part 10*. Letter 1454.

Berg, D.B. 1974k. *The Genesis Story Part 11*. Letter 1459.

Berg, D.B. 1974l. *The Genesis Story Part 12*. Letter 1464.

Berg, D.B. 1974m. *The Genesis Story Part 13*. Letter 1467.

Berg, D.B. 1975. *"Who to!"—Pushers or Problems?* Letter 334A.

Berg, D.B. 1977a. *Out of this World!* Letter 686.

Berg, D.B. 1977b. *Training and Shepherding Babes*. Letter 734.

Berg, D.B. 1978. *What Think Ye of Jesus?* Letter 1390.

Berg, D.B. 1979. *Frustrated?* Letter 835.

Berg, D.B. 1981a. *Backsliders Beware!* Letter 1045.

Berg, D.B. 1981b. *Get the Victory or Get Out!* Letter 1090.

Berg, D.B. 1981c. *Introduction to Revelation!* Letter 1169.

Berg, D.B. 1984a. *What's Wrong with Keda?* Letter 1739.

Berg, D.B. 1984b. *Keda's Penance*. Letter 1740.

Berg, D.B. 1984c. *Keda's Problem*. Letter 1747.

Berg, D.B. 1984d. *Exposing Keda's Problem*. Letter 1748.

Berg, D.B. 1984e. *Prayer Request for Keda*. Letter 1749.

Berg, D.B. 1985a. *Getting the Victory over DeepRooted Problems*. Letter 1887.

Berg, D.B. 1985b. *You've Got the Victory—Don't Give Up!* Letter 1925.

Berg, D.B. 1985c. *World Currents!—No.19*. Letter 2038.

Berg, D.B. 1985d. *Teaching Suspense and Our New Culture!* Letter 2320.

Berg, D.B. 1987. *Don't Be Discouraged!—Keep the Faith and Trust the Lord!* Letter 2386.

Berg, D.B. 1991a. *Grumblers Get Out!* Letter 2716.

Berg, D.B. 1991b. *Zach Attack Ultimatum!* Letter 2719.

Berg, D.B. 1991c. *Praise and Sing Your Way to Victory.* Letter 2833.

Berg, D.B. 1992. *Stop the World!—I Wanna Get Off!* Letter 2795.

Berg, D.B. and Kelly, S. 1989. *Victory over Depression and Drug Addiction!* Letter 2547.

British Association for Counselling and Psychotherapy. 2013. *Ethical Framework for Good Practice in Counselling and Psychotherapy.* Lutterworth.

Freeman, A. 2017. From the radical to the routine: the history and future of the Family International, in: Eugene V. Gallagher (eds) *'Cult Wars' in Historical Perspective.* Oxon/New York: Routledge.

Killeen, C. 1998. Loneliness an epidemic in modern society, *Journal of Advanced Nursing*, 28(4), 762–770.

Melton, J.G. 2004. *The Children of God: The Family.* Salt Lake City, UT: Signature Press.

National Health Service, Medical Causes of Tiredness. www.nhs.uk/Livewell/tiredness-and-fatigue/Pages/medical-causes-of-tiredness.aspx (Accessed 2 December 14).

National Health Service, Anorexia Nervosa. www.nhs.uk/conditions/anorexia-nervosa/Pages/Introduction.aspx (Accessed 1 December 14).

Shepherd, Gary and Shepherd, Gordon. The Family International (TFI) 2009 to Present. www.has.vcu.edu/wrs/profiles/TheFamilyInternational2009-Present.htm (Accessed 1 September 14).

The Family International. Statement of Faith 2010: Zurich, Switzerland.

The Love Charter 1995: Zurich, Switzerland.

Ward, Lord Justice Ward, W 42 1992 in the High Court of Justice, Family Division, Principal Registry in the Matter of ST (a minor) and in the Matter of the Supreme Court Act 1991. Available at www.xfamily.org/index.php/Complete_Judgment_of_Lord_Justice_Ward (Accessed 23 August 17).

Worden, William J. 1983–2010 *Grief Counselling and Grief Therapy.* East Sussex: Routledge.

Zerby, K. *The Letters.* Zurich: World Services.

Zerby, K. 1983. Love is the Most Important Thing! Letter 1793.

Zerby, K. 1991a. *Tony's Last Chance.* Letter 2714.

Zerby, K. 1991b. Different Strokes for Different Folks! Evaluating and Dealing with Problem Cases! Letter 2717.

Zerby, K. 1992. Overcoming the Past! More on How to Get the Victory over Bitterness! Letter 2877.

Zerby, K. 1996. Crisis of Faith!—More on Doubts! *Letters* 3088–3099.

Zerby, K. 1998. The Benefits of the Family! Letter 3172.

Zerby, K. 2000. Issues, Part 7. Letter 3350.

Zerby, K. 2001a. Full Possession! Letter 3376.

Zerby, K. 2001b. Fight for Life. Letter 3390.

Zerby, K. 2003a. Death to Depression. Letter 3464.

Zerby, K. 2003b. Issues, Part 17. Letter 3480.

Zerby, K. 2003c. What the Hell Is Lethargy? Letter 3482.

Zerby, K. 2004a. Choices and Consequences. *Letters* 3484–3486.

Zerby, K. 2004b. Shooting Straight, Part 3. Letter 3501.

Zerby, K. 2005. Positively Positive, Part 1. Letter 3581.

Zerby, K. and S. Kelly. *The Letters.* Zurich: The Family International.

Zerby, K. and S. Kelly. 2009. *Beyond Boundaries, Part 4: Building Bridges.* Letter 3810.

12 Scammers or saviours?

Nicola Laaninen

Deprogramme To free (a convert) from the influence of a religious cult, political indoctrination, etc., by intensive persuasion or re-education (in my case under physical restraint).

To deprogramme means that first one has to be programmed. When was I programmed by the Unification Church (UC)? Was I programmed by the UC? How did they programme me? How did the teachings of the Church affect me? Could these strange people throw some light on my soul searching and influence me? Was I indoctrinated into the Church? What does that mean anyway? These are questions I have thought about in depth, especially recently as my relationship with the UC has changed considerably. No matter what my relationship with the Church is now, it does not change my views on my deprogramming, other than being a little more enlightened about where the deprogrammers were coming from. I have always felt that I have good intuition, and I think this has helped me manoeuvre my way through the challenges of life.

To understand my attitude while I was with the deprogrammers I need to explain a little about my life and how and why I joined the UC. I am the third of four children in our family, my two brothers and sister went away to school, so most of my teen years I was the only one living at home. Though I had the normal teen ups and downs, I had a good relationship with my mum and dad. I was quite open and honest about my thoughts and views on life and they trusted me and afforded me more freedom than many of my peers. In my last year of studying physiotherapy, my dad had a stroke and almost died. It was a difficult time for our family and it started me on a journey of soul searching questions. I was raised in the Church of England, and though I had many questions and doubts, I had deep respect for my dad's faith and how he lived his life. But as he fought for his life, I saw him for the first time shaky in his faith, and fear was creeping in that I had been unaware of before. My rock, the place where my own faith was birthed, was struggling, and this set into motion deeper questions of my own. I decided that unless I could answer some of them I did not want to get married and have children, but slowly my dad improved, and he was soon out of the woods starting on the long road of rehabilitation. I returned to my studies, my sister gave up going to university for a year to help my dad with rehab, and my brother returned from New Zealand. As I slipped back into the routine of coursework and then work, the deeper questions about life slipped into the back of my mind.

After working as a physiotherapist for a couple of years in London, I decided to go and work in Canada, largely motivated by my love for skiing! My sister Fiona came out in the summer of that year, 1978, and we embarked on a short trip around the western United States. We had been travelling about a week when we hit San Francisco. It was there we met a member of the UC on Fisherman's Wharf. John Didsdury was standing at a table that had a large poster on it with beautiful photos of a farm in Northern California. I think the photos caught our eye and John quickly came over and introduced himself to us. We talked for a while, I can't even remember what about, but before we left he invited us to dinner that night. Having done a lot of walking, we were happy to have somewhere to relax and enjoy the company of some new people. We heard a short talk introducing some of the ideas the group was interested in, and Fiona seemed quite eager to check out their retreat up north. Fiona was more taken with our first experiences than I was. Quite frankly, I was ready to move on, but we were encouraged to stay. My initial scepticism about these people and what they had to offer, along with my reluctance to give up my travels, ebbed as I lingered and listened. The teachings struck a chord. Questions that had surfaced during my dad's stroke came flooding back, along with a renewed commitment to find answers. I was intrigued by the theology, and it did shed some light on my soul searching. I began to believe in the capacity for change, and maybe the chance of a more ideal world, something my dad and I had had lengthy discussions about. I thought about him constantly, convinced he would like many of these ideas, and to this day, I think he would have, except for the way I presented them. I decided to quit my job and not return to Canada. Fiona was going to give up another year of university. To make these decisions with little regard for our parents' opinion, when we knew they were anxious and afraid of what we had become involved in, was definitely out of character for us. Unfortunately, at that time I didn't realise the extent of the anti-cult movement. As soon as my parents voiced concern, in our absence, their answers were the exclusive truth for our family's anxious questions. This, along with my cousin's crusade to liberate us, only fuelled that fear.

I was unaware until after my deprogramming that my parents had attempted to kidnap us a year earlier in San Francisco. At that time we had been in the Church for two years. It had not worked as they would only allow it if the deprogrammers had been able to pick up Fiona and myself together and they were told, after they had invested thousands of pounds, this was not possible. There are countless questions I would have liked to have asked my parents about this attempt to kidnap us in San Francisco and my ultimate deprogramming in England. I was never able to; I couldn't bear to reopen a wound that had never fully healed. My relationship with my parents did improve, and they came to love Fiona's and my family very deeply. Both of my parents had a profound impact on our children's lives, such that my daughter's final message to my mum said, 'to Granny my Hero'. I am responsible for much of the pain my parents went through, but the exploitative methods of the deprogrammers and anti-cult movement amplified their hurt a thousand times over. I have come to see shortcomings in the political engine of the UC, but I still believe that what the deprogrammers encouraged my dad to do ate away at him till the day he died. It was something he could not talk about and it was hard for me to bring up. I did apologise for the hurt I had inflicted but it was never enough to completely eradicate all of the pain that was attached to that event.

I was living with a group of friends in a suburb of San Francisco in the fall of 1981. It was about 5 am when we were all woken by a loud banging on the door. Before we had a chance to open it, it was axed in and a slew of police and immigration officials flooded in. They ordered us to stay right where we were and they asked us our names and where we were from. When it got to me, right away they said 'Here's one; grab her'. Bewildered and exhausted, we were herded into a van and driven to immigration. There, we were individually interrogated. As I looked around there was a picture of Rev. Moon with devil horns on and, if I remember rightly, a set of darts to throw at it. I remember thinking *'boy, these guys really hate us'*. I, along with my friend, Pippa, were put into jail with prostitutes, armed robbers and drug offenders. As we became acquainted with the people in our cell they were shocked that we were incarcerated with them, for just overstaying our visas. We were eventually given voluntary departure and after ten days were put on a flight back to England. When we arrived in England, customs tried to separate me from Pippa and Chris (another friend who was asked to leave at the same time as me), but the two of them fiercely refused to leave my side. Eventually we got through, and we were greeted by a horde of press, family and friends all grabbing at us and wanting us to come with them. All of these events were completely out of character for my family, and because of this I was becoming more concerned about who my parents had been talking to. Having settled into the Church Centre, I started to communicate with my parents and even went home a couple of times for a visit. I have no idea why, but they never took these opportunities to restrain me.

It was a beautiful day in March of 1982 and I felt at peace and quite happy; I was on my way to visit an old school friend for tea. Chris walked me to the tube, and his presence thwarted the first attempt to pick me up. Looking back, I recognised two of the abductors while we were walking along Lancaster Gate in London. As I was going up the escalator of the tube station near my friend's flat, I felt an odd sense of unease. However, I dismissed it, as I was feeling too happy. Walking out of the station I saw two men who were vaguely familiar, but I didn't think much about it as my anxieties about being abducted had vanished having already been home. I had a nice cup of tea with my friend, though looking back maybe she had been a little on edge. I am not sure now what time it was when I got up to leave after saying our goodbyes. As I walked down the steps I was approached by two men, one who later told me he was in the Special Air Service (SAS), they grabbed me by my arms and legs and started singing happy birthday. My heart sank. I knew immediately what was happening, though I could barely believe it. My thoughts as I remember went straight to my mum and dad. Where were they? What were they going through, and what could be said that would have me recant my new faith? I had no idea where we were going and knew my captors would never divulge that. In the back of the van was my cousin, who I knew was opposed to my involvement in the Church. She, along with some other guy in the back of the van, anxiously tried to reassure me by informing me that they knew what I was thinking and that they were going to help me. It amazed me how she and the kidnappers professed to know what was going through my head, while in fact they were way off the mark. They searched to make sure I had nothing I could injure myself with, but thoughts of suicide were the furthest thing from my mind. Very quickly it was my urgency to go to the bathroom that bothered me, but they thought it was just a ploy to make an escape. They talked about finding something for me to pee in, which I promptly refused. I promised I would not run, but of course they didn't believe me. At the point I was about to explode, they pulled over. As I got out of the van I could see we were on a motorway. They tied some rope to me and told my cousin to stay right with me. I was so desperate, and as humiliating as it was, it was better than peeing in the van!

By the time we arrived at our destination, I was pretty disoriented, frustrated and anxious about what lay ahead. I was hustled into this small house to be greeted by my parents. I threw my arms around my dad, glad to see him and anxious to alleviate his fears about how I was. He immediately started to cry, saying 'I shouldn't have done this; she's okay'. My cousin, quickly piped in with, 'She is faking it; you can't trust what she's saying at the moment'. My cousin and the kidnappers had no idea what was going on in my head, but they thought they had. Once I had been picked up, I was not looking to run away, from them maybe, but not from my mum and dad. All I wanted was to be alone with my parents and talk to them. But that was obviously not going to be allowed, not for a long time. Once my parents had bought into this, fear and threats by these people had begun to control them.

The room I slept in was small and the tiny window there was boarded up. The bathroom window was also boarded and I was prevented from locking the door. That first night was long. Two guys rotated with each other to sit outside my door, chain smoking the whole time. I was not exactly scared, my parents were there and I knew I would not come to any physical harm, but I didn't sleep much at all that first night. I sensed fear all around me from my parents, the hired hands who had kidnapped me, and my cousin. The deprogrammers, who were former UC members, wanted to be sure it was safe before they came on the scene. They were always careful, with each move that was made, to make sure they could not be incriminated.

The following morning I was introduced to a tall, well-spoken man, who I assumed was the person hired to deprogramme me. After introductions, he quickly launched into his experience of being in the UC. Though there were things I could relate to, the way he thought and many of his choices whilst in the UC made little or no sense to me. I repeatedly reiterated this sentiment and he accused me of being dishonest. I quickly realised that this was a one-way debate and unless I agreed that his emotional torment had been my experience, then he was not open to anything I said. I remember him saying he had a tooth extracted as having it filled was too costly and time consuming. He felt this was how he had been taught to think. I responded by saying, 'That was your choice I would have made a different one'. He was there to break me – nothing less. It was certainly not a safe environment to have delved into questions I might have had about the Church. To extract me from the UC was what he had been paid to do. I noticed he constantly had to reassure my parents it was necessary. I knew convincing me to leave would also confirm for him that he had made the correct decision not to return after his own deprogramming.

The deprogrammers were constantly trying to reassure me they were there to help, to answer my questions and give me space to reflect on what I had become involved with. They were there to provide me with counselling and a chance to see a different side. But in my understanding of counselling, the counsellor is neutral and provides a *safe* place to reflect and come up with one's *own* answers. This was a far cry from my experience; in this environment I felt fearful, manipulated and unable to ask honest questions.

The following week I was barraged with questions, shown videos and, in a variety of ways, emotionally tormented. When my parents were not around, my captors would accuse me of hurting and abusing my parents. If they saw me waver or break at all emotionally, they quickly switched sides to become my comforters, turning events around to convince me that the Church was the real evil and that it had manipulated my mind to make choices I would have otherwise thought abhorrent. Even though I sensed what they were doing, still the constant barrage of questions and attacks on my character began to wear me down and I wanted out. I was never allowed time with just my parents, as I felt the deprogrammers knew I would be able to convince my already unsure parents that I was not 'brainwashed'. What the deprogrammers didn't know was I would not have run. As desperate as I was to get away from them, I did not want to run from my parents.

The days passed and another deprogrammer came to strengthen the attack. This way they could switch off, and at times it felt like they played good cop/bad cop with me. I joked, I laughed and I tried hard not to let it all get to me. At a certain point, they had to move me and I knew they were not at all sure where my mind was at. It was decided I would go to Europe but this time without my parents. Concerned, I got my parents to promise me that on my return I would be allowed to return to the Church. Much of my struggle within my deprogramming was rooted in my love for my parents and not having to cause them any more pain. At the same time, I needed to be free to make my own choices. I was taken to one of the deprogrammer's father's house in France. I was not allowed to go out unless I was with a deprogrammer or the one security person left. One deprogrammer kept a gun and a knife that looked much like a machete at the front door. According to their reasoning, this was in case the Church came to get me. In this way the deprogrammers attempted to paint a picture of a Church willing to go to any lengths to get me back, citing numerous occasions when they had used force in the past. While I was in France, the Church took out a *habeas corpus* order against my parents, asking them to produce me in court. During this time the deprogrammers pressured me into writing a letter saying I was with them of my own volition. They had already informed me that if I ran to get help from the French police (their friends), the police would just return me to them. They accused me of inflicting incredible pain on my parents and if my dad died I would feel responsible. They were right: I would have felt awful, and this was my most difficult time. I can't say I didn't wish the Church would drop the case, but these were not just Church members, they were friends and I knew they were concerned about me, despite what I had been told. All I wanted was to be with my parents alone: no deprogrammers and no Church. I knew together my parents and I could work things out. But it was a tough time for me with the deprogrammers and their friends all trying to wine and dine me at the same time as constantly belittling my faith choices and ability to make my own judgement. I felt bad about not trying to run away, but I still felt I would be running from my parents. Unless I made it through this, someone could come along and convince them to do this again. After a week in France and then another week in Spain, I was on my way back to England.

I was so happy to be back with my parents, we went away for a week to Wales. At this time I gently tried to break it to mum and dad that I wanted to go back to the Church. I felt all their fears, anxiety and pain come flooding back. It was no less than hell; I don't think I slept much that week. I had just gone through so much with the deprogrammers and was desperate for my parents to be completely supportive of my decision, which I think I knew was impossible. I can't say I didn't have plenty of questions I needed answered by the Church or at least somebody, because I was quite a mess. I was torn apart inside and losing faith in myself, though I was still able to give the external appearance of being together. As soon as I felt able, I contacted Pippa and Chris so they knew I was OK and started to help ease my parents into feeling comfortable about me returning to the Church.

It was a nice summer evening; both my parents were out and I was doing the dishes. It had already been a few weeks since I had returned from the deprogrammers the second time. Suddenly I heard this banging on the door and before I could get to the front door, the same security guy came in the back door brandishing a gun, closely followed by one of the deprogrammers. I was quickly rushed out and ushered into a car. I kept asking questions, 'What's happening, where are you taking me?' When in the car, they said that my parents had told them I had decided to go back. I was totally frustrated, angry, hurt and once again trapped and still emotionally exhausted. I don't think I put up much of a fight. Once again, I was on the way to a safe house, but this time one that was not for me but another person they were going to kidnap. Now I could see why the deprogrammers were so worried about my returning. They already had another job in the works and my returning to the UC had the potential of upsetting the plan, especially as I knew the person in question quite well. I believe that my presence in that house did help prevent that person from being kidnapped. Maybe this was in part because I got to meet his parents; though I am not sure I was in a state to coherently say, 'Don't do it'. Once I arrived at the safe house I insisted on talking to my parents and I burst into tears when I heard them on the end of the phone. My parents were furious the deprogrammers had taken it upon themselves to pick me up again. I was so relieved that it was not of my parents' doing, and they instructed the deprogrammers to return me home right away. The deprogrammer was concerned about what I would do when I got back to the UC – would I prosecute him? Convinced I would be pressured into taking him to court he launched into a speech about how this would affect my parents as I would have to take them to court also. I assured them I had no intention of pressing charges, but they were sure I would have no control over my circumstances once I reconnected to the Church.

I did return to the Church, sometime in June of 1982, though I went home a lot hoping to reassure my parents and rebuild my relationship with them and my brothers. I now have a beautiful family that has brought me infinite joy. Though like in any marriage, and raising children, it does not come without struggles and a certain amount of heartache. We did teach our children the UC theology and I taught Sunday School. One of the tenets of the Church was the unity of all religions and this was a large part of what attracted me to the Church. In this vein, as our children grew, we were always open to their own search for truth, and felt if our Church had anything to offer they would see it. My son is still young but feels Buddhism resonates with him. My eldest daughter is in college and is an activist on many fronts but also deeply searching for her spiritual roots. My middle daughter is in college having taken a gap year to participate in various volunteer projects in the USA and overseas. As in any Church, the UC has a political engine that I have come to see as being quite flawed. I am uninspired by the direction the Church is going at the moment. As Rev Moon aged, he became less in touch with the direction of the Church. His children have grown up and have far from embodied any of the ideals I hoped to see. At this point in my life, I am not about to follow any person, but see God and spirituality in a more personal way. I have no desire for my children to be involved in the UC, though they have many friends who are still connected, and there are important values that they have learned through our involvement with the Church. They are incredible human beings filled with love, compassion and a desire to make a valuable contribution to life. I am grateful to them and my constant friend and husband Matti who have enriched and bought infinite joy into my life, so how can I not say I am in some way grateful to Rev Moon?

13 Mindfulness and the YouTube channel of the mind

Maitreyabandhu

Introduction

In 2004 I co-founded the London Buddhist Centre's (LBC) 'Breathing Space' alongside Dr Paramabandhu Groves, an NHS (National Health Service) Consultant Psychiatrist. Both of us had been practising and teaching meditation and mindfulness for many years by then – we were ordained into the Triratna Buddhist Order in 1990 and had been meditating since the mid-1980s – and were inspired to find new ways of sharing mindfulness practice. We were intrigued by the work of Mark Williams, John Teasdale and Zindel Segal in creating Mindfulness-Based Cognitive Therapy (MBCT), derived in part from the work of John Kabat-Zinn. We wanted to learn from their approach and to bring our own experience of many years of Buddhist practice to the teaching and practising of MBCT. Breathing Space not only became a new 'secular' project for the LBC, it became a new venue: we created a dedicated space with its own access in the basement of the Buddhist Centre.

As I explored Williams', Teasdale's and Segal's approach to mindfulness, I was excited by the strengths of MBCT, and by how it could augment and enhance my own understanding and teaching of mindfulness. I also came to see how it differs from the Buddhist teaching of mindfulness. I tried to express both my understanding of MBCT and my experience of a more distinctly Buddhist approach in my two books: *Life with Full Attention: A Practical Course in Mindfulness* and *The Journey and the Guide: a Practical Course in Enlightenment.*

The following essay briefly outlines a Buddhist approach to mindfulness. As mindfulness is primarily something you *do* and not a scientific theory, psycho-educational tool or mental health intervention, I've tried to write it with the everyday, non-academic reader in mind.

Mindfulness and the Buddha

Buddhism begins with Siddhartha Gautama gaining Enlightenment whilst, as tradition would have it, sitting in meditation under a peepal tree on the full moon night of April/May, 2,500 years ago. In that moment Siddhartha became the Buddha: 'one who is awake'. The experience of Enlightenment transcends all egoistic clinging – it is a wordless, concept-less illumination. Most often it is said to consist in wisdom, compassion and unlimited energy. All genuinely Buddhist thought and practice derive from that experience and from the teachings that followed from it. The Buddha is not a theoretician; he's a *thinker*, yes, but not a metaphysician. In fact, the Buddha's teaching constituted a radical departure from the abstract, metaphysical and speculative thought of his day. The Buddha's teaching (most commonly referred to as the 'Dharma') is practical and pragmatic, method rather than doctrine.

The Buddha taught individual men and women how to make progress towards Enlightenment. He said his only concern was 'suffering and the end of suffering', so his teachings are addressed to the individual and to their psychological, social, spiritual and existential suffering. The Buddha's Dharma seeks to end *all suffering*, especially the suffering caused by egotism, selfishness and spiritual ignorance; it is not therefore a religion in the usual sense of the term. 'Religion' tends to be inseparable from belief in some sort of divine agency or God (which is alien to Buddhism). But then neither is it a philosophy in the abstract, academic sense. It is a path of human growth and change – from where we are now to Enlightenment itself. One vital dimension of the Buddhist path is mindfulness.

The model I introduce below is just one way of approaching the Buddha's experience. It is not an explanatory theory, although it does rather look like one. The best approach to it is *suggestive*: how might it help me make sense of my life? I have based my approach on an ancient Buddhist *sutta* (literally 'thread of discourse') called the *Honeyball Sutta*, which describes how our mind is patterned and structured.[1] I've kept quite a lot of the original Sanskrit technical terms for the sake of clarity, but I've tried to make the material of the *sutta* as relevant to today's world as possible. Primarily, I've wanted to stress the *practical* nature of mindfulness. Mindfulness is something you train yourself in, something you *practise*: its meaning and usefulness can be found only in that.

The YouTube of the mind

What pulls us away from our human depths – from a life of awareness, kindness and appreciation – is the mind's automatic, associative chatter. This self-talk is reflected in our technology. If I watch something on YouTube, the browser will come up with a whole selection of recommended related clips. Much of the time this is what our mind is like. We habitually click on our inner YouTube, building up our very own playlist of favourites. So when we're bored or not attending to lived experience, we'll automatically revert to our inner playlist – we play the kind of films we've played before. The more we get thoughtlessly preoccupied by our playlist, with its competing dramas, justifications, opinions and fears, the more divided and fragmented we become.

The Buddhist word for this is *prapañca*. It's a very useful word. It helps make a distinction between what we might call 'integrated thinking' and 'alienated thinking'. It helps us understand that it's not *thought* that's the problem; it's how aware or unaware our thinking is. *Prapañca* means 'mental proliferation'. It's the mind spreading out and connecting 'this thing' with 'that thing' – the present with the past, the past with an imagined future – and then coming up with a view or story to account for the experience we're having. *Prapañca* is associative, unaware and hankering. In Buddhist tradition, *prapañca* – whether expressed in happy inner burbling, or painful inner wrangling – is always limiting.

Prapañca is the mind ranging around trying to come up with reasons that 'explain' our experience – especially experiences we don't understand, find ambiguous or threatening. So, for instance, if we meet someone and ask them out, and they say 'Yes', we'll find our mind filling with stories about how it's going to go. Depending on whether we tend towards optimism or pessimism, we'll construct 'Happy Ever After' narratives or 'I Bet It Won't Work' stories. Let's imagine that we text them with a suggested venue. But they don't get back to us. We keep checking – an hour later, two hours later, a day – no reply. This is ambiguous. It's not clear what the text-silence means. So we find ourselves compelled to ruminate – to go over scenarios in our head in order to come up with possible causes, motivations and conclusions.

Then let's say he/she texts us back: 'Sory not bin well. Wil txt u later'. No 'luv', no 'x x'. This is painful (but still ambiguous). And, depending on our personal history, mental habit patterns and state of mind, we'll come up with blame narratives, or 'I'm too good for him/her'. If one of our mental habits is to feel down, we'll start to think 'Why does this always happen to me?'

All this is our mind trying to be in control of painful feelings – the assumption being that if we can *just sort them out in our head,* they won't hurt. We feel compelled to think, but our thinking is prejudiced, even contaminated, by our underlying assumptions, life history and worldview: much of which will be unconscious. The *prapañca* we drift into will tend to take place just below the level of our awareness, so it will be difficult to spot. And the fact that our thinking is automatic and habitual increases the likelihood of our not noticing it *as thinking.* Because our inner monologues are so familiar, we take them to be self-evidently true.

We assume the clips we play on our inner YouTube channel are reliable accounts of our experience. So when we say to ourselves 'Nobody fancies me' or 'Why did I make that stupid joke?' we think the situation itself has caused our painful emotions, when in fact it's our *interpretation* of the situation we're reacting to. How we interpret varies enormously, depending on how we feel. If we're feeling low, for instance, we'll pick up on and elaborate the most negative interpretations. Even being tired will distort how we interpret things – we'll see things differently in the morning.

When I teach MBCT to prevent relapse into depression, I use the example of waving at someone in the street and them not waving back. I ask people how they feel when they imagine that scenario. Someone will tell me it makes them worry about the last time they saw that person and, 'Oh no! What did I say? How have I upset them? Now I'm losing another friend because I'm such a misery guts'. Someone else will insist 'It's their loss', while another participant will say, 'Don't be silly they just didn't see you!'. One class nearly got into an argument about what *really* happened in the imaginary scenario! We mistake interpretations for observations, thoughts for facts (Williams et al. 2007: Chapter 1).

Prapañca is 'alienated thinking'. It's not our fault. We're not *doing it.* After all, we don't wake up one morning and say to ourselves 'I was going to have a lovely day but I've decided to dwell on feelings of being thwarted and over-looked'. *Prapañca* is characterised by unawareness and is alleviated by an ongoing commitment to mindfulness.

'Integrated thinking' is founded on awareness. It means being in touch with our feelings of disappointment, indignation or dismay (in the case of our text message), and consciously deciding how best to act. Awareness means owning our habitual stories and interpretations and remembering that they are 'thoughts not facts'. So instead of firing off a curt text, or going into a big sulk, we notice what's happening, remind ourselves that what we are experiencing is an *unpleasant arising* and that as yet, we don't know the truth. We might even decide to text back: 'Hope U feel better soon (smiley face) x x'.

Cultivating a 'fit mind'

To live a valuable and fulfilling life we need to cultivate a 'fit mind'. Cultivating a fit mind is like cultivating a fit body: it's gradual. It can't be forced. If you decide to run a marathon, you need a training schedule to increase your stamina, you need to look for guidance, and you need to make sure you do enough stretches and warm ups. Developing a fit mind is even more demanding than developing a fit body – it takes time, perseverance and patience.

When I first came to Buddhism, I was all over the place! I could be the life and soul of the party or locked in depression. I could be charming or cruelly sarcastic. I was talkative and yet I harboured guilty secrets. I wanted to be famous and I didn't like myself. It took me years to develop a fit mind. So the first thing to emphasise is: our actions modify our life. If I train myself to act in a positive, helpful, intelligent way, I will gradually transform my future. Just as I can train for the marathon, I can train for a fit mind.

By cultivating a fit mind, we gradually become calmer, more focussed, friendlier and more uplifted. Our experience starts to feel smoother; there's more of a sense of inner harmony and continuity. We feel more aesthetically alive – we're quicker to appreciate nature, for instance. And as we make progress we start to feel clearer, less muddled by irrational guilt and inner conflict. We become less defensive and narrow-minded: our thinking becomes more pliable, flexible and creative.

Our first task, then, is to develop a fit mind. This begins with cultivating integration. Integration means being collected rather than dissipated, unified rather than fragmented. The experience of integration is the experience of wholeness. It is reminiscent of the afterglow we experience when we've been deeply immersed in something positive – that sense of everything coming together. Integration is the opposite of channel-hopping or flicking through newsfeeds. It's inner fullness, as opposed to the emptiness we can feel when we finally turn off the computer.

Mindfulness: learning to step out of thought

Cultivating mindfulness is the royal road to integration. By 'cultivating mindfulness' I mean being aware of our present-tense experience rather than being lost in *prapañca*. The practice of mindfulness unifies our energies and gives us access to a much more direct and full-blooded experience of life. Mindfulness is something we *do* – imperfectly, inadequately much of the time – but something that gradually transforms our life.

Mostly we're not mindful. We want to savour the food we're eating but we keep slipping into daydreams; we try to enjoy our morning shower but we get obsessed with winning an argument in our head – in other words we endeavour to be aware, to be truly alive, but we keep drifting off. So the first thing to emphasise is: '*That's what human minds are like*'. The fact that we keep sliding into fantasy or rumination is not a personal problem; it's just *prapañca* doing its thing. So we need to nurture an amused, benevolent attitude to the 'stuff and nonsense' that goes through our head. We need to acknowledge it and train ourselves in coming back to a more direct mode of being.

We need to train ourselves in noticing *prapañca* (mental proliferation), without inner criticism. This might sound easy enough, but we so often jump in with habitual (and again, automatic) judgements about the contents of our mind – criticising ourselves for having 'bad' thoughts, worrying about them, telling ourselves we shouldn't be thinking them and so forth. This exacerbates our *prapañca*. It sends us into a spin. We think something, then think we shouldn't think like that, then think we shouldn't be telling ourselves off for thinking that...*prapañca* bouncing off *prapañca* bouncing off *prapañca*. For some people, especially those who are prone to feeling low, harsh inner criticism becomes an automatic response to painful thoughts and unpleasant sensations. As we cultivate mindfulness, we start to realise that we cannot *think* our way out of thought.

The basic, elementary, practice of mindfulness is twofold: noticing the mind going off into *prapañca* (without condemning ourselves for it) and using *prapañca* as a cue to tune in to the direct sensations of our body. To step out of the YouTube channel of the mind, we need to tune in to the body. Each time we do this, we create more space around our repetitive, proliferating mind. This is the first practice: noticing the success fantasy or the sob story and stepping out of that into the direct sensations of the body. After all, our body is not a thought; it's a *sensation*. Telling ourselves 'not to think' is just another thought; wishing that our mind 'wasn't so noisy' or thinking 'If only I was less scatter-brained' only makes the mind noisier and more dissipated.

The answer to all those painful noisy, distracted, hankering, surplus thoughts is simply to *feel* the body, directly, over and over again.

As we train ourselves to notice *prapañca,* and to step out of it into mindful awareness, we start to develop a 'fit mind' – a mind that is unified rather than fragmented, focussed rather than distracted. At first all we're trying to do is notice when the mind goes and then, as best as we can, turn towards the direct feeling-sensations in the body. That's all. No 'trying to make the mind go blank', no trying to be a better person or solve the problem of our unhappiness (if we are unhappy), just this really simple practice. We're not even cultivating mindfulness in order to relax. We're not setting *any kind of goal* – because when we do that, we so easily become over-concerned with achieving that goal and this becomes another automatic judgement: 'I just can't relax', 'It's not working', etc. Mindfulness is a *'Just Do It'* practice.

Feeling-sensations: 'Martha says I can't draw'

I've been describing how most of the time, we're elsewhere – planning, wool-gathering, comparing, fantasying – and I've said that the Buddhist word for this is *prapañca.* I've said that *prapañca* is often taking place just below the surface of awareness, so it's hard to spot. It's as if we unthinkingly board a train of thought and only come to (sometimes with a jolt) when we arrive at the station called 'Depression' or 'Bad Mood' or 'Now Look What You've Made Me Do!'.

Our mind, turning over in *prapañca,* is under the influence of our underlying habit patterns, personal psychology and life history; and this distorts how we experience our experience. Eventually we come up with an explanatory story, a version of events that seems to 'justify' our version of things. The mind clicking into place like this, coming up with a rough and ready theory for why we feel the way we feel, has a very long Sanskrit name: *prapañca-saṃjñā-sankha* or 'settled construction'.

Prapañca-saṃjñā-sankha is how we make sense of experience, but it is extremely biased. Because we're looking at life through a filter of views and stories, we keep getting those stories confirmed. If something matches our stories, we'll notice it (and exaggerate it); if it doesn't fit, we *won't* notice it or we'll find reasons to discount or minimise it. So we end up with more and more evidence to back-up our assumptions and narratives. These 'secondary constructions', arise from old, overused modes of thinking (*prapañca*) but they can also be given to us from outside.

When Alex, my partner's eldest daughter, stopped drawing, she told me her best friend Martha had told her she couldn't draw (Martha was seven and hardly David Hockney!). I told Alex 'I went to art school so I *know* you can draw' but she wasn't convinced. Eventually I started doing a drawing myself and after a while she climbed on my lap and joined in. Finally she said 'I don't know why I believed Martha…'. Had someone not found a way of getting her to draw again, the idea 'I can't draw' might have become a statement of fact.

Confronted with being asked to draw, she would have felt uncomfortable and this would have confirmed her feeling that she couldn't draw. Her picture not looking good straight away would reconfirm her uncomfortable feeling and make it difficult to make mistakes and therefore learn. The constructions we have ('I can't draw') create the world we experience.

This is difficult to spot. We're trying to *use* our mind to *see* our mind. We're trying to step back and look at what's going on, instead of *being* what's going on. We can do this already to some extent – we can say to ourselves 'I'm stressed', 'It's my time of the month', 'I don't know why I believed Martha', but usually our awareness flickers like a badly fitting light bulb. The aim of mindfulness is to have the light on all the time.

We need to keep stepping out of our secondary, highly constructed stories (*prapañca-saṃjñā-sankha*) into directly felt experience. 'Directly felt experience' is made up of three things. Firstly, we come into contact with things – we see things, hear things, touch things, smell things. Buddhism includes 'thought' as something we come into contact with (the mind is the sixth sense in Buddhism). So we come into contact with a memory or an idea. The Sanskrit word for this contact is *sparsa*. Secondly, everything we come into contact with – the snow on the roof beyond my window, the smell of toast, the thought of phoning a friend – *feels* like something: feels pleasant, unpleasant, or somewhere in between (i.e. neutral). The Sanskrit word for this is *vedanā*. Thirdly, all experience entails some degree of interpretation or labelling – 'mummy', 'warm', 'dark'. This capacity to make distinctions is called *saṃjñā*. We share this primary reality with the animal life around us. When a bird sees a cat, for instance, there is eye contact (*sparsa*); that contact feels unpleasant (*vedanā*); and that unpleasant sensation is linked with the knowledge (*saṃjñā*) that this ginger tabby is a threat!

These three foundational elements of direct experience make it clear that every experience *has feeling tone* and this has far-reaching consequences. Everything we see, hear, taste or touch has *vedanā*. Not only that but every idea, thought or memory has *vedanā*. So when I write 'Margaret Thatcher' or 'Abraham Lincoln' or 'Joan Johnson' – coming into contact with those words will feel pleasant, unpleasant or neutral. All of life, from the most abstract theory to drawing a picture of a princess, has feeling-tone: and that feeling-tone will either be pleasant, unpleasant or neutral. Our underlying feeling-tones are patterned by our previous experience, such as being told we can't draw.

But we often don't notice: we unconsciously react. If something is pleasant, we instinctively want to repeat it; if something is unpleasant, we immediately want it to stop; if something is neutral, we distract ourselves or get bored. And reacting like this gets us into trouble: craving to repeat pleasure diminishes the pleasure we experience; pushing away pain (especially emotional or mental pain) makes it worse; distracting ourselves from boredom (neutral feelings) causes us to waste time and comfort eat. *Prapañca* is the mind trying to make sense of our underlying feeling-tone (*vedanā*). It's our mind planning and scheming for more pleasure; trying to work out the causes, meaning and consequences of our unhappiness; and figuring out what to do about our boredom.

Hopefully it's clear how our secondary constructions (*prapañca-saṃjñā-sankha*) – the subconscious theories we fix onto to 'explain' and 'justify' our experience – *distort* our experience. So when I write 'Margaret Thatcher' I experience unpleasant *vedanā*. But I don't really know anything about her. I'm just accustomed to thinking of her as being responsible for various problems in the UK. When I was shouting 'Maggie. Maggie. Maggie! Out. Out. Out!' I thought that *she* was the cause of my unhappiness. Conversely, I have a pleasant *vedanā* when I write 'Abraham Lincoln' but I don't know anything about him either – I've just seen the Spielberg film. And Joan Johnson? Well, you probably have neutral *vedanā* when you read that, but she's my mother!

Feeling-tone (*vedanā*) is the underlying *texture* of life. We build our emotions out of this primary hedonic quality. For example, when we give a dinner party we try to provide our guests with as many pleasant sensations as possible – tastes, sights, sounds, etc. – in the hope these sensations will help our guests get into a good mood. We know it won't guarantee a successful evening, but it is more likely to than burnt Stroganoff! We create our moods and emotions from our underlying *vedanā*. Enough jostling, crowding and having to stand next to someone talking into their mobile will fray our temper. But it doesn't have to. We can stay with the pleasant taste of cheesecake without hankering for seconds; we can feel the discomfort of being in a traffic jam without succumbing to road rage.

This then, is the second training in mindfulness: staying with the arising of pleasant, unpleasant or neutral feelings instead of reacting unconsciously to them by grasping for more pleasure or pushing away pain.

When I asked Alex to draw, she experienced unpleasant *vedanā*. That uncomfortable feeling was based on believing what Martha told her (something Martha herself probably didn't mean). This unpleasant *vedanā* meant Alex stopped drawing. How we behave is based on the mind-constructions we have, which in turn creates the person we become. So the *third* training in mindfulness entails stepping out of the subconscious net of views and stories that shape our interpretations of life.

How we see the world

What is happening in much of our lives is that our primary and, as it were, innocent experience of coming into contact with something (*sparsa*), having an immediate hedonic response to that something (*vedanā*) and labelling the experience (*sparsa*) is distorted by our secondary constructions (*prapañca-saṃjñā-sankha*). Let's look at this is in a bit more detail.

I have already suggested that we mostly can't stay with direct experience; we drift off into *prapañca*. This *prapañca* is really a kind of alienated thinking cut off from actual experience. It is our mind going around in circles trying to work out the meaning and significance of our discomfort. Our *prapañca* eventually clicks into a *view* of our experience, a kind of explanatory theory for why the date didn't work, or why I can't draw.

What is important to notice is that these 'views' or 'explanatory theories' are often given to us from the outside. If, for instance, we have been told 'immigrants are taking our jobs', and if we've come to believe that (perhaps our parents told us that when we were a child) then when we meet someone with a foreign accent or with a different shade of skin, we'll be experiencing those three basic elements of life (*sparsa, vedanã, saṃjñã*) but they will be distorted by our pre-existing 'view'. We'll come into contact with someone's skin colour (*sparsa*), we'll label them a migrant (*samya*) and this will give us an unpleasant aversive feeling (*vedanã*) because our 'settled construction', our *view* (*prapañca-saṃjñã-sankha*) has modified and distorted our experience.

Recently I met the poet Elaine Feinstein. She recounted her first experience of anti-Semitism as a child growing up in Leicester in the 1930s. She was in the school cloakroom having just won a silver medal from the Form Teacher for good work. 'As I was pulling off my coat' she writes 'with the medal proudly pinned to my tunic, a red-faced girl...came up to me and sneered: "My father says you are nothing but a dirty Jew"' (Feinstein 2013: 5). Because our experience is shaped by our views – 'I can't draw', 'Migrants are taking our jobs' 'My father says…' – our direct experience is modified, often for the worse. The common sense assumption is that we have experience with views floating around in it, whereas actually what we have are views with experience floating around in them. By 'views' I don't just mean everyday beliefs and opinions – though I include them – I mean something much more like the deep, pre-conscious assumptions and presuppositions that fashion our life. In this deeper sense, the views we have create the life we live. The world – Buddhism tells us – has the tendency to conform to our *view* of the world. If we've been brought up to think that 'immigrants are taking our jobs' for example, or that there's something wrong with being Jewish, we'll keep finding 'evidence' to back that view up.

It's interesting to note that the model I am drawing on for this exploration of mindfulness is from a *sutta* in which the Buddha was asked to explain the causes of social unrest, disharmony and violence. The Buddha obviously wanted to explain how our views shape the experiences we have. The world we live in is view-laden – from ideologies like Marxism to beliefs such as Christianity; from world views such as consumerism to the myth of Psyche and Eros; from the doctrine of transubstantiation to anti-Semitism; from Kant's *Critique of Pure Reason* to the opinion of our friends. The Twentieth Century especially was a century blighted by ideologies – from National Socialism to State Communism and Maoism. History shows how our natural human sympathies can be blunted by our ideas, so much so that even good people will act inhumanely just because of a thought they have.

Our views are not necessarily overtly stated or even consciously held, they are woven into the fabric of society and into the background noise of our mind. We imbibe them unconsciously and from an early age, and we take them to be statements of fact not world views and life-attitudes. The views we are haunted by change with changing history, from belief in a creator god to venture capitalism. This changing 'climate of opinion' powerfully influences how we make sense of life.

Holding Maitreyabandhu's hand

Recently I went to collect Alex from school. She walked out of the playground in front of me and wouldn't hold my hand. She said, 'I don't like you picking me up because no one knows who you are; you're not a daddy or a granddad'. I suggested 'uncle' but she said, 'I've already got three uncles'. She moaned 'Everyone's staring at us'. To ask her what *she* thought would have been fruitless. She thought what she thought the others in the playground thought. She was just eight – but when it comes to views, we never get much older than that. We pick up our beliefs from the playground of our social milieu – they'll determine whether or not we'll hold Maitreyabandhu's hand.

We have views that arise out of our personal history and psychology. We might think that there's something intrinsically wrong with us; we might have a hang-up about authority or neurotic views about our health; we might be aggressively sceptical or believe that all we need to do is *be*. Whatever our underlying views, they will linger like low-level viruses, shaping how we experience our experience. Our views are therefore difficult to spot and hard to change. Usually we don't realise how attached to our views we are until someone challenges them.

We also have views that are given to us by the social-political climate that surrounds us. Modern technology – with its Facebook feeds and Twitter accounts, its news channels and chat rooms – is particularly (and sometimes dangerously) adept at disseminating a vast plethora of views, opinions, prejudices, suspicions, rumours and theories, which we pick up unknowingly and often uncritically. Most of our thinking, from this point of view, comes from someone else. The views we pick up from the world shape our experience of the world, as Elaine Feinstein and millions of others have discovered to their cost.

And we also have innate views; views that are foundational to lived experience. We build our sense of ourselves around a deep instinctual view of being an 'I', a 'me'. Out of this fixed sense of 'me' comes the particular kind of 'me' – a man or a woman, a this-sort-of-person or a that-sort-of-person. We then go about trying to protect and enhance the self we assume we have, and this generates aversion for anything that seems to threaten 'me', and craving for anything that might enhance 'me'. Whatever suggests that the self *isn't* fixed and permanent we tend to ignore. And this ignorance is active – it's our instinct not to look at the facts of life: for instance, at sickness, old age and death.

Our views – whether 'swallowed' as propaganda, picked up from mass media, caught from our work colleagues, or imbibed with our mother's milk – dictate the sort of experiences we have. Experiences that match our underlying views will show up to us, whereas experiences that don't, won't. This is because we see our world through the constructions – *prapañca-saṃjñā-sankha* – we have about it. So if we have a view that states 'no one loves me', we'll keep finding evidence to support that. When friends insist they *do* love us, we'll find ways of disbelieving them. In this way our views govern our life.

When we become suspicious of someone, for instance, everything they do will seem to confirm our suspicions – we're on the look-out for signs that our suspicions are justified and this will prejudice our awareness. Take witchcraft, for example. If you suspect that a particular old lady is a witch, your suspicion will fatally (for them) affect your awareness. If she seems odd or forgetful, that will confirm your suspicion; if she tries to explain her behaviour you'll think she's explaining it away; if she denies it you will think she is lying; if she doesn't say anything you will think it is because the accusation is just; if she seems sweet-natured you might think she is hiding her sorcery behind a veil of charm. An estimated 70,000–100,000 executions of older women took place in the years between 1400 and 1700 because the idea of 'witchcraft' haunted the Western imagination.

The views we have are the net in which we *catch* experience, the way we make sense of the vast range of impressions bombarding us. If our views are cynical, paranoid or prejudiced, we'll see the world through those views. The question is how vehemently we hold on to our views. How irrationally or belligerently do we argue for them?

Some of the views we hold are inimical to human fulfilment, some are harmless enough, others are helpful. The Buddha had no views. He didn't live on the basis of a belief, assumption, or theory. But we are not Buddhas. We need to become aware of which views hold us back and which views help us. Helpful views tend to be held more provisionally, while unhelpful views tend to be more defensive and dogmatic. Like Alex not holding my hand on the way through the playground, how we behave depends on our views.

Mindfulness: three initial trainings

Let's review where we are in terms of the *practice* of mindfulness:

1 The first training in mindfulness is to notice our driven, unaware, associative mental chatter (*prapañca*) and step out of that into direct experience – especially body sensations.
2 The second training is to notice the direct feeling-sensation of experience (*vedanā*) and to learn to stay with those feelings instead of trying to push away unpleasant feelings, grab at pleasant feelings, or fruitlessly distract ourselves from neutral sensations. We train ourselves to *stay with* direct feeling-sensations instead of spiralling off into stories *about* them.

When I teach mindfulness at the LBC, for instance, I ask people to make one of their daily walks – to the bus stop or tube station, say – into a 'mindful walk' in which they notice their mind spinning off into *prapañca* and practise coming back to the simple building blocks of experience: *vedanā*. I also suggest that they should turn a daily mealtime into a 'mindful meal' – once again using it as a cue to learn how to step out of thought, planning and rumination into the actual *taste* of the food.

3 The third training is to see what 'settled construction', what 'view' is shaping our experience. This is hard to do and implies quite a high degree of awareness as well as emotional positivity. At the very least, on the basis of (a) noticing *prapañca* and stepping out of it into direct experience (especially the body) and (b) staying with the feelings (unpleasant/pleasant/neutral) we are experiencing, we can (c) make wise choices about how we act.

'I'm not going to be able to get off!'

I want to conclude by looking in a bit more detail at making 'wise choices'. I have already touched on this but I want to look at it in more depth. I want to emphasise that not all our thinking is *prapañca*. Sometimes we usefully reflect: we realise we're overtired and that that is why we're feeling grumpy; we realise we're stressed and need to calm down; we make the right decision to turn off the computer and go to bed! The Sanskrit word for this capacity to be self-reflective is *vitarka* – *'tarka'* means 'reason', the ability to make connections and distinctions, and '*vi*' means 'divided', in the sense of stepping back from something and reasoning about it. *Vitarka* is our capacity to reflect and make choices about how to respond and behave. This faculty of *vitarka* – which we could translate as 'integrated intelligence' – is what we are developing when we practise mindfulness. It is often underdeveloped, but it is our greatest gift.

In my experience as a mindfulness teacher, many people tend to get stuck in repetitive inner narratives and circular thinking. This ruminative tendency is our attempt, as mentioned above, to solve the problem of pleasure and pain – how can I have more pleasure? Why am I experiencing pain? What is its cause? How can I avoid it in the future? The more complicated our life is, the more pleasant/unpleasant/neutral feelings we experience, the more we will feel compelled to make sense of them in our mind. But our capacity to 'make sense' of our pleasure and pain is often distorted by pre-conscious views, prejudices, life-attitudes and habits.

But we also have *vitarka*: the capacity to step back from experience and decide how best to act. *Vitarka* can face in two directions – it can face *back* into direct experience, encouraging us to directly feel and experience it; and it can face *forward* into *prapañca* and *prapañca-saṃjñā-sankha* ('secondary constructions', 'settled views') and help us deconstruct the views and habits that are distorting our life. It can help us tune in to direct experience and help us deliberately stop ourselves going off into *prapañca*; and it can help unpack the assumptions, prejudices and views that are underlying our *prapañca*. As such *vitarka*, discriminating intelligence, is a vital and distinctively human quality.

An example might help. I live in London and often travel on the tube. The tube – as everyone who has travelled in London knows – is often very crowded. So it's not uncommon that when you get to your stop you find yourself marooned in the middle of the carriage a long way from the door. Not only that but through the windows you see more people jostling to get on. So we can start spiralling off into *prapañca*, into thinking 'I'm not going to be able to get off!', 'The train is going to leave with me still on it!', 'I'll be late!' Just to add to our discomfort the carriage is often hot and stuffy and we are standing in the aisle. Meanwhile those on the platform might also be in *prapañca* 'Oh no, the train is *packed,* I'll never get on!'. So we start using our elbows trying to get *off* while those on the platform do the same to get *on*. All this can lead to quite a bit of unpleasantness – I've even seen people hit in this sort of scenario. And it is all based on the basic feeling of discomfort (*vedanā*) that arises as our train arrives at our station.

I remember one occasion of *'I'm not going to be able to get off!'* very distinctly. I remember tuning in to my direct experience of discomfort (*vedanā*) and remembering that it is just a feeling of discomfort and that never, in all the years I have lived in London, have I *not* been able to get off at my stop. Even if I *didn't* manage to get off – well, what's the big deal? – I'd just have to get off at the next stop! Nobody dies. As soon as I thought like this my feeling of discomfort disappeared and I made my way in an orderly manner to the sliding doors.

This little story shows what *vitarka* is, what 'discriminating intelligence' means – it is this ability to feel what is going on and to intelligently reflect on what would be the best course of action. It is putting things into perspective. It is making choices, based on direct experience, about how to respond to experience rather than reacting to it along the habitual lines of our alienated, driven thinking (*prapañca*). As we develop mindfulness as we become increasingly integrated and aware, our *vitarka* becomes increasingly non-verbal and responsive. As we cultivate a 'fit mind' – a mind 'fit for purpose' of living a fruitful, fulfilling and helpful life – *vitarka* becomes more and more our established mode of thinking, responding and reflecting. *Vitarka* is 'integrated intelligence' – integrated with our direct sensory experience, our body and our feelings. *Vitarka* is also the faculty we develop that *challenges* our stories, the 'secondary constructions' and 'views' we've become identified with. Living in *vitarka*, this integrated and intelligent responsiveness, is the aim of mindfulness.

The Buddha's teaching of mindfulness

According to Buddhist tradition the Buddha's last words were *'Vayadhamma sankhara. Appamadena sampadetha'*. Those around him near the end would have waited for one last teaching; they would have remembered and treasured those words and repeated them often. Other people would have asked what the Buddha's last words were and, similarly, stored them in their hearts. So it seems to me quite possible that *'Vayadhamma sankhara. Appamadena sampadetha'* is what the Buddha actually said.

Even now, we're fascinated with last words. Our fascination surely stems from a sense that last words are *deepest words*: the summation, the view of the whole of life from the end of life. The Buddha must have known that his last words would be remembered and carried, quite possibly intact, through the centuries. And his last words were 'All conditioned things are impermanent. With mindfulness strive on'.

These last words have three essential elements: impermanence, striving and mindfulness. If we had to reduce the whole of Buddhism to one word that word would be *impermanence*. The fact of impermanence is the weak spot in reality. It's as if there's a great wall – like the Great Wall of China – between 'me-as-I-think-I-am' and 'reality as-it-really-is'. Mostly that wall is insurmountable. But it has a weak spot, and this weak spot is the fact of impermanence: if we see impermanence deeply enough, we'll find ourselves on the other side of the wall; or rather we'll discover there never was a wall in the first place. This might sound rather mystical; let me briefly try to explain.

Buddhism is not saying that 'all things are impermanent' in the metaphysical sense; it's not saying that impermanence *is* reality. Buddhism isn't advocating a kind of stoicism in which we simply learn to accept that things change, that we'll lose everything you have. It's saying that if we attend to our experience with that *attitude* – that everything is changing, is in a state of flux – then a new kind of consciousness arises, one that is freer, lighter, more liberated and more in tune with how things really are. Seeing things as impermanent is another view, another way of looking. Looking at life in this way helps us discover the nature of things. It is a doorway into a new consciousness; it is not a statement about the ultimate nature of things.

So the Buddha was stressing impermanence, for pragmatic reasons: to remind us of the urgency of our human situation. In his last words he also emphasised striving. The path of Buddhism is essentially one of effort. Of course we need to learn *how* to make effort in a mature, non-neurotic, non-driven way, but nevertheless we need to strive. The Buddhist life means taking initiative and then *keeping the initiative* through thick and thin, highs and lows, good times and bad.

But the word 'mindfulness' is potentially misleading. The word used is *appamadena* (a form of *appamada* in Pali, or *apramada* in Sanskrit). This word doesn't mean mindfulness of body sensations or *vedanā*. It doesn't mean noticing *prapañca* and stepping out of that. Important though they are, the Buddha didn't choose to emphasise *those* aspects of mindfulness at the end of his life. *Apramada* doesn't mean 'being in the moment', *apramada* means: to keep mindful attention in order to guard against unskilful/harmful/unhelpful actions of body, speech or mind. *Apramada* means 'being on the alert for interruptions, temptations, and unskilful states' (Sangharakshita 1998: 145–47). It means a keenness to get on with the things that really matter in the knowledge that there is no time to waste.

Conclusion

In this article, I have tried to give the reader a deeper understanding of mindfulness from a Buddhist perspective (which is, after all, the worldview mindfulness arose from). Mindfulness-Based Approaches (MBAs) – such as MBCT – have helped people discover new and valuable ways of working with stress, depression and addiction. This can only be a good thing. I'm personally delighted that mindfulness is now being taught in a wide variety of settings – from schools to prisons, hospitals to GP surgeries. However, there are problems when we divorce mindfulness from the worldview that mindfulness grew up in.

Mindfulness has always been a vital part of the Buddhist path and all Buddhist schools have taught it. It has always been taught, however, alongside Buddhist ethical practices (such as the taking of the Five or Ten Precepts) and alongside a variety of meditation techniques. Mindfulness is not a path in itself; it needs to be practised in conjunction with the development of positive emotion – such as loving kindness, patience, courage and honesty – and in tandem with a thoroughgoing exploration of the views and pre-conscious theories and assumptions that shape our experience (as I hope my article makes clear). Without this ethical and self-reflective context, without the vision of Buddhism – a vision of a practical path of spiritual growth towards transcendent wisdom, compassion and freedom from egotism – it would be quite possible to teach mindfulness to jewel thieves or assassins. What it perhaps more likely is that mindfulness – divorced from its context – could be treated as merely a relaxation technique or even as a way of ignoring the gross inequalities and suffering in the world around us.

Teaching mindfulness within its Buddhist context gives mindfulness its underlying meaning and value as part of a whole path of practice: a path that encompasses meditation, ethical training, study, reflection and altruism. Taught within its Buddhist context, mindfulness is part of the realization of one's human potential and thereby part of becoming a source of goodness for a suffering and increasingly divided world.

Note

1 *Madhupindika Sutta*: *Majjhima Nikaya*, 18. Pali Text Society.

References

Feinstein, E. 2013. *It Goes with the Territory – Memoirs of a Poet*. Surrey: Alma Books Ltd.

Sangharakshita 1998. *Know Your Mind: The Psychological Dimension of Ethics in Buddhism*. Birmingham: Windhorse Publications.

Williams, M., J. Teasdale, Z. Segal and J. Kabat-Zinn 2007. *The Mindful Way through Depression: Freeing Yourself from Chronic Unhappiness*. New York: The Guilford Press.

Part IV

Some current issues in the counselling field

14 Emotional exchange

Anxiety to hope in two new religious movements

Charlotte Shaw

Emotional transformation is a highly important issue in the two very different new religious groups in London where I conducted fieldwork in 2011 and 2012. In fact, of all the possible motivations and benefits of participating in these groups, emotional change appears to be the most significant. This significance is both quantitative (participants cite issues relating to emotional health more than any other objective or benefit) and qualitative (this type of well-being is readily understood as important for every area of a human being's life [Strauss 2005: 13, 31]).

One of the groups is a yoga collective called Shanti. It meets at the Shanti Yoga Centre in the heart of Kensington. At the time of fieldwork, Shanti offered a wealth of different types of yoga classes, the majority of which took place during standard working hours, i.e. 09.00 to 17.00, Monday to Friday. Some of these classes (such as *ashtanga*, *hatha*, *vinyasa* flow, gentle and *kundalini*) are permanent fixtures of the timetable and led by resident teachers. Other classes (such as anti-gravity, de-stress, naked, travel recovery, pregnancy and kids yoga) are workshops whereby an external teacher 'hires out' the centre. As a collective, the practitioners at the centre have numerous demographic factors in common. The vast majority of students are female and of white ethnicity. The age of most of the attendees falls within the late 20s to early 40s. The majority of the women I spoke with in this context (with two exceptions) are wives and mothers and not in paid employment; their families can afford for them not to work.

The other group is a Sufi dance group called the Sufi Order, which is part of the Sufi Order International. Fieldwork took place at the London centre in Warwick Avenue, which is the informal headquarters of the whole of the UK Order. The main classes at the centre take place one after the other, between 18.30 and 21.15 on Monday evenings. The first class is an hour of Sufi-dancing, during which the group attempts three or four dances each week. The message class, which follows the dance, is a form of verbal address, during which one of the leaders of the Order may focus on the teachings of Hazrat Inayat Khan, or cite other religio-spiritual sources, including scriptures from dominant world religions. At the end of the 'message', the group is encouraged to share their thoughts and impressions. This time of reflection might also incorporate practices such as meditation, visualisation, breath work or dervish whirling.

The dominant demographic factors of this collective are different from the common traits which are noted as 'typical' within the Shanti context. For instance, there is a greater balance between the genders; there is not notably more of one gender than the other. The Order is also more ethnically diverse, with more people of white ethnicity than any other single ethnicity, but not necessarily constituting a majority in comparison to all other minorities. The average age of the members is older on the whole, with most of the students being in their late 40s to late 50s. Unlike at Shanti, the Sufi practitioners I spoke with all work in full-time employment.

There are no fixed dogmas in either Shanti or the Sufi Order. Rather, these two groups encourage a flexible and eclectic approach, and reference spiritual ideas that derive from a multitude of traditions. The ability for each individual to pick and mix the ideas that appeal most is typical of organisations that are categorisable as New Age.[1]

Despite the clear import of the theme of emotional transformation in these two contexts, understanding the phenomenon is far from straight forward. Evans-Pritchard claims *any* discussion of emotion leads to chaos because of the inevitable variability, not only within cultures, traditions and collectives but also within a single individual (1965: 44; Asad 1997). Similarly, Durkheim and Mauss also both caution that emotions are difficult to identify with any sense of certainty (Rorty 1980: 104). Beyond the challenge of the complex nature of feelings and psychological states is the issue that, traditionally, researchers of religion often bypass the topic of emotionality. As Riis and Woodhead acknowledge, it is easier to study intellectual and ritualistic aspects of religion (rather than emotional ones) because 'the tools of the academy are honed for the task' (2010: 13).

This chapter seeks to embrace the complexities of studying feeling in religious contexts by addressing the comparative emotional transformations said to occur by the two groups of practitioners at Shanti and the Sufi Order. This enquiry asks: what may generate the alleged shift from initial feelings of anxiety, stress and dissatisfaction to the subsequent states of hope, acceptance and peace? What techniques facilitate an emotional transformation? What happens during a practice that shifts a person from an initial feeling to a desired one or, if not the desired state, the resultant state which is nonetheless different from the beginning one?

The discussion will open by exploring the emotional contexts of both sets of members at the points of entry into the respective organisations and after a period of involvement with the group. Following these descriptions, the analysis will consider two intervening factors that are enforced by both centres: shared spiritual tenets and dissociation from usual thought processes. It will argue that the techniques are aligned to (what many psychologists would call) mindfulness. However, the experiences of emotional change are interpreted through the language of the spiritual tenets, thereby endowing the transformation with a spiritual status. The chapter will close by assessing the role that this process may have in motivating maintained commitment to the group.

Emotional contexts

In both groups, the informants' descriptions of their experiences of emotion show some commonalities. For instance, many practitioners recall periods of intense upset which appear to prompt or propel attendance at the centre. The majority of informants also present evidence for more positive, favourable emotions which coincide with their involvement with the respective new religious group. This section will consider each emotional context in turn.

Heightened distress: a trigger for participation

During the fieldwork periods at Shanti and the Sufi Order, I began nearly every interview with an attempt to establish a narrative for each informant's involvement with the respective organisation. I hoped the interviewees' own emphases within their chronicles might reveal the elements of experience that were of most importance from their point of view. Sure enough, most respondents did include and prioritise some components more than others. What was unexpected, however, was the common theme of emotional turmoil at the point of entry into the group. The descriptions suggest that feelings of extreme anxiety and despair can move and motivate individuals to begin participating at the centres. Moreover, comparable feelings which arise after the point of entry can spur more regular, increased participation.

Shanti practitioners

The yoga participants did not necessarily use words such as 'distress' or 'turmoil' within their own recollections. However, the often acute portrayals of the time at which they began attending classes at Shanti do commonly indicate these forms of suffering. The experiences of affliction often occur in association with particular adversities, such as a bereavement, divorce or a period of sickness. For example, Micha, one of the participants, describes the turbulent feelings which followed her father's death:

> After my father died, my relationship with my existence changed. I started looking for new understanding. I had to... I had to change my assumption that 'nothing too bad will happen to me'. It changed my understanding of myself as a person. It changed everything... That's when I started to give it [yoga at Shanti] a go. I had to do something. Oh God, I had to do something.

This practitioner makes connections between her father's death, the thoughts and feelings she experienced in response to that event, and her decision to participate at Shanti. In this way, she suggests that an emotional reaction to an occurrence provoked her first attendance at the yoga centre. Five other interviewees also note a painful time of bereavement in conjunction with their early involvement at the centre.

Other informants recount the anguish and sadness from a divorce or other relationship breakdown in connection with the start of their participation at Shanti. During an interview with Audrey she alluded to the distressing circumstances surrounding the dissolution of her marriage:

> I wasn't in the best place when I first came here. [My husband] had met someone else and we're not together now... It was a shock. I was desperate for some peace and I started to do funny things like stare at candles and count in my head just to distract myself. Yoga seemed like a healthier alternative and this is the nearest centre to my house, so that's why I'm here.

Audrey sought out yoga at Shanti as a 'healthy' means of distraction from the 'shock' and pain surrounding a shift in her marital relationship. Four other practitioners spoke about divorce or a 'break up' in association with why they began attending yoga classes. Other common triggers include the anxiety caused by a sick parent (which two students note) and the practitioner having a serious illness or near-death experience (which three informants described).

Many interviewees identify the emotional stimulants that increased participation at the yoga group (post entry) as being of a lesser intensity than the ones at the time of initial involvement. Ironically, the notion that a person would make time to do yoga when they are at their busiest or most stressed is not uncommon. These insights suggest that a more mundane type of anxiety or stress can boost the desire and will to practise yoga. The suggestion here is that yoga can help one to cope with such 'everyday' emotions and experiences.

The Sufi Order practitioners

Many participants at the Sufi Order also reference times of emotional suffering in their descriptions of deciding to become acquainted with the centre. Hence, the Order members indicate similar patterns between unwanted feeling and the inclination to attend. Like much of the Shanti group, many informants from the Sufi group cite specific forms of adversity in their descriptions, such as bereavement, separation, illness or losing a valued job.

Six Sufi Order members note redundancy as the primary explanation for their anxiety and low mood at the time of entering the Sufi group. One informant had been employed by HSBC in the financial centre of London. He depicts how losing his job during the recession impacted his emotions:

> I felt lost in all the aspiration and chasing of the City. Then I got made redundant and realised I wasn't lost before. That aspiration and chasing and my job – that was my identity. *Now* I was lost. That was my spiral going to the bottom. No job. No money. Failure...I knew I had to learn from it to survive it and I started to go to the Order. All of my questions were answered there.
>
> (Andrew)

This practitioner clearly states how his sense of crisis coincided with his decision to join the Sufi Order. Another example of this tendency to associate a time of distress with joining the group occurred during a conversation with another member:

> It's a year this week since I first started coming to this group. I know that because a couple of weeks ago it was the anniversary of the day my wife, well, since my separation and yeah, so I know I started with this lot three weeks after. That stuff gives you a jolt, you know. Pain makes you question what it's all about. You can't just keep moseying along all the time.
> (Matthew)

This participant makes an explicit link between the 'pain' of his separation and the 'jolt' it gave him to seek out a greater sense of meaning, or in his words 'question what it's all about', which we might assume he is attempting at the centre (where he 'started... three weeks after' the separation). The other emotions which informants note in the chronicles of their attendance at the Order include the anxiety caused by severe sickness (which four participants mentioned) and the sorrow of bereavement (which three interviewees spoke about).

The majority of my informants were regular attendees at the site, who were taking part in most of the sessions which the centre offered; however, some of the other members suggested they only attended, or at least attended more often, due to 'day-to-day' tribulations. For example, one practitioner believed her participation at the centre increased due to 'the weekday madness ... when everything's starting to get a bit too much' (Keri). These types of feelings and experiences that spark a rise in motivation to go to the centre are different from the more discrete reactions to a particular change (for instance in connection with a redundancy, separation or bereavement), but similarly result in the individual's desire to attend Sufi classes.

Favourable emotions as a result of participating

The majority of informants described a shift in emotional experience which was brought about by their involvement at the respective centre. Many of the portrayals of the new, welcomed feelings and mental states exude enthusiasm and even a sense of wonder at the efficacy of taking part in the sessions. Even in cases when a practitioner returned to the centre after a long absence, there is typically an expectation that the change in mood and self-perception will surely occur again. Thus, many participants perceive the relationship between participation and favourable emotional outcomes to be a very reliable one.

Shanti practitioners

During an interview with Oscar, who attended two classes a week at Shanti, he asserted that partaking in the yoga lessons transformed his emotional state, his 'relationship with himself' and how he feels about the major components of his life:

> I don't know how [yoga] works, but I know that I'm in my forties and suddenly I have a different relationship with myself … Suddenly I have a different relationship with my mind and how I feel about myself, my work, my wife – all of it feels a lot more positive, a lot easier. I'm a lot happier.

Even though Oscar cannot say why attending lessons at Shanti improves how he feels, he stated that yoga at the centre 'does seem to work' to this end. Oscar recalled a beneficial emotional response and recounted a more positive outlook.

Many other yoga participant insights offer comparable examples of emotional renewal. Arabella, for instance, considers the practice to be her 'secret antidepressant'. She explained:

> I was feeling a bit down for a while. I actually went to the doctor at one point and he said I could go on these antidepressants, or whatever, which I was a bit dubious about because my mother was never able to get off them. And I guess I just thought I'd try this. And I have to say it is quite extraordinary the difference that it can make. All of the heavy sadness, the second guessing yourself, the fears – all of that just lifts. It was such exquisite relief. This is my secret antidepressant.

Arabella's view that Shanti helped her feel better is explicit. She stated that 'it is quite extraordinary the difference it can make' and that yoga can provide 'exquisite relief'.

The emotional developments which Oscar and Arabella described have points of concordance with many other informant accounts. Each participant might employ distinct words and phraseologies, but the notion of a welcomed shift in feeling is a common denominator in all of these descriptions. For instance, terms like 'happier', 'more peace', 'lifted' and 'better' all indicate a sense of a positive emotional change. As the next section shows, the association between participation and improvements in mood is prevalent amidst the Sufi Order participants as well.

The Sufi Order practitioners

Another practitioner from the Order who works as a counsellor spoke about depression from the perspective of an insider who has experienced depression herself as well as from the perspective of a professional observing others. She says a lot of people 'starting on [the Sufi] path' share debilitating feelings, but emotionally transform because 'the teaching [at the centre] is therapy'.

> When I was going through [depression], I just wanted to sleep all the time and everything was too much effort. A lot of people here felt like that before starting on this path. It takes a little while but then there's this turning point and people start having a bit of a spring in their step and their tone of voice changes; it's like a rebirth. The teaching here is therapy. It's more than that as well, but, at least from my professional understanding – and I know because I was here when I was in a bad place – this is, I mean, it can be a lifeline.
>
> (Michelle)

In reaching the assessment that the Sufi Order teaching 'can be a lifeline', the participant refers to some of the psychosomatic changes she perceived in people who attend the centre; according to her they gained 'a spring in their step' and a change in 'their tone of voice'. Although this interviewee states that the change in feeling she identified in other attendees takes a little while, some other informants implied that the change can occur quite quickly, or even that once the change happens the first time, partaking in lessons at the centre is sure to bring about the same shift in emotions again. As one Sufi Order attendee said during a message class: 'I haven't been [to the Order] for a few years but it's the anniversary of my mother's death today and… this place always helps me climb out of my head and helps me feel present and ok again' (Bisma).

This attendee's renewed participation with the Sufi Order coincided with a time when she experienced the 'trigger' of the anniversary of a family bereavement. She recounted the reliability of the experience at the Sufi Order when she noted that the centre *'always'* helped her 'feel present and OK again'. It seems likely that the anticipation of these positive emotional outcomes inspired her attendance on this occasion. Many other members of this group also alluded to a perception of the relationship between participation and emotional benefits. Some of the terms which arose in statements of this kind include: 'calmer', 'more upbeat', 'happier' and 'more optimistic'. Thus, like a large proportion of the Shanti attendees, many Sufi informants utilised words that indicate new advantageous emotional states. This indicates that in both spiritual groups many of the informants recall similar emotional contexts at points of entry into the group and after being involved with the group for some time. It seems likely or at least possible that feelings of heightened negative emotions inspire the participant to explore, or even attempt to transform, his or her felt experience. In this way, negative feelings might motivate participation in the group. Just as the individual's response to external structures and relations had led to unwanted emotions, so the individual sought external structures and relations to change the emotions 'back', or generate new, more preferable thoughts and sensations. Sure enough, in both populations many respondents credited participation in the spiritual group for welcomed changes in mood and thought patterns.

These observations lead to some crucial questions. What sources of solace might the practitioners grasp by partaking in yoga at Shanti or Sufi dance at the Order? How might those sources affect the person's feelings in positive ways, and how might the person's positive feelings affect the sources? The findings from the two sites suggest that significant parts of the answers to these questions relate to shared narratives and techniques that encourage a change in the practitioner's habitual thought processes. The next section will show how these two factors could inform a more positive emotional experience.

Transformation tools

Shanti and the Sufi Order both propound shared notions of 'positivity', 'energy', and 'positive energy' in modes that encourage the practitioner to place hope in systems of social and even cosmological significance. The organisations also emphasise sensual and somatic felt experience in modes that appear to inform a shift in the participant's usual cognitive processes. According to my informants, this shift results in a change in focus that is beneficial for mood and mental health more generally. The descriptions of the cognitive shift highlight many similarities with mindfulness methodologies in the field of psychotherapy. However, participants at the centres most typically speak about the new favourable feelings as evidence for the 'positive energy' tenets.

Shared tenets

Both of the organisations that I studied implement discourses and practices that encourage the student's awareness of three collective tenets: 'positivity', 'energy' and (the combinative) 'positive energy'. Although the nature of the concepts allows some room for individual appropriation, for the most part the members of both groups mutually hold the main components of the concepts in common. As such, the tenets are shared amidst the communities of practitioners, and this generates collective support for the meaning system that the tenets create.

With regards to the tenet of 'positivity', many of the yoga participants and the dance practitioners commonly referred to a 'positive ethos' almost like a theodicy: as a means of making sense of suffering. One part of the shared ethos is the view that suffering is a useful opportunity or 'blessing' from the universe to help the person develop. The other part of the ethos implies that suffering is not inherently negative but is 'merely' the outcome of the individual projecting negativity on to an inherently positive situation from which the person can learn and flourish.

According to the 'energy' tenet, energy exists in absolutely everything. Arguing that energy is the common feature of the wider system of the cosmos, some informants from each group suggest that people can harness energy to achieve higher states of being. Perhaps the most common phrase regarding the nature of energy is: 'like attracts like'. This notion proposes that the quality of one's own energy (i.e. positive or negative) will attract the same quality of energy from the external world. A positive outlook will attract positive outcomes, and a negative outlook will attract negative outcomes. Thus, energy has an almost 'infectious' quality according to this view. The conceptualisations of positivity and energy conjunctively relate to a third tenet: 'positive energy'. This principle is indicative of a cosmological system of attraction in which the positive energy of the person will create a positive life for that person. An outcome of this mutual understanding is the claim that for the good of the self, people should strive to generate, identify and 'give off' positive energy. Some participants' views imply that this conception can result in a subtle collective expectation about how the individual should understand and express emotions. Positive emotions (such as joy and serenity) are indicative of positive energy and are thus welcome at the centres; negative emotions (such as rage and grief) are indicative of negative energy and are thus not welcome at the centres. Teachers will at times suggest that such emotions are anomalies to be 'worked on' through the practices. In both groups, different emotions have different social and public statuses in addition to being an individual, embodied experience (Appadurai 1990: 92).

The yoga and dance organisations promote teachings, anecdotes, courses, readings, quotes and 'mantras' which encourage faith in the three precepts. For instance, with regards to the positivity tenet, on numerous occasions at Shanti, yoga teachers console the group that nothing is inherently negative by assuring that adversity is a 'gift' from the universe to spur spiritual evolution. Comparably, courses at the Order (such as the paradoxically titled 'The Power of Vulnerability' seminars) propound that vulnerability is useful rather than a cause for despair.

The teachers and resources of the two centres also support shared awareness of the energy and positive energy tenets. At Shanti, all of the instructors at times describe the practices as a way of generating more positive energy, which will in turn 'attract' good things. Many of the books for sale in the yoga studio also increase shared consciousness of 'positive energy', including Orloff's text *Positive Energy: 10 Extraordinary Prescriptions for Transforming Fatigue, Stress and Fear into Vibrance, Strength and Love* (2006). At the Order, Sufi teachers frequently interpret textual sources in modes which enforce the infectious quality of energy. For example, during a message class, one leader deduced from a text: 'Rumi wants us all to surround ourselves with positive energy and be wary of the people who drain us'.

These organisational tendencies support hope in the positivity, energy and positive energy precepts. The compatibility of the three tenets allows for faith in a type of system in which suffering is meaningful, being positive is rewarded and energy is cultivatable for one's own benefit. Hope in this system has the potential to console the disheartened practitioner that all is well, and if it really seems that all is not, there are methods available that can cultivate the right energy and in turn attract more prosperous circumstances. Hope in this meaning system might assure, calm and encourage a sense of empowerment.

Encouraging felt experience

In addition to promoting faith in the reassuring tenets, the two organisations also contribute to the participants' emotional shifts by focusing on felt experience. Specifically, the centres encourage the practitioners to 'feel more and think less' by emphasising praxis, heightened sensual awareness and discourses relating to 'heart over head' or 'true self over everyday self'. This approach shows parallels with theories of Mindfulness-Based Cognitive Therapy (MBCT) which claim that breaking away from habitual thought patterns can generate emotional benefits (Segal, Williams and Teasdale 2013). However, the participant often interprets any subsequent experiences of feeling happier as evidence for the 'positive energy' tenets and thus, in this way, the accentuation of felt experience may function not only as an important facilitator of mood improvement but also as a means of motivating continued commitment to the respective groups that promote the tenets.

Taking each organisational tendency in turn and starting with the prioritisation of praxis, at both centres, involvement with the group is very participatory. There are no intellectual requirements. One need not read voluminous books, learn doctrine or even declare hope in positivity and energy. The only expectation is engagement with the (yoga or dance) practice. As Shanti's manager Per says to one group of his students: 'Yoga is a practice. It's about calming mental activity, not increasing it'. Comparably, a teacher at the Sufi Order instructs practitioners to 'not be too cerebral', to 'let your mind have a rest', to 'try to feel it' and to 'come into your body'. It is possible (and to my mind, likely) that it is harder to pursue a chain of thought during active practices like yoga and dance because one is at least partially concentrating on moving and balancing. In consequence, the participant may inevitably 'think less', or, if not less, at least in a different way.

In addition to the prioritisation of praxis, the multisensory stimulants that the organisations present are also likely to enforce the 'feel more, think less' disposition. For example, both contexts engage the sense of smell by lighting scented candles. Some yoga teachers also use scented 'chakra balm', whilst some Sufi teachers bring out incense sticks on ceremonial occasions. The two sites' potentially 'exotic' seeming décor is likely to stimulate the sense of sight. Shanti is filled with statues of Hindu deities, and the Sufi Order space exhibits Persian rugs and Islamic art. The two sets of teachers heighten the sense of touch by making physical contact with the students, either when altering a yoga posture or giving a short massage (as occurs at Shanti), or when encouraging the collective to hold hands during the dance practice or during the dance tuition itself (which takes place at the Sufi Order). Teachers at each centre also heighten audio experience. At Shanti, Sanskrit mantras, a gong and music (such as simulated sounds of the rainforest or Indian devotional songs) are prominent. At the Order, Farsi mantras and live music (using guitar, the grand piano that is on site or an accordion) are popular tendencies. The mentally overwhelmed 'sensation-gatherers' (Bauman 1998: 70–72) might stop thinking in quite the same way while immersing in such a sensually rich environment. The stimulation to the senses brings relief by momentarily distracting the mind from primary causes of concern.

The organisations also encourage the participant to 'think less and feel more' by verbally espousing a distinction. On one side is a superior, experiential truth linked to 'the heart' (at Shanti) or 'the true self' (at the Sufi Order) and on the other side is the fallible mental knowledge of 'the head' (at Shanti) or 'the everyday self' (at the Sufi Order). These dichotomies of 'heart and head' or 'true self and everyday self' suggest an attempt at dividing the felt and the mental. Yoga teachers like Dora encourage students to let go of everything the practitioner was 'thinking about before this lesson', and to instead, focus on the heart and 'to feel [their] way into the present moment'. At the Sufi Order, guides often explain to the attendees that the participant can access beyond the 'error-prone and finite realm of the mental' (Sean) by focusing on the somatic techniques which the Order prescribe.

As has been shown, both field centres accentuate praxis, multisensory stimulation and discourses which divide 'head and heart' or 'everyday self and true self'. These tendencies might support the student in engaging more with feeling and less with thinking, or at least encourage the student to think in a different way. The relationship between thought and emotion has been, and continues to be, thoroughly explored. A dominant claim amongst many cognitive scientists and psychoanalysts (such as Segal, Williams and Teasdale 2013) is that emotion is often inherently joined to thought, with thought typically preceding the emotion. In extension, many of these thinkers state that techniques to break free from usual thought patterns and to 'calm the mind' can be very advantageous for mental health, especially for people who are distressed or depressed (Csikszentmihalyi 1975; Beck et al. 1979; Jacobson and Dobson 1996; Williams and Garland 2002).

MBCT supports the suggestion that shifts in thinking patterns can be very beneficial for happiness levels. This type of therapy uses meditation and other techniques, including breathing and yoga-based exercises to help people 'quiet the mind' and enhance acceptance. MBCT has been clinically proven (Kuyken et al. 2015: 63–73) to be at least as effective as drugs for depression and it is recommended by the UK's National Institute of Clinical Excellence. According to Segal, Williams and Teasdale 'It is also thought to be extremely effective for people who are not depressed but who are struggling to keep up with the constant demands of the modern world' (2013: 278).

The prioritisation of felt experience at Shanti and the Sufi Order might turn the practitioner's attention away from his or her habitual thought processes in comparable ways to what is said to occur during mindfulness practices. This new kind of thinking seems like a probable contributor to the improvements in emotional experience which the informants recount. As such, by encouraging changing cognitive patterns, the organisations are likely to contribute to the favourable feelings which the informants describe.

However, none of the informants I spoke with employed the language of mindfulness therapies to explain the transformations in their emotional states. Instead, many participants cited the changes in feeling as part of their validations of the 'positive energy' system. As Aya, a yoga student at Shanti, explained, her welcomed change in feeling functioned as 'proof': 'The pain actually stops. That's how you know it works. That's your proof. You have to keep that discipline. Keep spreading the word and telling others who are stressed. Keep spreading the positivity. And attracting good energy'.

Aya's assertion that the ceasing of emotional pain is how she knows the system works encouraged her to socially perpetuate the tenets by 'spreading the word and telling others'. Similarly, an infrequent attendee at the Sufi Order said:

> It's like a new perspective. I understand now that I am not my pain. That isn't me. If I'm having a bad week – someone said something hurtful or whatever – and I can feel the dip coming, I make time to go [to the centre] and usually that's all it takes to get me back, feeling alright again, to reconnect to the teachings and feel the energy again.
>
> (Luke)

Like Aya, this Sufi participant associated his 'new' feelings and perspectives with the tenets. According to this view, the principle can impact the feeling and also *vice versa*, the nature of those new feelings informs the maintenance of the tenet. The Sufi Order informant would 'make time to go' to the place where he could access the 'teachings' and 'reconnect' with the tenets in order to feel happier once more. Hence, the new gratifying perspective encourages continued engagement with the precepts and specifically with the spiritual organisation that espouses them.

Although it is only possible to assess expressions of emotion (as opposed to privately felt sensations), these informants' expressions suggest that the centres' therapeutic functions have a profound effect on emotionality and, in turn, the practitioners' desires for involvement with the respective organisations. This effect often inspires regular participation, which can function as a kind of peace-maintenance and misfortune-management. At a time when 'the burden of vulnerability has been recast as an individual problem' for which there is 'minimal social support' (de Botton 2013; see also Riis and Woodhead 2010: 211), Shanti and the Sufi Order offer a helpful approach to managing the human condition in a way that is comparable to how more dominant religious groups (like the Church of England, for instance) do so: providing shared principles and communal practices. However, significantly, Shanti and the Order offer this collective support without requiring the practitioner to affiliate with a religious group or abide by religious rules. This approach is likely to be attractive for many people in a context where affiliation with religious institutions continues to decline and the search for alternative healing techniques continues to increase (Murcott 2005: 36; Heelas 2008: 67–68).

To conclude, at Shanti and the Sufi Order, the practitioners' descriptions of their emotional worlds alluded to a complex and rich area of experience. In both groups, many informants recounted enduring periods of intense undesirable feelings at the time of joining the new religious group and at times of increased involvement with the centre. Intriguingly, informants from both sites also described emotional transformations for which they credited the respective organisation. Nobody can claim with certainty that exactly the same emotional transformation would or would not have happened had the informant never attended classes at the centre or had adopted an alternative approach altogether. When discussing the complexity and variability of the emotional contexts of a collective of individuals, there is no control group for those individuals and their precise emotional circumstances that can offer comparative findings. However, the vast majority of informants (85 per cent from Shanti and 76 per cent from the Sufi Order) are convinced that the gratifying shifts in their sentiments and perceptions are due to their participation in the centre.

A reason why participation may lead to improvements in mood is the combination of the two 'transformation tools' taught at the organisations, which seem to encourage hope and shift habitual thought patterns. The organisations' promotion of faith in the tenets provides a collectively held framework which has emotional benefits for the individual. The centres' prioritisation of felt experience probably accelerates those emotional shifts in ways that resemble mindfulness therapies; however, the shifts are typically 'explained' by employing the framework of the tenets. In this way, the two field centres provide means of addressing some very serious emotional challenges and are said to offer valuable forms of solace and relief.

Note

1 Between October 2011 and April 2012 I collected qualitative data from Shanti; and between May 2012 and November 2012 I gathered qualitative data from the Sufi Order. This amounts to twelve months of field work, with six months spent at each site. The data was collected as part of a PhD study. The methods were: participant observation, conducting interviews (n = 128), and taking notes during group conversations (n = 9). Research participants have been given pseudonyms to preserve anonymity and confidentiality.

References

Appadurai, A. 1990. Topographies of the self: praise and emotion in Hindu India, in: L. Abu-Lughod and C. Lutz (eds) *Language and the Politics of Emotion*. Cambridge: Cambridge University Press, pp. 92–112.

Asad, T. 1997. Remarks on the anthropology of the body, in: S. Coakley (ed.) *Religion and the Body: Comparative Perspectives on Devotional Practices*. Cambridge: University of Cambridge Press, pp. 42–52.

Bauman, Z. 1998. Postmodern religion?, in: P. Heelas (ed.) *Religion, Modernity and Postmodernity*. Oxford: Blackwell, pp. 55–78.

Beck, A., A. John Rush, B. Shaw and G. Emery 1979. *Cognitive Therapy of Depression.* New York: Guilford Press.

Csikszentmihalyi, M. 1975. Introduction, in: M. Csikszentmihalyi and I.S. Csikszentmihalyi (eds) *Optimal Experience.* Cambridge: Cambridge University Press, pp. 3–14.

De Botton, A. 2013. Spirituality and Commercialism (lecture). Southbank Centre, London. November.

Evans Pritchard, E. 1965. *Theories of Primitive Religion.* Oxford: Oxford University Press.

Heelas, P. 2008. *Spiritualities of Life: New Age Romanticism and Consumptive Capitalism.* Oxford: Blackwell.

Jacobson, N. and K. Dobson. 1996. A component analysis of cognitive-behavioural treatment for depression. *Journal of Consulting and Clinical Psychology,* 64(2), 295–304.

Kuyken, W., et al. 2015. Effectiveness and cost-effectiveness of mindfulness-based cognitive therapy compared with maintenance antidepressant treatment in the prevention of depressive relapse or recurrence (PREVENT): a randomised controlled trial. *Lancet,* 386, 63–73.

Murcott, T. 2005. *Alternative Medicine on Trial?* Basingstoke: Macmillan.

Orloff, J. 2006. *Positive Energy: 10 Extraordinary Prescriptions for Transforming Fatigue, Stress and Fear into Vibrance, Strength and Love.* New York: Three Rivers Press.

Riis, O. and L. Woodhead. 2010. *A Sociology of Religious Emotion.* Oxford: Oxford University Press.

Rorty, A. 1980. *Explaining Emotions.* Berkeley: University of California Press.

Segal, Z., M. Williams and J. Teasdale. 2013. *Mindfulness-Based Cognitive Therapy for Depression: Second Edition.* New York: Guilford Publications.

Strauss, S. 2005. *Positioning Yoga: Balancing Acts across Cultures.* Oxford: Berg Publishers.

Williams, C. and A. Garland. 2002. Identifying and challenging unhelpful thinking. *Advances in Psychiatric Treatment,* 8(5), 377–86.

15 Attachment

Buddha and Bowlby

Joe Copestake

Introduction

How do Buddhist beliefs relate to beliefs about close interpersonal relationships? And how do Buddhist practices relate to the experience of counselling? These questions might arise when the counsellor is Buddhist: for example, they may practise meditation in the belief that this will support them to be a better counsellor. Or they might arise when the individual seeking psychological support is Buddhist: perhaps their Buddhist beliefs and practices are affecting their close relationships or *vice-versa*, and this is a cause of confusion or distress. In this chapter I will explore some lay accounts of such situations, and try to relate them to more technical concepts of 'attachment'. This word has weighty implications in this context both for Buddhism and for counselling: but the two use it in distinct senses, conceived independently from each other, and I will illustrate the importance of avoiding potential misunderstandings.

Several studies have shown that the practice of mindfulness[1] in the secular and increasingly fashionable form that has been adapted into a Western psychological framework, is correlated to secure attachment relationships (a term that I will define shortly) and greater compassion.[2] In my experience a mindful quality of attention has parallels with non-judgemental listening, a skill which I developed through being trained as a Peer Supporter by Oxford University Counselling Service. Many therapists and counsellors are integrating mindfulness practice and teaching into their work, finding that an embodied awareness helps to pinpoint problems – a fascinating topic which unfortunately I do not have space to explore here. Unlike most of my fellow administrators of the Oxford Student Mindfulness Society, which runs classes that are entirely secular and science-based,[3] I have spent considerable time exploring Buddhism. Secular mindfulness deploys terminology from cognitive behavioural therapy and neuroscience, rather than the language of non-attachment that is found in Buddhism. In this chapter I will be concerned only with the latter.

I am not a counsellor, meditation teacher or psychologist – my academic training is in religious studies – and this should be borne in mind by the reader. In writing this chapter I have drawn upon a 5,000 word essay that I wrote during my Masters in the Study of Religion at Oxford University, which was entitled 'Attachment, Indifference and Equanimity: An analysis of attempts in recent dialogues between Buddhism and Western Psychology to relate notions of "attachment" to the health of interpersonal relationships'.[4] This essay was concerned with psychological research and ancient Buddhist texts, and in the conclusion to this chapter I will show how it relates to the themes which I will explore here.

The first two sections of this chapter will be theoretical (drawing upon my earlier essay), briefly introducing first attachment theory (a pillar of western psychotherapeutic approaches to relationships) and second Buddhist ideas of attachment. The following sections will explore the interplay between these ideas using a variety of empirical examples. In these latter sections, all sources quoted are primary: they are either reflections on personal experience by myself or an author, or materials that are used in the context of counselling/therapy sessions or in Buddhist meditation instruction or dharma talks.[5]

Unfortunately, I do not have space here to look at different understandings of the self (including the Buddhist idea of not-self),[6] or to explore the research into the extent to which attachment theory holds true across cultures. In the West there is often a divide between the Buddhism of immigrants from Asia to the West, which may attempt to transplant Asian forms of Buddhism unchanged, and forms of Buddhism practised by and for people who may have never been to Asia, that have been created by Westerners who went to Asia and then on returning to the West, tried to adapt what they had learned about Buddhism to their native contexts.[7] My focus in this chapter is on the latter, and as such is largely on meditation – their central Buddhist practice – and its context.

Buddhism often refers to compassion, 'letting go' and the inevitability of change, while when discussing relationships, we hear more about passion, 'holding on' and constancy. This chapter will illustrate how the difficulty that an individual faces is resolved after they find a way to balance these (which does not mean trying to have their cake and eat it). They become complementary rather than contradictory.

Attachment theory – a brief introduction

John Bowlby, a London-based psychiatrist who worked with many emotionally disturbed children, developed attachment theory from the 1930s onwards. The theory's central propositions have received strong empirical support (Gomez 1997: 160), and it continues to be of enormous influence today. Bowlby argued that 'Individuals whose primary attachment relationships in childhood were satisfying and provided emotional security view themselves as lovable, expect positive interactions with others and value intimate relationships' (Goldberg 1999: 362). Bowlby saw infants as alternating between two behavioural systems that he termed 'attachment' and 'exploration' ('caregiving' and 'sexuality' are two other systems described in Bowlby's theory). When an infant's attachment system is activated, they seek proximity to, and security and affection from, the parent; when the exploratory system is activated, the infant is free to play and explore away from the parent. The emotional and physical bonding of healthy attachment behaviour provides stability and security without which the infant cannot engage in the branching out, risk-taking and personal growth of healthy exploratory behaviour. Bowlby's theory was influenced by the theory of evolution through natural selection: infants who form healthy attachments, he held, are more likely to survive. His theory contradicted the previously dominant notion that infants attach to their mother because the mother is the source of food. In 1958, Harry Harlow's study of infant rhesus monkeys which had been separated from their mothers provided experimental support for Bowlby against this older theory. These monkeys were given two substitute 'mothers', one made of wire and one made of cloth. Even when the wire substitute was the only source of food and heat, the monkeys still spent most of their time attached to the cloth substitute, showing that their need for affection and closeness went beyond meeting solely physical needs.

Mary Ainsworth, Bowlby's colleague, devised the famous 'Strange Situation' experiment. This involves an infant, their parent and another adult who is friendly but unknown to the infant. The infant is put through a standard sequence of separations from each of the adults, and the infant's distress and coping strategies are observed. Ainsworth divided these into three main categories, as Susan Goldberg describes:

> In the secure strategy, the attachment system is activated only when the infant's security is threatened (for example, the caregiver departs and the child is left in an unfamiliar place) and subsides to give the exploratory system free rein when the attachment figure (the secure base) returns. In the avoidant (dismissing) strategy, the attachment system is defensively suppressed so that the child appears to be exploring without concern for security, although he carefully monitors the attachment figure. In the ambivalent/resistant (preoccupied) strategy, the attachment system is continually activated at the expense of the exploratory system, even when to all outward appearances the child should be safe and comfortable (i.e. the attachment figure is present).
>
> (Goldberg 1999: 363)

When the attachment figure re-entered the room, the avoidant infant would, for example, play with toys away from them while monitoring them warily. By contrast the ambivalent infant would seek proximity, but also show signs of wanting to punish the attachment figure for the absence. Later research has suggested that it is also possible for one individual to be high in both ambivalence and avoidance: 'such individuals deny support needs, but still experience anxious ambivalence and a desire for proximity' with the attachment figure (Crisp et al. 2009: 116).

Attachment strategies are determined by the quality of caregiving that the infant received. In simplistic terms, securely attached infants had a parent who was sensitive to their needs and distress; avoidant infants had a parent who was more distant and impersonal; ambivalent infants had a parent who was insensitive to their needs and responded unpredictably; children with disorganised attachment styles have had neglecting and/or abusive caregivers which meant they could not develop one of the other attachment strategies (Gomez 1997: 160).

Patricia Crittenden, Ainsworth's student, characterised the behaviour patterns associated with the different styles.[8] In brief, avoidantly attached individuals alternate between compliance (being overly quick to anticipate the desires of others in order to divert attention from themselves, and not disclosing their own feelings out of fear of rejection) and pathological self-reliance, whereas ambivalently attached individuals alternate between feigned helplessness (in order to incur assistance from the attachment figure) and aggressive demands that their needs be met (beneath which lies a fear that they might not be). 'Detachment' as described by Bowlby occurs when an infant is separated from the caregiver for a sufficient length of time such that, after passing through denial and then despair, they repress or disinvest from their relationship with the lost parent and begin to become attached to a new and available attachment figure (Gomez 1997: 162). Such infants tend to attach to whoever is available, rather than to form close bonds with particular others.

These habitual attachment behaviours, and their relationship to the exploratory system, persist outside the contexts of the relationships that formed them. The insecure attachment styles may have been the best strategies that the infant had available at the time, but can be very unhelpful in the context of the adult's relationships in later life, and when they are passed down between generations. Cindy Hazan and Phillip Shaver (1987) were the first to show that attachment theory could be used to understand romantic attachment between adults. Adults who are avoidantly attached to their romantic partner appear to be little concerned with the relationship and to be uncomfortable with intimacy, wary of depending upon them and being depended upon. Adults who are ambivalent towards the romantic partner are particularly prone to worrying that their partner does not love them completely and can be easily frustrated or angered when their attachment needs go unmet. Detachment can also occur among adults experiencing the bereavement of an attachment figure, although they are less vulnerable to it than infants (Gomez 1997: 167).

In therapy, the therapist who works with attachment becomes an attachment figure for the patient/client, and at the same time aims to direct the patient's attention towards painful attachment-related experiences, in order that the patient/client becomes more aware of their own attachment behaviours and better able to regulate them. This is a difficult task as the patient/client will often be highly invested in avoiding doing so and in denying that their attachment style is unhealthy (Muller 2010: Chapter 2).

Buddhist ideas of attachment – a brief introduction

Upadana,[9] or attachment, is a central concept within Buddhism. Richard Gombrich writes that

> the word *upadana* has both a concrete and an abstract meaning. In the abstract it means, attachment, grasping; in this sense it is much used in Buddhist dogmatics. Concretely, it means that which fuels this process... so when the context deals with fire it simply means fuel.
>
> (Gombrich 2009: 114)

In Gombrich's view the Buddha deliberately puns on these two meanings of *upadana* (Gombrich 2009: 114); at one point the Buddha compared the mind being swayed by attachments to a bonfire upon which someone throws fuel (*upadana*).[10]

In Buddhist teachings attachment and craving are delusions, in that they wrongly treat phenomena as permanent, substantial and satisfactory, when in fact they are empty (*sunya*) – that is, they are in fact only conceptual constructs, with no irreducible, primary existence (Williams 2012: 101). The doctrine of *anatta* or *anatman* ('no-self'/'non-self') is the application of this to the self. Living under these delusions is the cause of suffering (*dukkha*): by abandoning them one abandons suffering and, if this is perfected, achieves *nirvana*.[11] Elsewhere, *upadana* is defined as fourfold: grasping sense pleasures, rituals, views and ideas about the self.[12]

Research psychologists Sahdra, Shaver and Brown consulted eighteen 'Buddhist experts', all of whom agreed that:

> Attachment, in the Buddhist sense, can take the form of possessiveness (e.g. in relationships), a sense of ownership of persons or things; jealousy; preoccupation; clinging; defensiveness; compulsion; obsession; acquisitiveness; defensive avoidance; competitiveness; and anxiety about gaining, escaping, or being able to avoid. When people are attached (in the Buddhist sense), their sense of well-being is contingent, that is, dependent, on a particular state of affairs. Phenomenologically, they feel stuck or fixated on ideas, images, or sensory objects and experience an internal pressure to acquire, hold, avoid, or change.
>
> (Sahdra, Shaver and Brown 2010: 118)

They also agreed that non-attachment, from a Buddhist perspective, is the opposite of all of this, and that: 'Rather than being aloof, indifferent, uncaring, or unengaged (which are common misconceptions about nonattachment in the West), the non-attached individual genuinely cares about, is engaged in and responsive to the present situation without falling into self-aggrandizement or self-degradation' (Sahdra, Shaver and Brown 2010: 118). Furthermore, the researchers argued that

> there is no reason to assume that the quality of nonattachment is unique to Buddhists... There are likely to be multiple determinants of nonattachment, many of which may be present in life circumstances other than engaging in a formal meditation practice.
>
> (Sahdra, Shaver and Brown 2010: 117)

According to the eighteen experts, while some attachments are better than others – an example given by Rupert Gethin is that attachment to the Buddhist precept of not harming living creatures is not as bad as attachment to the habit of killing living creatures (Gethin 1998: 71) – none are ultimately good and the goal is to abandon all attachments.

Spiritual bypassing

Acclaimed Buddhist teacher and psychotherapist Tara Brach (2014) tells the story of a boy who was scared in the night by a thunderstorm. His father said it was OK, because God was with him. 'I know' said the boy, 'but right now I need somebody with skin on!'

For the father to reject the boy's entreaty, and reassert what he said originally despite the boy's continuing fear, would be an example of 'spiritual bypassing' – a term first coined by psychologist John Welwood in 1984. Welwood defined it as 'the use of spiritual practices and beliefs to avoid dealing with our painful feelings, unresolved wounds, and developmental needs' (Masters 2010: 5). This constitutes attachment (*upadana*) to a particular technique, or to a particular false idea of nonattachment, so that one tries to use it to solve a problem to which it is not suitable and will be inefficient or ineffective at yielding a solution. Robert Masters, a psychotherapist who specialises in spiritual bypassing, describes one form that he sees in some spiritual teachers as follows:

> If a spiritual teacher is asked by his students about difficulties they are having with integrating their spiritual practice and the demands of intimate relationship, and he provides them with only big-picture answers/truisms, waxing eloquently about the finite and the infinite, the nature of self, and so on, then he is engaged in spiritual bypassing, no matter how articulate and precise his answer may be, for he is, however inadvertently, avoiding dealing directly and relevantly with his students' personal and interpersonal pain, and probably his own as well.
>
> (Masters 2010: 12)

One can imagine the mirror of this phenomenon, in which a psychologist or counsellor attempts to use attachment theory to understand aspects of life beyond the theory's scope, perhaps through an overly reductive approach that dismisses the intrinsic importance and emotional resonance of philosophical ideas or religious symbols. This problem is of course not limited to spiritual teachers and counsellors – it also applies to lay individuals who may or may not seek appropriate help.

In order to avoid spiritual bypassing, Buddhist teachers might benefit from being aware of which types of needs they can address, and of when to refer on to a counsellor who might be more specialised and experienced in dealing with particular unhealthy attachment behaviours. Conversely, and particularly when dealing with Buddhist patients/clients, counsellors and psychotherapists may also find it helpful to understand how Buddhist teachers deal with patterns of attachment (in a Buddhist sense) that do not correspond to their own areas of expertise, and to develop guidelines on how and when to refer patients/clients to Buddhist teachers. This might be useful in cases of addiction (which is often correlated with insecure attachment) for example, given Buddhist approaches to alcohol and food. A joined-up approach is also possible. Insight Meditation (*Vipassana*), a Buddhist tradition associated with influential teachers such as Jack Kornfield and Tara Brach, is a case of a Buddhist tradition in the West that has become highly integrated with psychotherapeutic perspectives. For example, half of the teachers at Spirit Rock Insight Meditation centre in San Francisco are also psychotherapists.[13]

I suggest that the phenomenology of caregiving, and the ideas and images which different lay individuals associate with it, become important at this point. Some people might associate caregiving with purity and goodness, others might associate it with an ironic affection for individual foibles and the animal side of human nature (perhaps this depends on the types of threat that one has encountered in the past). What seems ethereal to one person may seem demeaning to another: such associations affect perceptions of, and behaviours towards, attachment figures. In a post on Facebook,[14] Zen teacher and psychoanalyst Barry Magid said that he is not the type of Buddhist teacher who inspires others by his example of a simple, disciplined and kind life (a life which tends to revolve around commitment to spiritual practice). Instead, he emphasises that rather than attempting to achieve self-reliance or purity, meditation can be about developing emotional honesty and an appreciation of the weaknesses and vulnerabilities of ourselves and others, and that the goal is to learn to 'be dependant intelligently' upon other people (whether or not these other people are Buddhist, incidentally). He writes elsewhere:

> Traditionally, spiritual practice opens us up to the universal and non-exclusive, *while psychotherapy* helps us to tolerate the vulnerability of being exclusively attached to a single person. But the two practices can and should dovetail… Once we can learn [in meditation] to accept each thought, one after another, just as it is, we accept each person, one after each other, just as they are. And that is something that makes living with, and depending upon, that single special individual a much less threatening proposition.
>
> (Magid 2008: 101)

Self-reliance and transcendence

In an interview with a Somatic Trauma therapist called Staci Haines and David Treleaven, an academic from the California Institute of Integral Studies, Haines said that to survive her own trauma it was important for her to follow certain intuitions and physical sensations, rather than viewing them non-reactively and equanimously which seemed to dissociate her from them. She advocates that meditation should be 'a deeply embodied experience – not just an observing sensations experience. And I really hold a distinction between those two'. This is an important point when defining nonattachment. She adds that

> I also – with all due respect – have met deep meditation practitioners where I cannot feel their humanity. I can't feel their warmth; I can't feel their love. They might be very nonreactive but how it looks to me is they have numbed, they have numbed to a point of nonreactivity almost by bypassing their human healing work by taking the route of the observer. What I notice is it's hard for them to build and sustain intimacy.
>
> (Haines and Treleaven 2011)

Similarly, Treleaven said that 'So much of the hurt from the people that I've met in *Vipassana* has been that a lot of us were running away from contact because it was terrifying' (Haines and Treleaven 2011). He notes that,

> It is my understanding of the traditions where Western teachers were taught [i.e. in Asia] that meditation was taught far down the road. The first steps were ethics and connections to community, before you would ever be asked to sit on a cushion.
>
> (Haines and Treleaven 2011)

This contrasts with the frequent Western practice of meditation alone. Part of the problem may be that equanimity has not been sufficiently balanced with warmth and kindness, the latter also being states which Buddhists can attempt to cultivate through meditation.[15] Another problem is insufficient attention to personal life. Meditation teachers who are not also counsellors or psychotherapists, while they obviously encourage awareness of emotions and physical sensations, often refrain from initiating discussion with practitioners about contemplation of personal history. This may be particularly true in traditional Southeast Asian Buddhism (Haines and Treleaven 2011). In such circumstances practitioners may in turn be less likely to discuss their personal history with meditation teachers – they might say for example 'there is a pain in my back' but not go into any emotional factors in their personal lives that might be connected with it. I do not think that this is necessarily a fault on the part of the meditation teachers, and may well be a helpful professional boundary for them, but it is a limitation on what they are offering that it is important for practitioners and teachers to be aware of in order to manage expectations. There is the danger that an avoidantly attached person, who may deeply need to talk about their personal history but has inhibitions about doing so, is encouraged to bypass their own need for the interpersonal honesty and direct communication that is found in secure attachment.

Several Zen teachers, such as Barry Magid (Rosenbaum and Magid 2016) and Thich Nhat Hanh, have highlighted the problems of removing mindfulness from a social framework – in the Buddhist case, from the context of ethics, community, doctrine and ritual. One should not be attached to these, yet they are very helpful in the development of nonattachment, the Zen teachers assert. The Zen teachers argue for instance that individual alertness, even when developed by mindfulness practice, must be balanced by the need to restore and refresh through rest, and that personal happiness cannot be complete without taking into account the happiness of others. Such points illustrate the pitfalls that an avoidantly attached person may fall into, if they try to use meditation techniques to make themselves more self-reliant and to lessen their need to depend upon others (in other words, if they are attached, in the Buddhist sense, to these techniques). Secular mindfulness is often taught in eight-week courses, but it is much rarer to find support groups for people who wish to continue the practice after graduating them, a situation which may encourage such misuse (Rosenbaum and Magid 2016).

In Buddhism, meditation is often seen as leading to insight, and individuals may believe it to be capable of doing so all by itself, without consideration of the type of insight that may be yielded. This misunderstanding may encourage a meditator who is avoidant (or for that matter, reluctant to seek psychological help for other reasons) to believe that they can understand their psychological problems all by themselves, without seeking the support of a counsellor. The notion of mindfulness as 'bare attention', a mental faculty capable of simply revealing whatever is present through direct experience unmediated by concepts, has been criticised (Rosenbaum and Magid 2016: epilogue by Robert Sharf). Furthermore, to paraphrase Jack Kornfield, the mind is only semi-permeable to awareness: thus there are great athletes who know their bodies well but are emotional idiots, and professors with brilliant minds but rudimentary relationships to their bodies (Kornfield 2011: 247). This being said, in light of the research that shows correlation between secular mindfulness and secure attachment,[16] I think it reasonable to expect that research on mindfulness in a Buddhist context would demonstrate the same correlation. It seems logical that by helping the meditator to tune into their own feelings, the practice of mindfulness can challenge the suppression of emotion that is typical of unhealthy attachment styles (Buddhist teacher Thich Nhat Hanh describes mindfulness as the middle way between expression and repression).

Meditation and relationships

How might attachment theory shed light upon relationships that are formed and sustained in the context of Buddhist activities? On the face of it some of the things that attract some people to, and result from, Buddhist practices seem to be the same things that people seek from attachment relationships. Gillath, Shaver and Mikulincer (2005: 145) write that secure attachment promotes caregiving because it 'provides a solid and stable psychological foundation for a form of empathy that is not overwhelmed by others' suffering or threatened by the interdependence entailed by caregiving' (Gillath, Shaver and Mikulincer 2005: 145). They write that therefore, particularly in a securely attached individual, caregiving: 'can be extended to include care and concern for other people in need, perhaps even compassion for all suffering creatures – an important Buddhist ideal', (and a characteristic of nonattachment) (Gillath, Shaver and Mikulincer 2005: 144).

However, such relationships often lack features such as verbal interaction or romance which might be associated with healthy relationships. This challenges therapists to articulate the connections between these features and secure attachment. Sumi Loundon, author of two anthologies of personal stories by young Buddhists, describes her motivations for writing the first book:

> I had a really practical need which was that I needed friends and I needed to date somebody [Laughs]. So, in a certain way we could say these anthologies all come about as a form of lust, but I'm just kidding about that [Laughter].[17]

Lacking a peer group, she says, young Buddhists may feel that their close relationships and their Buddhist practice pull them in different directions. Loundon sees this as a problem affecting other age groups too:

> Buddhist communities in the West generally tend to be pretty asocial. I am not sure if it is because Buddhism in the West draws people who are inherently introverted and asocial or whether when the people come, they are social but then Buddhism or the meditation makes them a little bit asocial. I suspect it is the first, that people who are already a little bit introverted and quiet, and you know, it is hard for them to be in community or work towards a community feeling. Those kind of people are drawn to Buddhism.

Such people may be healthily solitary or independent, and some may be avoidantly attached. It seems to me that the Buddhism to which Loundon refers probably revolves around intensive individual meditation, unlike some traditions such as Triratna or Plum Village.

Although meditation can be a solitary activity focused upon individual inner experience, many meditators prefer to meditate with others, finding that this supports their personal meditation. Fully silent group retreats, a format held to assist nonattachment, offer a unique interpersonal dynamic, in which individuals may form surprisingly strong emotional bonds despite never having spoken with each other, raising questions about the role of verbal or written communication in adult attachment. At Gaia House, an Insight Meditation (*Vipassana*) centre in Devon, silence usually begins about an hour after retreat attendees arrive, and lifts only an hour before they leave. 'Distractions' such as reading material or electronics are absent (in order to reduce *upadana* towards them), and the environment is dedicated to embodied mindfulness of everyday activities, which can give participants an enhanced sensitivity. Connection happens through shared activities like washing up, through body language, or just passing by in a corridor, all of which provide vehicles for emotional communication. Some teachers speak jokingly about '*vipassana* romances'. Then you find, when speaking at the end of the retreat, that they may in some respects be very different to the person who you had perceived them to be. This offers an opportunity to observe, free from everyday demands upon our attention, how our attachment patterns transfer onto people around us.

In a chapter entitled 'The Perfect Buddhist Boyfriend', from one of Loundon's anthologies, one contributor describes how she and her partner had both learned outward 'Buddhist' behaviours, such as wearing a serene facial expression, which actually caused problems in their relationship. She recounts a fight, caused because she interrupted his meditation, which ended with her screaming 'asshole' at him. She continues:

> Granted, we argued about different things than your typical couple might, but the anger, fear, and grief were just as potent as with any couple. Power struggles, territoriality concerns, abandonment wounds, control issues – all the things that arise from a bad childhood – appeared... Even though we both strove for insight, peacefulness, and compassion, our practice manifested itself selectively. If anything, our practice might have forced our issues to the surface more dramatically and much earlier than in a conventional relationship because we were so intensely aware of every flicker of negative emotion... Maybe we believed our Buddhist masks so much that we held each other to very high standards. When one of us would explode, the other was supposed to be a Buddha, with infinite understanding and wisdom. And, just as [her boyfriend] was hiding from himself by sitting on the cushion, I was hiding from myself by not meditating.
>
> (Loundon 2001: 8)

She concludes that 'it now seems to me that the fundamentals of relationship – love, care, kindness, respect, honesty – are the foundation of being Buddhist' (Loundon 2001: 9).

Conclusion

To conclude, I have found, first, that there is considerable overlap in the issues to which the two concepts of attachment are, and can be, applied. In Buddhism, *upadana* is relevant when considering the mind in relationship to any object of mind, but one context in which it is applicable is that of interpersonal relationships, the subject matter of attachment theory in Western psychology. While at first glance attachment styles as understood by Western psychology might seem to be concerned solely with close interpersonal relationships, in fact the impulses towards and away from solitude and community, transcendence and intimacy, can all become intertwined with them. Second, I have found that the Buddhist concept of nonattachment does not, if correctly understood, suggest any standard for, or approach towards, good relationships that conflict with secure attachment in the sense first developed by Bowlby and his students. Indeed, when properly understood the two approaches seem to be complementary. The characteristics of insecure attachment strategies, such as avoidance of, or ambivalence about, caregiving, are also characteristics of *upadana*. Just as Buddhists try to liberate themselves and others from *upadana*, healthy attachment relationships involve cutting down on the behaviours that characterise insecure attachment strategies. Buddhists should not fear that a good counsellor well versed in attachment-based approaches will be guiding them in a way that conflicts with their Buddhist beliefs and practices. At the same time, Buddhist meditation practices, community and wisdom about relationships, may be of real support for individuals with problems related to insecure attachment behaviours.

However, I have found, third, that if this is not understood, there is potential for harm. The well-known Buddhist teacher and psychotherapist Jack Kornfield describes certain emotional states as 'near enemies' to those which Buddhists may seek to cultivate. A 'near enemy' is a harmful state that is relatively easy to mistake for a desirable one: for example, compliance and kindness, or indifference and equanimity. It will have become clear by this point that avoidant attachment is, in my opinion, a particular 'near enemy' for some Buddhist practitioners, arising out of overattachment (*upadana*) to particular meditative techniques or from an imbalanced approach to relationships with oneself, friends and partners. I think that when exploring such issues, whether as a counsellor, a Buddhist or neither, it is as ever essential to be deeply compassionate, and to be discerning but not judgmental. As with the young woman searching for 'the perfect Buddhist boyfriend', such issues can be worked through.

I believe that there are fascinating points of contact between Buddhism and attachment-based counselling beyond those that I have discussed here. My previous essay (which I mentioned in the introduction to this chapter) explores some of these issues further in a more theoretical manner, drawing upon ancient Buddhist texts which nonetheless illustrate practices and beliefs that are not uncommon today. It discusses further the questions explored above about kindness and compliance and about what constitutes caregiving, by looking at how Buddhist ideas and practices around *metta* (translated as loving-kindness or friendliness) relate to secure attachment. It also looks at Buddhist ideas and practices around *upekkha* (equanimity) and how this relates to emotional numbness, self-reliance and other features of the different attachment styles. Finally, it looks briefly at how monasticism relates to ideas about the role of sexuality in secure adult attachment, and at the question of whether attachment theory can be applied to supernatural attachment figures. The effects of different ideas of the self, attachment theory across cultures and the question of how attachment strategy relates to the tendency to identify with groups are all areas for future research.

Notes

1 Mindfulness is commonly defined as paying attention, on purpose, in the present moment, with an attitude of curiosity and kindness. It is cultivated through meditation in which one takes an object, such as the breath or bodily sensations, as a focus for attention.
2 For example, Shaver, Lavy, Saron and Mikulincer (2007).
3 An account of the society can be found online here: http://mindfulnessforstudents.co.uk/counsellors/.
4 This essay is available on my academia.edu web page.
5 A dharma talk is a talk about Buddhist theory that is at the same time a meditation instruction. Listeners are encouraged to listen meditatively, in an embodied way rather than just with their intellect, in order to feel in an embodied fashion where the talk resonates with them. While these talks certainly draw upon preconceived Buddhist ideas and upon prepared materials, they tend to have a spontaneous aspect in that the teacher will be, in part, responding to the particular audience at hand, and the teacher will often later record this in the form of books or articles.
6 For a case study on this topic, about a Zen master who sought therapy to deal with childhood abandonment issues, see Brown (2009) and Nordstrom (2010).
7 For example, see the introduction to Aronson (2004).
8 Patricia Crittenden's website, section on the DMM Model, http://patcrittenden.com/include/dmm_model.htm.
9 I will italicise non-English Buddhist words.
10 Samyutta Nikaya (an ancient Buddhist text) 12.52.
11 Khandhavagga-Sutta, Samyutta Nikaya (an ancient Buddhist text).
12 Sammaditthi-sutta (an ancient Buddhist text).
13 According to its website www.spiritrock.org.
14 Ordinary Mind Zendo New York Facebook page. Post dated 22 May 2015.
15 I explored this issue in my previous essay, mentioned in the introduction.
16 For example, Shaver, Lavy, Saron and Mikulincer (2007).
17 Buddhist Geeks interview with Sumi Loundon (2010).

References

(All online material was retrieved 31st May 2015.)

Aronson, H. 2004. *Buddhist Practice on Western Ground: Reconciling Eastern Ideals and Western Psychology*. Boston, MA: Shambhala.

Brach, T. 2014. 'Refuge in Loving Relationships', a dharma talk by Tara Brach. www.youtube.com/watch?v=8cuMryutjOo.

Brown, C. 2009. Enlightenment therapy. *The New York Times*, 26 April. www.nytimes.com/2009/04/26/magazine/26zen-t.html?pagewanted=all&_r=0.

Crisp, R.J., C.V. Farrow, H.E.S. Rosenthal-Stott and N.M.K. Penn 2009. Interpersonal attachment predicts identification with groups. *Journal of Experimental Social Psychology*, 45(1), 115–22.

Crittenden, P. Dynamic Maturational Model. http://patcrittenden.com/include/dmm_model.htm.

Gillath, O., P.R. Shaver and M. Mikulincer 2005. An attachment-theoretical approach to compassion and altruism, in: P. Gilbert (ed.) *Compassion: Conceptualisations, Research and Use in Psychotherapy*. London: Routledge, pp. 121–47.

Goldberg, S. 1999. Recent developments in attachment theory and research, in: A. Slater and D. Muir (eds) *The Blackwell Reader in Developmental Psychology*. Oxford: Blackwell. (Chapter previously published in 1991 in the *Canadian Journal of Psychiatry*, 36(6), 393–400).

Gombrich, R. 2009. *What the Buddha Thought*. London: Equinox. (Chapter 6: 'The Buddha's Positive Values').

Gomez, L. 1997. *An Introduction to Object Relations*. London: Free Association Books. (Chapters on Bowlby and Winnicott).

Haines, S. and D. Treleaven 2011. 'Possibilities and Limits' interview by Turning Wheel Media. www.turningwheelmedia.org/somatics-interview/.

Hazan, C. and P. Shaver 1987. Romantic love conceptualized as an attachment process. *Journal of Personality and Social Psychology*, 52(3), 511–24.

Kornfield, J. 2011. *Bringing Home the Dharma*. Boston, MA: Shambhala.

Loundon, S. (ed.) 2001. *Blue Jean Buddha*. Boston, MA: Wisdom Publications.

Loundon, S. 2010. Interview by Buddhist Geeks. www.buddhistgeeks.com/2010/04/bg-166-what-young-people-want/.

Magid, B. 2008. *Ending the Pursuit of Happiness: A Zen Guide*. Boston, MA: Wisdom Publications.

Masters, R.A. 2010. *Spiritual Bypassing: When Spirituality Disconnects Us from What Really Matters*. Berkeley, CA: North Atlantic Books.

Muller, R.T. 2010. *Trauma and the Avoidant Client: Attachment-based Strategies for Healing*. London: W. Norton.

Nordstrom, L. (Mitsunen) 2010. A response to enlightenment therapy – Setting the record straight. www.hokorizencenter.org/dharmatalks.html

Rosenbaum, R.M. and B. Magid (eds) 2016. *What's Wrong with Mindfulness (and what isn't): Zen Perspectives*. Somerville, MA: Wisdom Publications.

Sahdra, B.K., P.R. Shaver and K.W. Brown 2010. A scale to measure nonattachment: A Buddhist complement to Western research on attachment and adaptive functioning. *Journal of Personality Assessment*, 92(2), 116–27.

Shaver, P.R., S. Lavy, C.D. Saron and M. Mikulincer 2007. Social foundations of the capacity for mindfulness: An attachment perspective. *Psychological Inquiry: An International Journal for the Advancement of Psychological Theory*, 18(4), 264–71.

Williams, P., with A. Tribe, and with A. Wynne 2012. *Buddhist Thought: A Complete Introduction to the Indian Tradition*. 2nd ed. London: Routledge.

16 Twelve step mutual aid

Spirituality, vulnerability and recovery

Wendy Dossett

There are similarities between Twelve Step fellowships[1] and programmes[2] and new religious movements. There are also differences. There are similarities between Twelve Step fellowships and programmes and counselling. There are also differences. Through exploring these intersections and interrelationships, this chapter attempts to shed light on some of the numerous controversies surrounding the Twelve Step phenomenon. Controversies include the debate about whether addiction, or substance use disorder (SUD)[3] is a disease. If SUD is classified as a disease, the legitimacy of the Twelve Step claim that the problem is 'spiritual' in nature is in doubt. As neuroscientist and addictions journalist Maia Szalavitz (2012) puts it:

> If addiction really is a disease, why is it the only one where having it makes you qualified to treat it? For no other medical disorder is meeting and praying considered reimbursable treatment: if a doctor recommended these religious or spiritual practices for the primary treatment of cancer or depression, you would be able to sue successfully for malpractice.

Here Szalavitz refers to the professionalisation of the Twelve Steps in an addictions treatment setting for which clients or taxpayers pay.[4] Twelve Step programmes practised in the context of independent anonymous mutual aid fellowships like Narcotics Anonymous and Alcoholics Anonymous are not remunerated. They are provided free by self-governing groups of recovering people committed to corporate poverty.

A historically and cross-culturally informed account of medicine would properly highlight the fragility of constituting addiction entirely in secular terms, evacuated of all relationship with human knowledge structured by religious or spiritual epistemologies. Nonetheless, this presentation clearly highlights the apparent absurdity of the Twelve Step approach from the perspective of secular mainstream medicine. Medical anthropologist Natalie Tobert, for example, notes that 'In India the use of a multiplicity of medical, alternative, complementary, religious and/or spiritual strategies to address human suffering is not controversial' (2014: 9). The allopathic or mainstream model of medicine is as culturally specific as any other, though it draws on the legitimating discourse of secular science. Harold Koenig (1998), Kenneth

Pargament (1997) and others (Porche et al. 2015) have proposed positive, empirically testable correlations between some forms of religious and spiritual involvement and physical and mental health. All this notwithstanding, the case for the relevance of a spiritual approach to addiction recovery remains highly controversial – in allopathic medical circles[5] in which addiction is considered to be a brain disease (Wise 2000), as well as in other psychosocial discourses which prioritise community and individual psychological approaches.

The intention here is not to defend the case for a spiritual approach to addiction recovery, nor to critique it. This would be ill-advised for several reasons, including the problem that such a case would depend upon unhelpfully essentialising the category of spirituality. Rather, through drawing on accounts of people in Twelve Step programmes who use the language of spirituality to describe their recovery, the intention is to consider their language in the light of the twin foci of this volume, namely counselling and new religious movements, in the hope that such an investigation illuminates Twelve Step experiences in new ways.

The fieldwork upon which this chapter draws was undertaken by myself and a colleague, John Stoner,[6] between 2012 and 2017, and remains ongoing. The Higher Power Project,[7] based at the University of Chester, is a large qualitative research project comprising data from 107 participants so far, all of whom responded to a questionnaire, and around half of whom have, at the time of writing, spoken with one of the researchers in a semi-structured telephone interview. Participants in the project are members[8] of Twelve Step mutual aid fellowships,[9] with six months or more continuous abstinence from the relevant substance or behaviour, or in the case of Al-Anon,[10] six months of membership or working the programme. The longest abstinent person to participate to date was 48.5 years without taking a drink or other drug at the time he was interviewed. The researchers have attended Twelve Step meetings, other mutual aid meetings (such as SMART Recovery, and Buddhist 'sit and share' meetings) and numerous other events and activities within the wider 'recovery scene'. They have both worked in the past as key workers at a residential rehabilitation centre for drug and alcohol addiction, which used the Twelve Steps combined with Reality Therapy and other addictions counselling modalities.

Expertise, experience and vulnerability

Addictions counselling and the Twelve Step approach may appear to have little in common. Key differences include the primacy of 'expertise' in counselling, contrasted with the primacy of 'personal experience' of Twelve Step fellowship members; the contrasting remunerative arrangements and the power dynamics these reflect; the disease model (tacitly assumed in Twelve Step, and either embraced or eschewed in different counselling models); the concept of powerlessness (largely challenged in counselling models); and the notion of a 'spiritual' approach (often considered irrelevant or inappropriate in counselling models).

Counselling is undertaken by trained professionals. Whilst contemporary counselling models commonly assign expertise, along with agency of change, to the client, a helper-helped differential inevitably still operates, and the counsellor is the 'professional' and sometimes even the 'expert' in the room. It is common for people in recovery (who may or may not be 'abstinent')[11] to become addictions counsellors or support/recovery workers of various kinds[12] and these professionals may draw on their personal experiences in positive ways, but their own recovery status is not a necessary or essential component of their work. By contrast there are no 'experts' or 'professionals' in addictions recovery in Twelve Step meetings; only people with first-person experience of addiction, relapse, abstinence and recovery. Whilst trained counsellors may happen to be amongst them (there because they identify as 'addict' or 'alcoholic' and they are seeking help to become or remain abstinent, or to deepen their recovery), meetings are likely also to include people of other professions and none, and a range of levels of education, including high levels of functional illiteracy. The professional and educational background of those present is entirely irrelevant to their presence in the meeting, and no one is authorised to give professional advice. It is the norm and tacit expectation that people speak only about their personal experiences. A further dimension of the contrast here, is that even experienced members of the fellowship are considered to be 'vulnerable'. In the Twelve Step approach, addiction has no 'cure'. In other words, the individual is unlikely ever to be able to drink, or use drugs, or gamble, or consume pornography (or whatever the primary addiction happened to be) without excessive and harmful behaviour returning. As such, even long-time 'clean' or 'sober' members are vulnerable to relapse. Some of our participants spoke about a growing sense of ease about their condition as months and years went by, but they also spoke of the need to avoid complacency, to preserve an awareness of the presence of their 'disease', and to continue to 'work a daily programme' to address it. Thus there is a sense of equality in Twelve Step communities, and a common expression is that the person who is most clean or sober in the room is merely the one who got up earliest that day. This is taken to reflect the contention that 'sobriety' is a condition which must be renewed every day, whether the individual is a day, a week or a decade away from their last drink or drug. Thus the fellowships might be understood correctly as groups of vulnerable people helping each other. This is indeed one of the sources of anxiety that professionals who have not seen these groups in action reported having about them.[13]

Counsellors are both insured and paid (by clients, endowments, and/or taxpayers). Twelve Step groups and programmes are free. Members may make voluntary contributions to cover the cost of refreshments, room rent and group literature, but they are not compelled. Twelve Step groups are not financially dependent upon a client list. When a group is not viable owing to too few voluntary contributions to meet room rent, or too few people to fill the three or four 'service positions'[14] required for a group to run, it may simply close down, but no one's livelihood is affected, and meetings nearby may swell in size. According to the Traditions, a set of guidelines developed from the experience of the early members of Alcoholics Anonymous (the prototype Twelve Step fellowship, founded in 1935), the 'public relations policy is based on attraction rather than promotion'.[15] The fellowships are not 'recruiting' in the same way that treatment centres or counsellors might be. There is nothing, financial or otherwise, to gain from membership increase. The groups simply have something to offer, which they consider potentially helpful to those who might be interested. In the second, and all subsequent, editions of the main text *Alcoholics Anonymous* (known as 'the Big Book') it is acknowledged that AA does not have a 'monopoly' on 'therapy for the alcoholic' (Alcoholics Anonymous World Services 2001: xxi). In fact, Twelve Step fellowships do not offer 'counselling' or 'therapy'. Instead they offer the twin approaches of 'mutual aid' fellowship combined with a programme or framework of recovery in the Twelve Steps which encapsulates a particular (and contested) theory of addiction and recovery.

Counselling is time-bound; the weekly 50 minutes in the room, the six or twelve sessions. Twelve Step meetings are available daily, and those living in urban areas may have access to dozens of meetings daily. Members may go on attending meetings for years, even for life, 'putting back' (as several of our participants put it) what they had 'taken out'. Supportive relationships develop outside of the formal meetings, and members are encouraged to socialise with other members. Many avail themselves of sponsorship by established abstinent members. A sponsor is (usually) someone who uses the steps as their framework for recovery, and shares their experience of this with a sponsee, offering guidance, typically in the form of reporting experience rather than issuing instruction. While a close relationship develops between sponsor and sponsee, it is not usually considered 'friendship' as such (conventional friendship can be seen as risking collusion with and enabling of addictive behaviour), though it does have features in common with 'spiritual friendship' found in some religious traditions. The sponsorship relationship, when it is fruitful and successful,[16] is reported by both parties as a significant source of strength, and even as a way of being in touch with a 'higher power'. Therese's[17] comment is typical:

> I am very aware that I cannot rely on my own will and direction and that I must actively seek the guidance of and connection with a natural force outside of myself. I see this force in the fellowship, in conversations with my sponsor, in my actions of helping others.

While counsellors may experience profound fulfilment from their work, it would not normally be seen as helping to support their own recovery. It may do so incidentally, in cases where the counsellor is a person in recovery from an SUD, but it would be considered unprofessional if the motivation for engaging clients was explicitly to secure the counsellor's own recovery. It is not uncommon for sponsors and other established fellowship members to receive phone calls from vulnerable members during unsocial hours, nor for that contact to enable the individual to remain abstinent during a challenging period or experience. Alan W wrote in a questionnaire response:

> I was in so much mental torture and emotional pain that I was on the verge of committing suicide ... Whatever it was, I had a 'light bulb' moment, when I phoned the man who became my sponsor. I saw – through him – that there had to be another way...

Evidence suggests that the close relationships developed in fellowship settings, in which this kind of support is freely available, are one of the mediating factors of AA's efficacy, especially in the longer term (Kelly et al. 2011). Intra-fellowship relationships are a powerful source of 'bridging' social capital (Putnam 2000), developing beneficial connections amongst people across the divides of education, social class, experience of the criminal justice system, relative wealth, gender, family-type, religion and other social markers. However, this type of 'out of hours' contact with counsellors would be rare, and, in most cases and for good reasons, considered unprofessional. Outside of the counselling contact, clients must make their own way, drawing on whatever other resources the counselling sessions have supplied or highlighted.

Powerlessness

These practical differences are further complicated by the range of significantly contrasting counselling philosophies which inform and underpin addictions counselling. Christine Lê and colleagues (Lê et al. 1995) explored common features of addictions counselling philosophy, drawing on person-centred, humanistic, analytical, neo-Freudian, existential, Gestalt, rational-emotive and cognitive approaches, and concluded that, despite differences, central to them all was the facilitation of change, growth and development of the individual, emphasising self-direction, self-efficacy and empowerment. Had they explored so-called third wave and mindfulness-based approaches, their conclusions in this regard would likely have been similar.

Given this emphasis, much addictions counselling inevitably rejects the 'powerlessness' starting point of the Twelve Steps.[18] Most counselling models would set out to build a sense of empowerment and self-efficacy, and would not begin with the apparently negative starting point of facing the client with their powerlessness. This is particularly the case in feminist critiques of the Twelve Steps, some of which have informed counselling practices (Bepko 1991; Briggs and Pepperell 2009), and some of which have resulted in the development of women-specific programmes of recovery, such as Women for Sobriety[19] and 'The 16 Steps for Recovery and Empowerment' (Kasl 1992).

When women experience addiction, their power, which is already diminished by virtue of their gender, is diminished further. In broad terms, most research suggests that the consequences of addiction for women can be more costly socially, psychologically and physically than they are for men (Wilsnack et al. 1994; Sanders 2009). When people seek the help of Twelve Step fellowships it is usually because they are experiencing some kind of crisis. One participant, Katherine, described herself as being 'desperate' when she 'first came into the fellowship'. Crises faced by women are particularly marked by the consequences of unequal power dynamics; rape, abuse, domestic violence, poverty, the pressures of child care or the crisis of loss of children – all exacerbated by the presence of addiction in individuals and families. The large-scale study undertaken by Jolene Sanders and published in 2009 as *Women in Alcoholics Anonymous: Recovery and Empowerment* discovered that despite feminist critiques of AA, female members of AA tend to be 'substantially more feminist on measures of gender roles, feminist identification and attention given to women's issues' than the wider population (Sanders 2009: 123). Furthermore, she claims that her research demonstrates that 'both collective and personal empowerment is beyond doubt a primary outcome of participation in the Twelve Step program of AA' (Sanders 2009: 134). Whilst a programme that focuses on powerlessness may seem intuitively wrong both for women and for feminism, Sanders provides evidence that it supports both.

The disease model

Despite the recent re-emphasis on addiction as a brain disease in the work of the current Director of the USA's National Institute of Drug Abuse, Nora Volkow (Volkow and Fowler 2000), and in the most recent, fifth, edition of the *Diagnostic and Statistical Manual of Mental Disorders* (DSM) (American Psychiatric Association 2013), neuroscientists with an interest in neuroplasticity, for example Marc Lewis (2011, 2015), argue that the so-called 'disease model' is misleading, since brain changes resulting from substance use are not permanent. Alcoholics Anonymous has implicitly legitimised the disease model by assuming it.[20] The assumption, however, was unrelated to competing theories in neuroscience, but emerged from the need to counteract the negativity of the 'moral model' prevailing in the puritan environment in which AA emerged. Freedom from guilt and shame derived from the realisation that their addiction was not the result of their immorality or weakness of will, but that they were suffering with a disease that simply strikes down a proportion of the population, released energy that people badly needed to drive their recovery. Thus the disease model may be instrumentally powerful. However, some counselling theories reject it because they consider it to be (instrumentally) disempowering and self-defeating. It is negative to think of oneself as a 'victim' of a random disease, to which, if the AA account is to be accepted, there is no 'cure'. The territory of this debate is highly complex, with promoters of either view frequently misreading and misrepresenting their opponents. Twelve Step members often assume that scientific opponents of the disease model are implying that they are weak and immoral, when they may be doing no such thing (Orford 1985). Some opponents of the disease model are implying that addiction is indeed a moral failing (for example, Hitchens 2012), but not all (Lewis 2015). Sometimes scientific, psychotherapeutic or community-recovery oriented opponents of the disease model find the language negative (for example, Wilbanks 1989) whilst completely ignoring, or at least potentially undervaluing, its liberating power for those who have built their recovery upon it.

Fellowships as NRMs

The most controversial feature of all in Twelve Step discourse is the idea that addiction is at root a 'spiritual malady' (Alcoholics Anonymous World Service, 1939 [2001]: 64), and that the solution, therefore, is a spiritual solution. The spiritual approach derives from AA's origins in the Oxford Group, an American evangelical organisation that modelled itself on its construction of 'first century' Christianity, and identified fear and selfishness as driving human problems (B 1992). The first few years of Alcoholics Anonymous saw an implicit rejection of the narrowness of the Oxford Group approach, and an explicit move away from the assumption that members would have a Christian conversion experience.[21] However, the centrality of 'spirituality' was reaffirmed in the correspondence between Carl Jung and Bill Wilson in 1961, which introduced the eye-catching phrase '*spiritus contra spiritum*' ((holy) 'spirit' against (liquor) spirits).[22] 'God as we understood him', a 'Higher Power' and 'a power greater than ourselves' became the transcendent focus of the Twelve Steps, at once distancing them from mainstream Christianity and at the same time ensuring (for many) compatibility between them. Inevitably, these terms have an unstable and ever-shifting history of interpretation. Analysis of the Higher Power Project data, gathered from amongst contemporary fellowship members, has demonstrated divergent interpretation of the notion of Higher Power across a wide secular/spiritual spectrum. The project has explored the function of the relationship between external sources of authority (fellowship texts, slogans and performative language) with internal personal autonomy and discernment in the construction of higher power language, and concludes that despite the presence of strong authoritative sources, the scope for individual interpretation is significant (Dossett 2013).

In the USA, an increasing number of federal courts have ruled that mandating the attendance of probationers at Alcoholics or Narcotics Anonymous meetings is a violation of the First Amendment of the US Constitution in terms of both the Establishment Clause – 'Congress shall make no law respecting the establishment of religion...' and the Free Exercise Clause – '... or prohibiting the free exercise thereof' (Peele et al. 2000). As yet there has been no Supreme Court ruling on this, but significant sectors of the US legal system consider Twelve Step fellowships to be religious organisations of a Christian character. Interestingly, numerous Christian authors and related treatment programmes consider the Twelve Step approach to be problematically secular, for example the work of the Bobgans (1991) which present the steps as a form of 'psychoheresy' which prevent people with addictions finding the love and healing of Christ.

There are significant differences in the practice of the Twelve Steps in the USA and the UK. In the USA, meetings commonly conclude with the recitation of the Lord's Prayer, which is unusual in the UK. In the USA, atheist members report negativity and judgement from theist members, and some atheist meetings are not accepted as *bona fide* AA in a small minority of local regions (Scrivener 2011). In the UK, the Twelve Step fellowships appear, at least anecdotally,[23] to be more comfortable for atheist and agnostic members than they are in some areas of North America. One of the UK-based atheist participants in the Higher Power Project research, Keith, who was 35 years sober when he was interviewed, said:

> I have two sponsors, one a devout practising Roman Catholic and the other a high-church Anglican; both of them accept my views and do not love me any the less.

One of the most striking titles in the literature critical of Twelve Step programmes is anarchist Charles (Chaz) Bufe's *Alcoholics Anonymous: Cult or Cure*? (2nd ed. 1998). In this volume, Bufe highlights what he considers to be AA's cultic features. He makes a distinction between 'communal AA' (the kind that naturally occurs within communities) and 'institutional AA' (the use of the Twelve Steps in the professional treatment sector). He is more alarmed by the latter, and notes that 'communal AA' is exempt from many of what he views (simplistically) as characteristics of 'brainwashing cults'. For example, he says that communal AA does not, 'for the most part', employ 'mind control techniques', does not have 'a charismatic leader', does not have 'an authoritarian hierarchical structure', does not 'economically exploit its members', is not 'possessive of its members', does not provide 'a closed and all-encompassing environment', is not 'millenarian' and does not 'employ violence, coercion or harassment' (Bufe 1998: 147–56). He claims, however, that it does have some 'cult-like' tendencies, in which he includes the fact that it is 'religiously oriented', that it 'discourages scepticism and rational thinking', that it is 'dogmatic', that members have 'a "chosen people" mentality', that it 'elevates its own ideology over experience, observation and logic' and that it 'see[s] itself as the exclusive holder of the truth (at least in regard to the treatment of alcohol abuse *[sic]*)' (Bufe 1998: 143–56). Evidence can be presented both in favour and against these claims. The Higher Power Project data tends to show people grappling with some of the ideas of AA, often finding them difficult or even offensive; in some cases rejecting or significantly reinterpreting core ideas; reading authoritative texts yet making their own judgements and developing personal versions of central messages with the help of a wide variety of other sources of inspiration (Dossett 2013, 2015). It is difficult to imagine any other large organisation with a singular focus which (mostly comfortably) contains such diversity of world views. In any given Twelve Step meeting a member is likely to sit with atheists, agnostics, Christians of various stamps, Deists, people who believe in interventions from supernatural realms (be these by God, angels, spiritual forces or the deceased); people who believe that their power to be abstinent comes from communitarian rather than supernatural sources; practitioners of Mindfulness, practitioners of Buddhism; people who identify across a wide range of religious traditions; people who use Native American ceremonies and ideas; people who use Positive Thinking or programmes such as 'The Secret' or 'A Course in Miracles'.[24] Twelve Step programmes describe themselves as 'spiritual but not religious'.[25] Whilst they entertain statements of belief, ritual, communal prayer and other features associated with 'religion', the core notions are so widely interpreted, and the motivation for involvement does not reach beyond the goal of abstinence and recovery, it is hard to agree entirely with the assessment that they are 'religions' in any formal sense. The term 'New' has some valence of course, in the sense that the fellowships and the Twelve Steps did not emerge until the 1930s, though some writers (B 1992) emphasise how the Steps draw on traditions dating back to the Early Church. In support of Bufe's account, a number of people interviewed in the project certainly spoke of initial alarm about the apparent religiosity of the fellowship. Anne, for example, said, 'My initial reaction to the mention of God (Higher Power) at my first Al-Anon meeting was fear. I was concerned the organisation may be some sort of cult'.

Lynden similarly described her experience of initial dissonance on encountering the idea, then a reinterpretation:

> When I first saw 'God' in the 12 Steps I thought 'This is not for me. This will be full of evangelists trying to convert me. I don't want to be saved thank you. I don't want to dedicate my life to Jesus. I don't trust these people, they have another agenda.' When I saw 'Higher Power' I thought 'This is just the Christian God by another name. I know this because it has capitals – like He and Him … – and I am not going to be taken in by this'. When I saw 'power greater than ourselves' I thought 'This is interesting. There must be a power greater than myself because I am not doing a very good job of being in charge, but I don't know what this 'power' can be. And if it is not myself then I am very suspicious of it and not inclined to trust it.' This has changed a great deal over time, and is still changing.

Others we interviewed spoke of their commitment to making sure their fellowship remains a site of religious freedom. Katherine for example:

> I still feel that there are many evils committed in this world in the name of religion, and do not, myself, subscribe to or follow any recognised

> religion … Whatever works for any individual is great, as long as that individual does not force their religious beliefs onto others or tell others (especially within AA) that their concept of God and the particular religion they follow is the only way to go, or the only way to get sober!

Jung's own insistence on a 'vital spiritual experience' has an undeniable rhetorical power. However, there is more in Jung's letter to Bill Wilson,[26] and commentators seem often to miss that Jung actually attributes Hazard's recovery to 'personal and honest contact with friends'. Jung states that the journey of what he calls this 'unrecognised spiritual need' into perdition can be arrested in two ways – either by 'real religious insight', or by the 'protective wall of the human community'. A spiritual experience in the conventional sense is therefore not the only solution to alcoholism. Engagement with other human actors is also a solution.

This perspective fits comfortably with contemporary clinical research, which names the role of friendship groups and the power of the taking up of service responsibilities in developing a healing sense of self-efficacy as the central planks of AAs effectiveness (Kelly and Greene 2014). While spirituality is generally positively correlated to well-being (Lun and Bond 2013) it is not usually thought by social and life science researchers to have much to do with why Twelve Step is successful to the extent that it is. This might be surprising to Twelve Step practitioners, who often assert that it makes no sense to speak of the 'spiritual side' of the programme, since that implies there are features of it which are *not* spiritual. Part of the issue here may be that social scientists are likely to define spirituality in terms of 'belief' whereas Twelve Step practitioners are very clear that for them spirituality is about action. Thus, they would count all the mediating factors to do with peer group involvement as spiritual rather than sociological factors. If 'belief' is prioritised and essentialised as the primary defining characteristic of spirituality, it becomes a little blunt as a tool of analysis in this context. Understanding precisely what Twelve Step fellowships are, what they do and how they should be valued is notoriously fraught with disciplinary biases and other difficulties. As Psychiatrist Mark Galanter points out in his 2016 volume on AA

> … other than long term members, few people are familiar with what the basics of what membership entails, such as the way people get involved, what the Twelve Steps are understood to mean, and the role that experiences such as 'spiritual awakening' play in the fellowship.
>
> (Galanter 2016: xiii–xiv)

The twin lenses of counselling and new religious movements shed some light. However, people who transition from hopeless-seeming addictive substance use to abstinence, recovery and a demonstrably enhanced quality of life, explain this experience in their own terms. Their narratives are central to the effort of better understanding this experience.

Notes

1 Addictions literature refers to these groups as Mutual Aid organisations. These groups describe themselves not as 'organisations' but 'fellowships'. Its problems notwithstanding, the term 'fellowship(s)' is used in this chapter as it accords with the language of research participants. The first, and still largest twelve Step Fellowship, is Alcoholics Anonymous. For a detailed history see Kurtz (1979).

2 'Twelve Step' is comprised of two 'disciplines': 'fellowship meetings' and the 'programme' of the 'Twelve Steps', (see footnote18 for the Twelve Steps) which members may choose to 'work' (emic vernacular), or not. The literature of AA is clear: full-blown alcohol addiction is the symptom of a 'spiritual malady' (AAWS 1939, 2001: 64) the solution to which is a 'spiritual awakening' (AAWS 1939, 2001, 567).

3 Terminology is problematic and definitions are contested. 'Addiction' can include process or behavioural addictions (to sex or gambling for example) which involve no substances. However, the term addiction is often problematically conflated with dependence or hazardous use. In relation to substances, the *Diagnostic and Statistical Manual of Mental Disorders*, 5th Edition: (DSM-V) uses the term Substance Use Disorders (SUDs.) (American Psychiatric Association 2013). Twelve Step fellowships and programmes which are the focus of this chapter are available for addressing both SUDs and process addictions.

4 This is widespread in the US, the so-called 'Minnesota Model' (Anderson et al. 1999) based on a mixture of Twelve Step and other psychotherapeutic interventions, dominates the professional treatment scene. In the UK, of the 96 residential treatment centres listed in the DDN Directory www.ddnhelp.com/residential/residential-treatment/, 47 offer what are described as 'Twelve Step Services'. Most of these take publicly-funded clients. However, funding is increasingly hard to come by. My thanks to Liam Metcalf-White for researching the DDN Directory.

5 The American National Institute on Drug Abuse, NIDA, website www.drugabuse.gov characterises addiction as follows: 'Addiction is defined as a chronic, relapsing brain disease that is characterised by compulsive drug seeking and use, despite harmful consequences'.

6 With transcription assistance from Tim Roberts and David Williams.

7 For more information on the project see http://csarsg.org.uk/research/the-higher-power-project/.

8 The only membership criterion for Twelve Step fellowships is the desire to stop drinking/using substances or other behaviours. Thus people are members if they say they are members, and they cannot be ejected for any reason.

9 The majority (88) of the project participants were members of Alcoholics Anonymous, 19 were members of Narcotics Anonymous; 13 were members of Al-Anon, six were members of Overeaters Anonymous, four were members of Cocaine Anonymous and there were also members of Gamblers Anonymous, Emotions Anonymous, Adult Children of Alcoholics, Families Anonymous, CoDA (Co-dependents Anonymous), Marijuana Anonymous and Workaholics Anonymous. The sum of these figures is greater than 107 because some participants identified as belonging to two or more fellowships.

10 Al-Anon Family Groups are for the friends and family of people with drinking problems. The fellowship was founded by Lois Wilson, the wife of one of the founders of Alcoholics Anonymous. Al-Anon is a Twelve Step fellowship, and members often choose to 'work' the steps themselves, seeing themselves as 'ill' as a consequence of their loved-one's addictive behaviour. Whilst they are not using a substance addictively, they see themselves as in need of recovery and change, regardless of whether the behaviour of their loved one changes.

11 There is no single definition of 'recovery'. In the context of Twelve Step fellowships it usually includes abstinence from alcohol and narcotics on the presumption that safe use is impossible. However there are vast expanses of respected recovery discourse which includes in the definition the reduction of substance use to below harmful levels, desisting from substance-related crime, being in substitution therapy, or even simply taking actions that may lead to decreased use, such as seeking help.

12 In a personal communication with Ray Jenkins, Director of Emerging Futures, I was told that in 2009, 19% of *Change, Grow, Live*'s approximately 2000 recovery workers were people who identified as recovered or being in recovery. *Change Grow Live* (formerly CRI) is one of the UKs largest providers of support for people seeking recovery from SUDs.

13 Day et al. (2015) explores this and other anxieties about Twelve Step groups acknowledged by treatment professionals, but notes that the majority of treatment professionals have never attended a Twelve Step meeting.

14 Service positions might include 'secretary of the meeting' (organising, 'opening' and 'closing' the meeting with formal statements, choosing a 'main sharer' and readings); literature secretary (ensuring that literature is available for members to borrow or purchase); tea/coffee person; treasurer to keep account of the voluntary donations, and in large meetings 'greeters' to welcome people at the door.

15 The Twelve Traditions of Alcoholics Anonymous are: (1) Our common welfare should come first; personal recovery depends upon A.A. unity. (2) For our group purpose there is but one ultimate authority – a loving God as He may express Himself in our group conscience. Our leaders are but trusted servants; they do not govern. (3) The only requirement for A.A. membership is a desire to stop drinking. (4) Each group should be autonomous except in matters affecting other groups or A.A. as a whole. (5) Each group has but one primary purpose – to carry its message to the alcoholic who still suffers. (6) An A.A. group ought never endorse, finance, or lend the A.A. name to any related facility or outside enterprise, lest problems of money, property, and prestige divert us from our primary purpose. (7) Every A.A. group ought to be fully self-supporting, declining outside contributions. (8) Alcoholics Anonymous should remain forever nonprofessional, but our service centres may employ special workers. (9) A.A., as such, ought never be organized; but we may create service boards or committees directly responsible to those they serve. (10) Alcoholics Anonymous has no opinion on outside issues; hence the A.A. name ought never be drawn into public controversy. (11) Our public relations policy is based on attraction rather than promotion; we need always maintain personal anonymity at the level of press, radio, and films. (12) Anonymity is the spiritual foundation of all our Traditions, ever reminding us to place principles before personalities. (Reproduced with permission from the General Service Board UK of Alcoholics Anonymous).

16 A minority of our participants spoke about relationships with sponsors that had been less helpful, or appropriate only for a particular period of their recovery. Not all of our participants had a sponsor. 81 (n. 107) currently had a sponsor, 14 used to have in early recovery, and 12 never had.

17 Participants chose how they are to be named in research outputs.

18 The Twelve Steps are: (1) We admitted we were powerless over [alcohol/drugs]—that our lives had become unmanageable. (2) Came to believe that a power greater than ourselves could restore us to sanity. (3) Made a decision to turn our will and our lives over to the care of God as we understood Him. (4) Made a searching and fearless moral inventory of ourselves. (5) Admitted to God, to ourselves, and to another human being the exact nature of our wrongs. (6) Were entirely ready to have God remove all these defects of character. (7) Humbly asked Him to remove our shortcomings. (8) Made a list of all persons we had harmed, and became willing to make amends to them all. (9) Made direct

amends to such people wherever possible, except when to do so would injure them or others. (10) Continued to take personal inventory, and when we were wrong, promptly admitted it. (11) Sought through prayer and meditation to improve our conscious contact with God as we understood Him, praying only for knowledge of His will for us and the power to carry that out. (12) Having had a spiritual awakening as the result of these steps, we tried to carry this message to alcoholics, and to practice these principles in all our affairs.(Reproduced with permission from the General Service Board UK of Alcoholics Anonymous).

19 www.womenforsobriety.org/ (accessed 30.08.15).

20 Alcoholism is described as a disease or an illness in numerous places in the 'Big Book'. *Alcoholics Anonymous* 1939, 2001: 18, 30, 64, 92, 115, 139, 142.

21 Seen in Appendix II of the second and all subsequent editions of the book *Alcoholics Anonymous*.

22 In the late 1920s before the founding of AA, Jung had treated an American patient at his Swiss clinic, a Harvard educated Rhode Island textile magnate called Rowland Hazard III. (Bluhm 2006). Jung diagnosed Hazard as suffering with alcohol dependence so extreme that he was 'beyond the help of medicine'. His only hope was what Jung described as a 'vital spiritual experience' and announced that he was unlikely to find such a thing in the church. Nevertheless Hazard sought out the Oxford Group and stopped drinking. Hazard along with fellow religionists then managed to bring Ebby Thatcher, a former drinking partner of Bill Wilson, to sobriety. Ebby's example became influential in the later founding of AA, which emerged from the friendship of Bill and Dr Bob Smith, a surgeon from Akron, Ohio, and was built by the first 100 members. In 1961 Wilson wrote to Jung to thank him for his role in the course of events which had led to the development of AA, and Jung replied immediately. The text of Jung's letter may be read at: www.silkworth.net/aahistory/carljung_billw013061.html.

23 This conclusion is drawn from observing social media pages and websites for atheists and agnostics in AA, such as 'We Agnostics and Freethinkers' www.facebook.com/waaftcentral?fref=ts (accessed 31.08.15) and AA Agnostica http://aaagnostica.org/ (accessed 31.08.15).

24 *The Secret* is a film and book package authored by Rhonda Byrne (2006) which promotes positive thinking and the law of attraction, in order to attain health, wealth and happiness. It is based on the idea that 'like attracts like' – thus the person who thinks positively accumulates positive experiences. *A Course in Miracles* (Schucman, 1975) is an allegedly 'guided' text and spiritual work programme which is based in a non-dual cosmology and the development of self-forgiveness and love. Author Marianne Williamson popularised 'the Course' and is herself an author frequently read by twelve step practitioners. http://marianne.com/.

25 Fuller (2001: 112) credits AA with introducing the concept of SBNR into the lexicon.

26 www.silkworth.net/aahistory/carljung_billw013061.html.

References

Alcoholics Anonymous World Services 1939, 4th edition 2001. *Alcoholics Anonymous. The Story of How Many Thousands of Men and Women Have Recovered from Alcoholism.* New York: Alcoholics Anonymous World Services.

American Psychiatric Association 2013. *Diagnostic and Statistical Manual of Mental Disorders.* 5th ed. Washington, D.C.: American Psychiatric Association.

Anderson, D.J., J.P. McGovern and R.L. Dupont 1999. The origins of the Minnesota model of addiction treatment–a first person account. *Journal of Addictive Diseases,* 18(1), 107–14.

Bepko, C. 1991. *Feminism and Addiction*. New York: Haworth Press.

Bluhm, A.C. 2006. Verification of C. G. Jung's analysis of Rowland Hazard and the history of Alcoholics Anonymous. *History of Psychology*, 9(4), 313–24.

Bobgan, M. and D. Bobgan 1991. *12 Steps to Destruction: Codependency Recovery Heresies*. Santa Barbara, CA: EastGate Publishers.

Briggs, C.A. and J.L. Pepperell 2009. *Women, Girls, and Addiction: Celebrating the Feminine in Counseling Treatment and Recovery*. New York: Routledge.

Bufe, C. 1998. *Alcoholics Anonymous: Cult or Cure?* 2nd ed. Tucson, AZ: See Sharp Press.

Byrne, R. 2006. *The Secret*. New York: Simon & Schuster.

Day, E., R. Wall, G. Chohan and J. Seddon 2015. Perceptions of professional drug treatment staff in England about client barriers to narcotics anonymous attendance. *Addiction Research & Theory*, 23(3), 223–30.

Dossett, W. 2013. Addiction, spirituality and 12-step programmes. *International Social Work*, 56(3), 369–83.

Dossett, W. 2015. Reflections on the Language of Salvation in Twelve Step Recovery 'in return for a bottle and a hangover we have been given the keys to the kingdom', in: H. Bacon, W. Dossett and S. Knowles (eds) *Alternative Salvations: Engaging the Sacred and the Secular* (pp. 21–30). London: Bloomsbury Academic.

Fuller, R.C. 2001. *Spiritual, But Not Religious: Understanding Unchurched America*. Oxford: Oxford University Press.

Galanter, M. 2016. *What is Alcoholics Anonymous?* Oxford and New York: Oxford University Press.

Hitchens, P. 2012. *The War We Never Fought*. London: Bloomsbury Continuum.

Kasl, C.S. 1992. *Many Roads, One Journey: Moving Beyond the Twelve Steps*. New York: HarperPerennial.

Kelly, J.F. and C.M. Greene 2014. Toward an enhanced understanding of the psychological mechanisms by which spirituality aids recovery in Alcoholics Anonymous. *Alcoholism Treatment Quarterly*, 32, 299–318.

Kelly, J.F., R.L. Stout, M. Magill and J.S. Tonigan 2011. The role of Alcoholics Anonymous in mobilizing adaptive social network changes: a prospective lagged mediational analysis. *Drug and Alcohol Dependence*, 114(2–3), 119–26.

Koenig, H.G. (ed.) 1998. *Handbook of Religion and Mental Health*. San Diego, CA: Academic Press.

Kurtz, E. 1979. *Not-God: A History of Alcoholics Anonymous*. Center City, MI: Hazelden Educational Services.

Lê, C., E.P. Ingvarson and R.C. Page 1995. Alcoholics Anonymous and the counseling profession: philosophies in conflict. *Journal of Counseling & Development*, 73(6), 603–609.

Lewis, M. 2011. *Memoirs of an Addicted Brain*. New York: PublicAffairs.

Lewis, M. 2015. *Biology of Desire: Why Addiction is Not a Disease*. New York: PublicAffairs.

Lun, V.M.-C. and M.H. Bond 2013. Examining the relation of religion and spirituality to subjective well-being across national cultures. *Psychology of Religion and Spirituality*, 5(4), 304–15.

Orford, J. 1985. *Excessive Appetites: A Psychological View of Addictions*. Chichester and New York: Wiley-Blackwell.

Pargament, K.I. 1997. *The Psychology of Religion and Coping: Theory, Research, Practice*. New York: Guilford Press.

Peele, S., K. Ragge and C. Bufe 2000. *Resisting 12-Step Coercion: How to Fight Forced Participation in AA, NA or 12-Step Treatment.* Tucson, AZ: See Sharp Press.

Porche M.V., L.R. Fortuna, A. Wachholtz, R.T. Stone and R.T. Stone 2015. Distal and proximal religiosity as protective factors for adolescent and emerging adult alcohol use. *Religions*, 6(2), 365–84.

Putnam, R.D. 2000. *Bowling Alone: The Collapse and Revival of American Community.* New York: Simon & Schuster.

Sanders, J.M. 2009. *Women in Alcoholics Anonymous: Recovery and Empowerment.* Boulder, CO: FirstForumPress.

Schucman, H. 1975. *A Course in Miracles.* (W. T. Thetford [ed.]). Mill Valley, CA: Foundation for Inner Peace.

Scrivener, L. 2011. Does religion belong at AA? Fight over 'God' splits Toronto AA groups. *The Toronto Star*, June 3.

Szalavitz, M. 2012. Do the Twelve Steps belong in Addiction Treatment? *The Fix.* Available at www.thefix.com/content/do-12-steps-spirituality-effective-addiction-treatment8221 (Accessed 6 June 2017).

Tobert, N. 2014. *Spiritual Psychiatries: Mental Health Practices in India and UK.* London: Aethos.

Volkow, N.D. and J.S. Fowler 2000. Addiction, a disease of compulsion and drive: involvement of the orbitofrontal cortex. *Cerebral Cortex*, 10(3), 318–25.

Wilbanks, W. 1989. The danger in viewing addicts as victims: a critique of the disease model of addiction. *Criminal Justice Policy Review*, 3(4), 407–22.

Wise, R.A. 2000. Addiction becomes a brain disease. *Neuron*, 26(1), 27–33.

Index

For Product Safety Concerns and Information please contact our EU representative GPSR@taylorandfrancis.com Taylor & Francis Verlag GmbH, Kaufingerstraße 24, 80331 München, Germany